THE TEACHERS' HANDBOOK

THE TEACHERS' HANDBOOK

TO

THE SYLLABUS OF RELIGIOUS INSTRUCTION

FOR USE IN
SCOTTISH SCHOOLS

BY

The Rev. JAMES SMITH
M.A., B.D. (Abdn.), Ph.D. (Edin.)

DIRECTOR OF RELIGIOUS INSTRUCTION
St Andrew's Provincial Committee for the Training of Teachers

AUTHOR OF
The Book of the Prophet Ezekiel: A New Interpretation

EDINBURGH:
THE CHURCH OF SCOTLAND EDUCATION AND YOUTH COMMITTEES,
121 GEORGE STREET;
AND
THE EDUCATIONAL INSTITUTE OF SCOTLAND,
46 AND 47 MORAY PLACE.
1936.

" A mind not instructed can no more bear fruit than can a field, however fertile, without cultivation."—CICERO.

TO THE

Rev. ROBERT VENTERS, B.D.,

FOR THIRTY-FIVE YEARS MINISTER OF
THE CHURCH AND PARISH OF BELLIE.

FOREWORD

In 1927 the Church of Scotland, the United Free Church of Scotland and the Educational Institute of Scotland appointed a Joint Committee to prepare a new Syllabus of Religious Instruction for use in Scottish Schools. The work of the Joint Committee received the approval of its parent bodies in 1929, and the new Syllabus was accepted by Education Committees generally throughout Scotland until it now forms the basis for religious instruction in the great majority of Scottish schools.

While the work of preparation was going on, it was felt that a series of Teachers' Handbooks would add greatly to the value of the Syllabus. The comprehensive Bibliography, which was added as an appendix, met to some extent the need thus foreshadowed. The desire for some form of Handbook, however, found strong expression in the results of an enquiry made last year into the working of the Syllabus, in which it was made clear that a companion Manual to the Syllabus would be welcomed by many teachers.

The Joint Committee considers itself fortunate that it is in a position at least partly to satisfy this demand, and desires to express its gratitude to the Rev. Dr James Smith, the Director of Religious Instruction at St Andrews-Dundee Training Centre, for placing at its disposal the MSS. of a manual which he had recently prepared in response to many requests for a comprehensive text-book relating to the Syllabus. The book is now issued by the Joint Committee of the Church and the Institute, with confidence that it will commend itself to the teachers of Scotland as an invaluable aid in the moral and religious training of the rising generation, in so far as that is based upon the teaching of the Scriptures.

W. M. WIGHTMAN,
JOHN WISHART,

Secretaries of the Joint Committee of the Church of Scotland and the Educational Institute of Scotland.

EDINBURGH, *July*, 1936.

PREFACE

RECENT psychological research has confirmed the belief that man is by nature a religious being and that, if he be not led to revere the God and Father of our Lord Jesus Christ, he will worship a god of his own invention. Our Lord came to reveal to us the living God and to unite us in fellowship with Him. The aim of religious education is to guide children from the earliest age to seek God and to learn that only through Him can they enjoy full, rich and satisfying lives.

We are told that religious instruction is not religious education and that a man may con the Bible from its first to its last page without having any contact with the divine presence. That may be; but beyond question much of the moral sickness of our age is due to religious ignorance. It should never be forgotten that no man by searching can find out God. The Bible is a revelation, not the record of a human quest. The function of the teacher is to awaken the child's mind to the thought of God and to lead him on step by step by methods that will arouse his interest to those aspects of revealed truth which his budding intelligence can grasp.

The purpose of this book is to supply to the teachers in Scotland such a knowledge of the background of the lessons in the Syllabus of Religious Instruction as will enable them to make these lessons throb with vitality. No attempt has been made to " work out " lessons for no one can teach a lesson prepared by another. The writer knows after fifteen years' experience in a Training College that no two students, from the same material, will prepare a lesson in the same way.

Although these notes deal only with the lessons in the Syllabus from Junior I. to Senior III., they will be useful also to teachers of Infants and of pupils in Advanced Division and Secondary Schools.

The writer is most grateful to the Educational Institute of Scotland and to the Education and Youth Committees of the Church of Scotland for issuing this book as an official publication, to the National Sunday School Union for permission to reproduce their illustrations, to the Rev. G. Ogg, D.Litt., of Anstruther, and to Mr John Hutcheson, M.A., Headmaster of Maryhill Public School, Glasgow, for their helpful advice and criticism, to the Rev. W. M. Wightman, B.D., F.E.I.S., and to Mr John Wishart, M.A., F.E.I.S., for their kindness in writing the Foreword, to Mr Alexander Sivewright, M.A., F.E.I.S., (of Lindsay & Company, Limited), for his personal interest and many helpful suggestions, and above all to the Rev. Dr Alex. Andrew, Convener of the Education Committee of the National Committee for the Training of Teachers and Convener of the Education Committee of the Church of Scotland, whose many illuminating comments have greatly enriched this work.

JAMES SMITH.

THE TRAINING COLLEGE,
DUNDEE, *June,* 1936.

TABLE OF CONTENTS

LIST OF ILLUSTRATIONS

xiii

Reference
Pages

INTRODUCTION.

THE GOSPELS.

The four Gospels which stand at the head of the Books of the New Testament are our primary authorities for the life of Jesus. Our purpose is (A) to tell how they came to be written and (B) to state what are the broad characteristics and what is the special value of each of them. The first three, while each has its own peculiar features, in many respects agree closely with one another and are markedly different from the fourth. Because they give in one common view the same general outline of the ministry of Jesus, i.e., the same conspectus or synopsis, the first three are known as the Synoptics and require in reference to many points to be considered together. The Fourth Gospel, while it needs to be set in relation to the Synoptics, being different not only in contents but also in style and method presents many features which call for separate consideration.

(A)

(1) In following the growth of the Gospels we must think first of the time before any of them had been composed and before any of the sources used in their composition had yet been written. That is the interval reaching from *c.* A.D. 30 to A.D. 50 or a little later. To penetrate into this hinterland is the aim of one of the most recent German schools of Gospel Criticism. The pathfinder has been M. Dibelius. He and those who follow him start from the assumption that in this period of oral tradition the material now in our Gospels existed in the form of single isolated elements. These they not only attempt to classify according to their form; it is almost entirely from the point of view of their form that they treat of them. Hence the name of this school, the formgeschichtliche or form-historical.

That there are in our Gospels narratives and sayings that may very well have existed as separate units must be allowed. A good example is the account of the tribute

B

money in Mark xii. 13 ff. It is a story that can be lifted
out of its present setting without loss to itself, which is
complete in itself, which in the oral period may, therefore,
have been transmitted as an independent unit. To admit,
however, that narratives and sayings may thus at one time
have had an independent existence is not necessarily to
make way for the view of at least one representative of
this school who likens the material which came to Mark's
hand to a heap of pearls that he strung in the order that
pleased him most upon a string of his own spinning. To
entertain such a view is to assume that there are in Mark
more gaps than there actually are. It is to ignore the fact
that its Passion story is a relatively long continuous narrative and that several other sections of it have unquestion-
ably an historical unity.

In attempting to classify the separate units according
to form the representatives of this school have gone their
own ways. The result is a terminology which is neither
happy nor homogeneous. Indeed there is here a multi-
plicity of terms which suggests that there is in the Gospels
material that does not easily fit into the frames this school
has created for it. Peculiarly difficult to classify are
certain stories about Jesus, e.g., those of his Baptism,
Temptation, and Transfiguration. We may well believe,
nevertheless, that in the oral period a considerable portion
of the Gospel tradition did have certain definite forms.
There was the short story which had as its climax some
notable word of Jesus as, e.g., the story of the tribute
money referred to above in which everything leads up to
the saying, " Render to Caesar the things that are Caesar's,
and to God the things that are God's." There were longer
stories in which were recorded the mighty works of Jesus.
So far as concerns words of His not preserved in short
stories the one recognisable form is the parable.

What would seem to have taken place in this period
may now be indicated briefly. After the Resurrection
there were living those who remembered in order what
Jesus had said and done. In particular in the several
centres where He had laboured there were those who could
recall what had been the course of His ministry there. In
time, however, these connected reminiscences underwent
a process of dissolution. Portions of them ceased to be
remembered and were lost; other portions, oftentimes re-
called and told over and over again, survived as isolated
stories and sayings and groups of sayings. This process

was not indeed complete. Those sections of Mark which have historical unity and notably its Passion narrative testify that there were certain connected reminiscences the several parts of which did not loose apart either to be lost or to survive in isolation. But though not operative everywhere there was such a process and the explanation of it is to be found in the circumstances of the Christians of the time. In their assemblies, as at the services of public worship to-day, it was upon single stories and sayings of Jesus that they meditated and those established themselves most securely which, putting them in mind who He was and how He came to His Passion, confirmed them most in faith and obedience. In the world of their time, in contact with Jews and Gentiles, these early Christians found themselves confronted by many practical problems, solutions of which they often found by recalling some word or act of Jesus Himself. Because of their bearing upon conduct such isolated sayings and deeds were naturally treasured and transmitted. Yet again, while the Passion story was always required in its entirety, it was isolated stories and words of Jesus that the missionaries of those early days found most serviceable in commending Him to others. In short, in this period the demand was not for a connected account of Jesus' ministry but for self-contained stories, isolated sayings and sayings groups; and it was in these that interest was centred.

(2) We have now to consider the interval reaching from the end of the oral period to c. A.D. 65. There is reason to believe that in this interval and largely for catechetical purposes there were made and committed to writing at least three collections of the sayings of Jesus.

Of these the first in time and perhaps the most valuable is that which is now generally recognised as the source whence was derived the non-Markan material common to Luke and Matthew. It is known as Q (from Quelle = source) : its date which may be as early as A.D. 50 can hardly be later than A.D. 60: Antioch has been suggested as the place where it was compiled. Essentially Q is a collection of sayings, yet from the sayings it contains, much can be gathered as to the personality of Jesus and as to the sphere and purpose of His ministry. The question whether Q contained any narrative material, in particular whether it contained a Passion story, has been much debated. It has been thought that Q is the work referred to by Papias in a statement preserved in the Church History of Eusebius, " Matthew composed the Logia in the Aramaic tongue and each one interpreted them as he could." That theory would perhaps explain the connection of Matthew's name with the First Gospel but it is now less popular than it was.

The second collection of sayings is of later date than Q, was compiled at Rome and used as a source by Mark. To it there belong sayings in Mark which are parallel to, yet verbally distinctly different from sayings in Q. Until recently these sayings were taken as indicating that Mark used Q. According to the present theory he drew them from an entirely independent source.

The third collection, because it was used by the First Evangelist, is known as M. The date suggested for it is A.D. 65. From its Jewish tone and certain other features it would seem to have been compiled in Jerusalem. To it there belong portions of Matthew which, while having parallels in Luke, have yet little linguistic agreement with them. From M there have also been derived the parables peculiar to Matthew.

(3) Finally we have to consider the interval A.D. 65-100 within which the four Gospels were composed. The explanation of the emergence of these fuller accounts of the sayings and doings of Jesus must be sought in the apologetic, missionary, and religious needs of the now rapidly expanding church.

The earliest of the Gospels, it is now recognised, is Mark. Touching it the following statement of Papias has been preserved by Eusebius: "Mark, having become the interpreter of Peter wrote down accurately all that he remembered of the things done and said by Christ, but not however in order." This, there is little reason to doubt, is a trustworthy account of the origin of the Second Gospel. John Mark of Jerusalem, the companion of St Paul, after the death of that apostle continued in Rome where he devoted himself to St Peter. From him he learned what had been the course of the ministry of Jesus and into this framework, after the death of Peter, he inworked not only what he had heard Peter utter in public preaching but also stories he himself had been told by Peter, portions of the second of the three collections of sayings mentioned above and perhaps also one or two already existing small collections of " conflict stories." The evidence both external and

internal points to Rome as the place of origin of this
Gospel. The theory advanced by some that it is an unskil-
ful translation of a document originally written in Aramaic
is not required, the semitic colouring of its Greek being
sufficiently explained by the fact that Mark, a Jew, had to
translate his Aramaic thought into Greek. Since this
Gospel was written after the deaths of Paul and Peter and,
as appears from internal evidence, before the fall of Jerusalem it is to be dated within the period A.D. 65-70.

According to the more recent Proto-Luke hypothesis
there was a Gospel written earlier than Mark but it remained unpublished until it had been enlarged by considerable extracts from Mark. The theory—at least one form
of it—is that Luke who already possessed a copy of Q and
saw what need there was to supplement it, being in
Caesarea during the two years of Paul's imprisonment
there, took then the opportunity of collecting the oral
tradition of that centre. After his departure for Rome and
before A.D. 65 he worked materials from this collection (L)
and from Q into a single document—Proto-Luke—which,
however, while more nearly complete than Q, apparently
seemed to him to lack that completeness that would justify
his giving it to the world. Later in Rome in the Gospel
Mark had composed there, he found the extra material he
needed. Combining Proto-Luke with Mark and prefixing
an account of the Nativity he became, somewhere in the
period A.D. 80-85, the author of the Third Gospel.

For the author of the First Gospel, as for Luke, two
principal sources were Q and Mark. This is what largely
explains the remarkable agreement which the Synoptics so
often present not only in the sequence of events and
sayings but also in the actual words in which they are
recorded. Since Matthew makes many rearrangements of
Mark's order while Luke makes but few it is inferred that
the original order of Q is less well preserved in Matthew
than in Luke. Matthew made use, in addition to Mark
and Q, of the Jerusalem sayings collection mentioned
above. It is possible that he obtained his stories of the
Nativity and certain other stories peculiar to his Gospel
not from a written source but from the oral tradition of
the Church—possibly Antioch—for which he wrote. It
has frequently been suggested that he used a collection,
made by the apostle Matthew, of Testimonia, i.e., of Old
Testament prophecies that were believed to have been
fulfilled in Jesus. Such a theory might explain how

early tradition associates the First Gospel with the name of Matthew. But, however that description is to be accounted for, this Gospel, so largely dependent on earlier writings, cannot be the work of an apostle. Its author is unknown. Since he used Mark he wrote after A.D. 70. Indications in the Gospel of the thought and organisation of the Church of the time suggest that it was written towards the close of the century. Those who maintain that it must have been written not long after Luke date it in the period A.D. 85-90.

One of the latest commentators on the Fourth Gospel at the conclusion of his Introduction quotes these words, " If there was a great picture which tradition had affirmed to be painted by Raphael, and it was proved not to have been painted by Raphael, but by some otherwise unknown artist, the world would have not one great painting the less, but one great painter the more," and then he adds, " Whoever wrote it, the Fourth Gospel will always be the Holy of Holies of Christian literature . . . the book which is, as Luther puts it, ' the chiefest of the Gospels, unique, tender, and true.' " While occasionally there may have been the expression of some hesitation or doubt the tradition that John the son of Zebedee had lived in Ephesus in the reign of Trajan and there written the Fourth Gospel remained uncontradicted until the appearance in 1820 of the " Probabilia " of Bretschneider. In the years that have intervened, while many have come forward as champions of the Johannine authorship, the tendency has been to abandon it : yet increasingly the necessity is being felt of maintaining that, whoever the author of this Gospel may have been, he was one who, standing in intimate relation to John, was able to make such a full use of that apostle's reminiscences as made it possible for his work to become known and to be accepted as the Gospel according to John. To say more about this writer without stepping on to debatable ground is not easy. Many are agreed that he was a Jew; not all are persuaded that he was a Jew of Palestine.

Evidence has frequently been brought forward that John died a martyr's death at the hands of the Jews in the early days of the Church, probably at the same time as his brother James (Acts xii. 2). If this evidence must be accepted then possibly the view expressed above as to the authorship of this Gospel and certainly the tradition that John, removing to Ephesus, attained there a great age and was the last survivor of the company of the apostles must be abandoned. Certain scholars do accept this evidence: those who reject it as unconvincing give good reasons for their doing so.

It is now recognised that there is a more important question than that of the authorship of this book, the question namely of the historicity of its contents. There are two extreme views, the one that in all it reports this Gospel is an accurate historical record, the other that it is a theological treatise cast into the form of an imaginative biography of Jesus. Neither view is to be accepted. Nevertheless justice needs to be done to the truth for which each stands. On the one hand there is no reason to suppose that all that was remembered about Jesus found its way into the Synoptics. Much of the narrative material of the Fourth Gospel, though there is nothing parallel to it in the Synoptics, has all the appearance of being authentic. On the other hand the author of this Gospel appears to have passed much of the teaching of Jesus through the alembic of his own penetrating and deeply spiritual mind and to have set down the words of Jesus in many places not as they were actually spoken but as he himself interpreted them and developed them and translated them into the thought forms of his time. This, however, does not mean that he has not sometimes reproduced or that he has not always started from the actual words of Jesus. To-day the tendency even among critics who cannot be suspected of conservatism is to recognise that the author of this Gospel utilised tradition that is independent of the Synoptics and of excellent value, that therefore he provides material that cannot be neglected in any attempt to reconstruct the life and teaching of Jesus.

Related to this question of the historicity of the Fourth Gospel is that of its author's relation to the Synoptics. Parallel narratives and verbal resemblances make it fairly certain that he knew Mark. There are indications also that he knew Luke but no good evidence that he was acquainted with Matthew. Apparently his aim was to supplement the Synoptic record as he knew it, in certain particulars also to correct it. A more daring suggestion is that he sought to provide what would supersede it.

There has been a gradual recession from the view of an extreme criticism that dated this Gospel in the second half of the second century. To-day it is widely agreed that it was written in Ephesus not far from the end of the

first century. Its text appears in places to have suffered
dislocation. To the rearrangements given in Moffatt's
" New translation of the New Testament " many add the
transposition of Chapters V. and VI.

(B).

Generally it may be said of all four Evangelists that
they have sought to present a vivid picture of the historical Jesus. There is, however, this difference—whereas
the Synoptists have been content to leave that picture to
make its own appeal to mind and heart, the Fourth Evangelist, as he expressly affirms (xx. 31), has sought through
the picture he has presented to establish the true doctrine
of Christ's person. Thus, whereas the interests of the
Synoptists are essentially biographical, supremely the
Fourth Evangelist's concern is in what the events and
sayings he records mean and illustrate. Hence the statement of Clement of Alexandria, " John, perceiving that the
bodily facts had been made plain in the Gospel, being urged
by his friends, and inspired by the Spirit, composed a
spiritual Gospel."
In setting down what are the characteristics and what
is the special value of the several Gospels it will be well
to take them in chronological order.

(1) Mark.

Undoubtedly the most noticeable characteristic of this
Gospel is its graphic style. Mark's narration abounds in
vivid, life-like touches. In places the original words of a
speaker emerge in a striking fashion. The only possible
explanation of this feature, since the author himself was
not an eye-witness, is that he was dependent upon and
has faithfully reproduced the reminiscences of one who
was. Another characteristic of the record of this Gospel is
a certain activity or rapidity of movement. Mark is more
interested in what Jesus did than in what He said and he
hurriedly passes from event to event often with no connecting word save his favourite " straightway." Yet another characteristic of this work is its author's unhesitat-
ing acceptance of the supernatural and his interest in Jesus'
works of exorcism.
Supremely the value of this Gospel lies in the picture

it provides of Jesus in all the concrete reality of His historical life. This Gospel is not indeed chronological in detail. To borrow a well-known figure, there are stations at the end of not a few of its sections and the connections are not guaranteed. Yet neither Luke nor Matthew gives so simple, so orderly, or so consistent an account of the ministry. Throughout, the main stress is upon the humanity of Jesus. Mark does not hesitate to refer to His compassion and other emotions in terms which the other Synoptists omit or alter. But His Divinity does not remain unemphasised. He is presented as a supernatural person to whom witness is borne by voices from heaven, who claims superhuman authority, who works superhuman works, reads the secrets of men's hearts, and knows what the future has in store. A peculiarly valuable feature of this Gospel is the place given in it to the thought of suffering. The shadow of the Cross reaches as far back as the second chapter; from the crisis at Caesarea Philippi onwards the thought of approaching suffering and death keeps recurring.

(2) LUKE.

From the literary point of view this is the most beautiful of the four Gospels. Its author has command of a good Greek not possessed by any of the other Evangelists. He is also the only one of the four to set the record of Jesus' life in relation to secular history. Pervading his Gospel and distinguishing it from the others is an unmistakable spirit of gladsomeness and hopefulness. Particularly noteworthy is the place in it occupied by women, children, and young men. So prominent is its author's sympathy with the poor, it has been supposed, though quite wrongly, that it emanated from a body of early Christians known as the Ebionites or "the Poor Men."

The value of this Gospel lies in the priceless contribution it makes to our knowledge of Jesus. Not only does Luke afford us glimpses of His inner life, e.g., His habit of prayer, it is he in particular who makes it plain that in Him there is neither Jew nor Greek, bond nor free, male nor female. It is a mark of the liberality of the Evangelist's spirit that while thus stressing the universalism of Christianity he manifests practically no trace of bias against the Jewish Christian community. It is especially in this Gospel that we see the graciousness of Jesus, His sympathy with and His longing to save the outcast and the sinner. It alone preserves the matchless parable of the Prodigal Son.

(3) MATTHEW.

This Gospel is Jewish-Christian. That is its most outstanding characteristic. It is seen in the author's affectionate references to Jerusalem and in his preference for the Rabbinical phrase " the kingdom of the heavens " to that usual in the Synoptics, " the kingdom of God "; again it is seen in his interest in Christianity as the consummation of the Old Testament religion as revealed in his many citations of prophecies believed to have been fulfilled in the life of Jesus, in his conception of Jesus as the Messiah of the Jews, manifested, e.g., in the emphasis he lays upon His Davidic descent, and in the prominence he gives throughout his Gospel to the theme of the Messiah's kingdom. This Evangelist, however, was no Judaiser. He tells us indeed that Jesus said, " I am not sent but unto the lost sheep of the house of Israel " (xv. 24), but he also records the coming of the Magi, tells with what satisfaction Jesus beheld the faith of a centurion, and how He foretold that certain Jews would be cast out of the Kingdom and their places taken by many " from the east and the west." Another characteristic of this Gospel is its massing of the teaching of Jesus in large groups. Of these the most noticeable are the following: (a) Chapters v., vi., vii., (b) Chapter x., (c) Chapter xiii., (d) Chapter xviii., (e) Chapters xxiv., xxv. This rearrangement, while it makes for lucidity, has resulted in an over-emphasis on some matters and a neglect of certain others. Many hold e.g., that Matthew, because he has simply massed Jesus' statements about His coming again and omitted to show how He spiritualised the eschatological ideas of His time, gives the impression that He taught a nearness of His coming beyond what He intended. A minor feature of this Gospel is its author's fondness for the numbers 7, 5, 3, and 10.

Its special value lies (1) in the striking picture it presents of Jesus in all His majesty as the Messiah of God, and (2) in the insight it affords us into the thought world of early Jewish Christianity.

(4) JOHN.

This Gospel is characterised by a remarkable simplicity of style. Actually its ideas are few in number and are nearly all introduced in the Prologue (i. 1-18). They are, however, ideas of the profoundest order, yet are expressed in the simplest of terms. Such a statement as "I am the life" a child can read, yet the wisest cannot exhaust its meaning. A second characteristic of this Gospel is the mysterious spell it casts over all who turn to it. He who reads it has not merely a feeling that more is meant than is said, he is overawed: a sense of the divine is conveyed to his soul. If the view of not a few scholars is to be accepted it is a further feature of this Gospel that in it there are certain polemical aims. At the time it was written Judaism was attempting to ridicule the claims made by the Church for her Lord. Gnostic heretics, maintaining that the body of Jesus was only a semblance, were denying His true humanity and the reality of His suffering. A Baptist sect was exalting John above Jesus. The author of the Fourth Gospel, it is thought, had opponents such as these in mind as he wrote and sought to meet them. It is this perhaps that explains the strange vehemence and controversial tone of several of the discourses of Jesus as given in this Gospel. These polemical aims, however, were subsidiary. The great purpose of the author was that he mentions in xx. 31:—

The value of this Gospel lies—(1) In the supplement it makes to our knowledge of the Ministry of Jesus. The impression the Synoptics give is that that ministry lasted but a single year. This Gospel shows us that its duration was not less than two years and some months. The Synoptics, confining Jesus' ministry to Galilee and districts east and north of that, bring Him to Jerusalem only for the Passion Passover. From this Gospel we learn that He was in the Holy City on several earlier occasions.

(2) In the deeper understanding it affords of the significance of Christ's person and work. Here these are seen not in reference merely to the past or the present or the future but to eternity.

JUNIOR (First Year) — NEW TESTAMENT.

A.—STORIES OF JESUS.

THE BOYHOOD OF JESUS—*Luke* ii. 40-52.

LITTLE is told us directly of the boyhood of our Lord. But there is material enough in the Gospels (*see* Appendix II. of the Syllabus) to enable the teacher to give a series of inspiring lessons on the subject. According to the Gospel record our Lord grew in wisdom and in stature and in favour with God and man. It is well to consider the influences and external conditions amidst which He was brought up; for in His environment in childhood and youth is to be found, at least in part, the explanation of His understanding of, and communion with, God.

(1) It is said, not without truth, that God to the child is in large measure a projection of his parents or parental substitutes. The child's picture of God is inevitably coloured by his ideas of his parents and his first contact with God is, or should be, through worship in the family circle. Of all the influences playing upon the life of the Holy Child the most important were those of the home. In the home at Nazareth He saw human nature at its best. He was reared in an ideal home environment. Joseph and Mary belonged to the best section of the Jewish people, the quietist party, those who waited patiently for the redemption of Israel, humble and pious folks, merciful and full of loving kindness. Judaism is a religion of the home. A learned Jew when asked the question : " What is the explanation of the survival of Judaism? " replied : " The mothers in Israel." Daily in the home as a child our Lord must have watched Joseph and Mary performing numerous ritualistic acts. No doubt He enquired about the significance of these and so learned of the faith of the race to which He belonged. For example, Joseph on entering the home touched a little metal box at the door, called a Mezzuzah, and then put his fingers to his lips and uttered a blessing. The boy Jesus, seeing this, must have been told that the box contained an inscription from Deuteronomy (VI. : 4-9, XI. : 13-21). One of the first passages of Scripture, therefore, that He learned to lisp may well have been these words : " Hear, O Israel : the Lord our God is one

Lord : And thou shalt love the Lord thy God with all thine
heart, and with all thy soul, and with all thy might." The
Jew was not familiar with the word "project" but his
insistence that the religious rites of the home were to be used
as object-lessons to the children and that the child's instinct
of curiosity was to be aroused before an explanation of the
rites was given, shows that he knew the principles of
pedagogy. Our Lord must also have heard stories of the
great heroes of faith. As He listened and observed and
experienced He felt that whatever else God might be, He
must be like Joseph and Mary.

(2) Much of our knowledge of the educational system of
the Jews comes from the Mishna (200 A.D.) and if we can
infer—the inference is open to question—that conditions
were similar in the days of our Lord, then in matters educational the Jews of His time were in certain respects far
ahead of us to-day. For example, not more than twenty-five
boys might be taught by one master and if there were over
forty children there must be two assistants. As the teachers'
salaries were paid by the community which made a levy upon
itself for the purpose, no child was debarred by poverty
from receiving instruction in the Law. There was a unique
system of universal education (for boys) and it is not altogether surprising that the Pharisees looked with contempt on
the ignorant section of the Jewish community holding that
those who did not know the Law were wilfully blind and
wilfully ignorant. To every synagogue there was attached
an elementary school to which boys were sent at the age of
six. The school was known as "the house of the Book"
because the only book studied was the Old Testament. The
children literally sat at the teacher's feet. They squatted on
the floor while he sat on a platform. Learning was by repetition. Our Lord acquired a thorough knowledge of the Old
Testament and learned something of the traditional interpretation. In later life the knowledge of God thus acquired
availed Him time and again in His hour of need. He
repelled the Temptations by an appeal to the Old Testament.
Twice He quoted Hosea's great saying about mercy, and on
the Cross He repeated the opening words of the twenty-
second Psalm. It is clear that He regarded Himself as the
fulfilment of Old Testament prophecy.

(3) No Jewish boy's education was complete without
manual training. The study of the Law must, the Jews
wisely decided, be accompanied by the learning of a trade and

as a rule a boy followed the trade of his father. Our Lord
was a carpenter. In the workshop He learned about timbers
and their uses. He must also have learned about house-
building for in Palestine in these days a carpenter was also
a mason. (*See* Holtzmann : *The Life of Jesus.*) He knew
the fate that would befall a house built upon sand in contrast
to what would be the fate of the house built upon a rock.
This manual labour made for physical development. St Luke
tells us that He grew in stature. But the workship did more
than develop strength of limb. St Luke tells us that He grew
in wisdom. Our Lord came to realise that God can be as
effectively served through conscientious labour as through
the worship of the Synagogue and the study of the Law.
In the workshop too He acquired an insight into human
nature. The workshop was a centre for the exchange of
ideas and the airing of opinions on religious and political
questions, and our Lord would hear much of the Messiah who
was to come, the Messiah who would set up a new kingdom,
the Messiah for whom His people were eagerly awaiting.

(4) One of the best avenues of approach to God is that of
Nature. Through contact with Nature the child can find an
answer to many of his questionings. If he is given a religious
training in conjunction with his nature-study he comes to
realise something of the majesty and the mystery and the love
of the Creator. The purpose of nature-study in schools
should be to secure not utilitarian but religious values. Jesus'
heart was always open to God through the channel of Nature.
His sayings abound in references to Nature. In His rambles
among the hills of Nazareth He watched with eyes of wonder
the unfolding of the buds, the springing of the flowers, the
nesting of the birds, the retreat of the fox to its den, the
trustfulness of the sheep in the guidance of the shepherd;
and He knew that God was a Father who made provision for
all His creatures.

Mention must be made of the influence upon our Lord of
the geographical position of Nazareth. From the hills surrounding the village our Lord could see Mount Carmel, the
scene of Elijah's contest with the priests of Baal; Mount
Tabor, the scene of the victory of Deborah and Barak over
Sisera and the Canaanite hosts; Mount Gilboa, where Saul
met his death; the Valley of Jezreel, " the scene of so much
of Israel's glory and crime "; the Valley of Megiddo, where
" the never-ending battle between light and darkness, between
good and evil, was still being fought, as it had been in the

past, and would be in the future." He saw the merchantmen
going down into Egypt with their carpets and silks and spices,
and the Roman troops whom His people hated filing past.
Living in such an environment He learned that religion was
the secret of His nation's greatness. (The teacher might
quote Hilton Young's *Christmas*.)

THE VISIT TO THE TEMPLE—*Luke* ii. 42-52.

A Jewish father was responsible for the religious education of his son until he reached his twelfth birthday.
Thereafter the boy became a " Son of the Law," as in our
own Church the adolescent before his first Communion
voluntarily repeats the vows taken on his behalf by his
parents at Baptism. He himself assumed full responsibility
for keeping the Law of Moses and became "bound to the
Law " as a man by reading in the Synagogue the portion of
the Law appointed for the day.

The Synagogue.—The origin of the Synagogue is lost in
obscurity but may be found in the new situation created by
the fall of the Temple in 586 B.C. With the destruction of
the Temple and the temporary cessation of the sacrificial
system, worship, as understood by the Israelite, came to an
end. If the worship of the God of Israel were to survive
it was essential that something take the place of the Temple
system. And so during the period of the Captivity the
Jewish exiles met together for worship and instruction on the
Sabbath. A living prophet would address the assembled
exiles, confession would be made of the sins that had led to
their captivity and prayer offered to God for restoration to
the home-land. With the institution of the Synagogue there
was associated a more spiritual worship than with the Temple
as prayer took the place of sacrifice and the congregation met
for worship and instruction in the Law. By the time of the
return from exile synagogues had been established in every
Jewish community throughout the world and even after the
rebuilding of the Temple the synagogue retained its prestige.
To the Jew it was the bond of union throughout the whole
world. Wherever there were ten male householders there was
a synagogue and where the Jewish community was too small
for a synagogue there was a place of meeting under the open
sky. There were synagogues all over Palestine and in
Jerusalem they were arranged according to crafts. " By the
beginning of the Christian era, the synagogue was no longer

a surrogate for worship in the Temple but had attained an independent position as the seat of a worship of a different character, and regular instruction in religion had now found a place as an organic part of worship."

As an instrument of religious education the Synagogue was most effective. There the Pharisees expounded the Law to the people, maintaining that the Law had been given to the whole of Israel and that therefore its interpretation was not the exclusive privilege of the priests. The synagogue " was essentially an institution of laymen. Priests were not excluded and no doubt many of the Pharisees were priests. But no priest as such had any controlling function in the management of the synagogue. There the sole qualification was piety, knowledge of the Law and ability to communicate that knowledge; and that was not confined to any class of men. There was no one who held the same position in regard to the synagogue as is held by the minister of a Christian congregation. A Rabbi was only a layman; and such authority as he exercised rested on his own personal character and mental gifts. A Rabbi was ordained to his office; but that meant that he was recognised as competent to interpret and teach the Law. The worship of the synagogue was regulated by the members themselves under the leadership of those who, by gifts and character, were best fitted to lead. The prayers may have been usually recited by one person appointed for that duty, but members were called up to take part in the reading of the Law and the portion from the prophets. If a discourse was given after the prayers, it was given by someone in the opinion of the ruler of the synagogue best qualified to give it. There was no stated preacher. When Paul and his companions went to the synagogue in Antioch of Pisidia they were given the opportunity of speaking to the congregation, being merely visitors, not regular members, much less its appointed officers. It was in some such way that Jesus had his opportunity of speaking in the synagogue at Nazareth." Great importance was attached to the address and the synagogue was crowded on the occasion of the visit of a popular speaker. Because He spoke with authority and not as the scribes our Lord, as a synagogue preacher, must have exercised a tremendous power over the masses. It is worthy of note that He never gave up the custom of attending the synagogue on the Sabbath day.

The Temple.—On the occasion of the Passover Feast, falling immediately after His twelfth birthday, our Lord journeyed to Jerusalem to take part in the great service in the Temple. A conjectural restoration of the whole complex of edifices in the Temple in the time of our Lord is given as a frontispiece to Sanday's *Sacred Sites of the Gospels*. In 2G B.C. Herod set about the rebuilding of the Temple, and to allay Jewish fears collected all the material for the new building before the work of demolition on the old building was begun. The house and the inner court were built by a thousand priests in eighteen months, but the building of the other portions was not completed until 62-64 A.D. "Its eastern front was covered with plates of gold, which threw back the rays of the rising sun, and formed an object of rare beauty for miles around. The stone of which it was built was white marble, and a large part of the side walls were covered with gold." The outer court, five hundred and eighty-five feet East to West by six hundred and ten feet North to South, was enclosed by a wall pierced by eight gates, four on the western side, two on the southern, one on the northern and one on the eastern. The outer court surrounded by this wall was the Court of the Gentiles. On the inner side of the wall were built porticoes or porches, that on the east being "Solomon's Porch," so called because it was believed to be part of the original Temple of Solomon. The Court of the Gentiles was open to anybody and it was there that the animals for sacrifice were bought and sold, and the tables of the money-changers set up.

The inner court was a rectangle, including the women's court, the men's court (court of the Israelites), and the "house." Round the women's court was a stone parapet and on the 3 gates in the parapet were notices warning Gentiles not to pass this boundary. "No Gentile may enter within the balustrade and embankment round the sacred place. Whoever is caught will be answerable for his death, which will ensue." Just as the Gentile might not pass beyond the Court of the Gentiles, so a Jewess might not pass beyond the Court of the Women. The inner court was surrounded by a wall with 9 gates, with folding doors covered with gold and silver. The Gate Beautiful, the central one, measured 56 by 40 cubits and required the combined efforts of 20 men to open and close it. Within the women's court were some of the 13 boxes for contributions to the "treasury"—the remainder being in the court of the men. The boxes were narrow at the top and wide at the bottom and were therefore known as "trumpets." Into one of these the widow cast her mite. In the corners of the court of the women were 4 enclosures, one for priests who, owing to some temporary

c

defect, had to withdraw from duty, one for cleansed "lepers" who washed before showing themselves to the priests at the Nicanor Gate, one for the Nazirites who shaved their heads and prepared their peace-offering, and one for oil and wine to be used as drink-offering.

The Court of the Women was separated from the Court of the Israelites by a large gate, "Nicanor's Gate," where those who came to be pronounced free from uncleanness of any kind "stood before the Lord." There Simeon took our Lord in his arms and blessed Him. Within the men's court was the Priests' Court with enclosures for sacrificial victims, for storing salt and wood, for changing vestments, etc. Normally this court was reserved for priests but occasionally a layman might, in accordance with the Law, enter this court to lay his hands upon a victim about to be slain. In the east of this court was the altar of burnt-offering, with 2 holes for the sacrificial blood and refuse which passed underground to the Kidron. To the altar also were attached rings for fastening down the sacrificial animals and near-by were tables on which they were cut up.

The actual "House of God" was divided into two parts, "the Holy Place" and "the Most Holy Place," the latter being entered only once a year by the High Priest on "the Day of Atonement" on behalf of the Jewish race. Only priests might enter "the Holy Place" and bring in the incense, place fresh bread on the Table of Shewbread and trim the lamp. The priests and Levites were responsible for the sacred enclosure and were grouped into 24 courses, each course doing duty for a week. They were many in number; Josephus (born in 37 A.D.) states that there were 200 for the gates alone. "The qualification for the priesthood was severe. Family history was very important, and the first inquiry by the Sanhedrin always related to the candidate's genealogy. If he failed to satisfy the court about his perfect legitimacy he was veiled in black and removed. If he passed this ordeal, he was examined for bodily defects, of which 140 were tabulated as permanent disqualifications and 22 as temporary. Those who stood the twofold test were dressed in white raiment and their names were entered on a roll."

In this lesson stress should be laid on the impression made upon the mind of our Lord by His first visit to the Temple and His all-absorbing interest, even at that early age, in religion. Daily in the Temple porch during the Passover week the rabbis expounded the Law and gave every opportunity to the pilgrims to raise objections, ask questions and take part in the discussions. Joseph and Mary set off for home after the third day of the festival but our Lord was so absorbed in the Temple discussions that He did not note the absence of the Nazareth caravan. He felt that He must respond to a higher call than that even of His parents. " Wist ye not that I must be in my Father's house?"

The teacher should stress the fact that already as a boy our Lord realised that the one thing He must do was the will of His Father. (A simple sketch of the Herodian Temple such as the teacher might reproduce on the blackboard is appended.)

JOHN THE BAPTIST—*Matthew* iii. 1-6.

To understand the significance of John the Baptist and to interpret his message we ought to know something of the background of his preaching : we must trace out the development of the Messianic Hope. From the beginning Israel had but one king, Jehovah. God entered into a covenant with Abraham and the history of Israel is the story of this covenant relationship. As far back as the age of the Patriarchs there is the idea of a kingdom of God, a kingdom in which God is sovereign. In Abraham shall all the families of the earth be blessed. Israel is to form a kingdom whose members are consecrated to God and Israel will be the medium of divine blessings to the Gentiles.

In the period of the monarchy the kings of Israel reigned as the representatives of God. They embodied the divine rule and were set over Israel by God. But the expansion of the kingdom meant a change in the administration of justice. In place of the tribal elders who administered the law of God in the interests of the whole community the king and a governing class acted for purely selfish ends. Between rich and poor there was a great gulf fixed. The weak and the helpless were at the mercy of those who sat in the seats of the mighty. As the champions of the oppressed there appeared the prophets who in the name of an outraged God demanded justice. In the reign of Jeroboam II.—a period of great material prosperity—Israel looked for the " Day of the Lord," a day of triumph for the nation, a day of still greater prosperity. The smoke of the sacrifices that rose to the sky attested the devotion of the people to God's service and was a guarantee of the continuance of divine favour. But God's Moral character was overlooked and Amos came forward with a message of doom, of a Day of the Lord that would be darkness and not light. To Amos and his prophetic

successors in the 8th and 7th centuries B.C., the " Day " which
is near is one in which God will manifest Himself in His
full power and glory. The wicked will be destroyed, but
because God chose Israel He will not make a full end of
His people. By their faithfulness a remnant of the righteous
shall live and form the nucleus of a kingdom of God, and at
the head of this new kingdom of the future will be a
descendant of David.

With the return from Exile—a period when the religious
life of the Jews took on new forms—faith in the ultimate
triumph of God's kingdom became a fixed idea. The post-
exilic prophets proclaimed that God would deliver His people
and establish His kingdom for ever. Jerusalem would arise
from her ruins, peace would reign throughout the earth even
in the animal kingdom. Israel as a righteous nation would
walk in the statutes of God and her oppressors would be
swept away. But prior to the advent of God as Redeemer
there would be vast world-movements, portents in the earth
and in the heavens, trials for Israel and visitations upon the
Gentiles. As the precursors of the Messianic Era there
would be Messianic Woes, times of tribulation and distress
before Israel could enter into her inheritance.

The hopes that centred round the Second Temple were
not realised. Israel, crushed under the heel of the nations,
gave way to despair. But she was the chosen of God and
God, it was believed, would vindicate her in the eyes of the
peoples. But how was vindication to come? In one way
only—by the intervention of God. God would bring in the
Golden Age, the supernatural order, the Kingdom of Heaven.
Thus beginning with the Book of Daniel (165 B.C.) there grew
up a vast literature called Apocalyptic that dealt with this
coming Kingdom of Heaven. With this expectation of a
new kingdom was associated the belief that it would be
founded by the Messiah, the Anointed. His function would
be that of ruling the new kingdom in justice, wisdom and
goodness. In His days the knowledge of God would be
poured out on the earth as the waters of the sea. There
would be a society delivered from all spiritual evil, while in
the material world pain would cease and toil be marvellously
rewarded. " Healing will descend in dew and anxiety and
anguish and lamentation will pass from among men and
gladness will proceed through the whole earth. The reapers
will not grow weary nor those that build be toilworn. The
earth will yield its fruit tenthousandfold, and those who have
hungered will rejoice." The Messiah as the supreme repre-

sentative of God, having the Spirit of God dwelling in Him, would be a worker of miracles and, fulfilling all the functions of a true prophet and loyal king, would make known God's will to mankind. Through Him God would break in upon the world to lighten its darkness and to effect the regeneration of man. Through Him not only Israel but all the nations of the earth would find salvation for His kingdom would embrace all peoples. The world of nature and of man would undergo miraculous transformation. The wilderness and the solitary place would be glad, the desert would rejoice and blossom like the rose. The eyes of the blind would be opened and the ears of the deaf unstopped. For the new kingdom, the heavenly city, would be ushered in by the Superhuman Son of Man, endowed with the fulness of wisdom and righteousness, of glory and might, exalted above all other spiritual beings.

When a Jew heard the message "the Kingdom of God is at hand" he understood that message to mean the establishment of God's rule upon earth. But there were varying conceptions as to the meaning of God's rule. In addition to the spiritual conception of the Messiah outlined above there was the nationalistic conception. The Jews were the chosen people. "Us and us only hath God known of all the families of the earth," they said. They prided themselves on their exclusiveness. Moreover they had suffered grievous persecution at the hands of the Gentiles, and in many minds the hope of a Messiah was centred on a Messiah, a descendant of David who would set up a Jewish kingdom with its central seat of worship and rule in Jerusalem, a Messiah who would bring destruction upon Israel's enemies. Such Gentiles as escaped destruction would but live to show the triumph of God's people.

In the century preceding the birth of our Lord the Jews not only looked for the coming of the Messiah but they drew a sharp cleavage between this age and the age that He would introduce. The most decisive characteristic of the Apocalyptic is the contrast between "this age" and "the age to come." The present order is altogether under the power of evil, of Satan and his hosts. Evil spirits hold mankind in thrall and cause sickness, disease and death. In the coming kingdom God will reign supreme in the person of His Messiah. Thrones will be set and before the Messiah will be gathered men of all kindreds and tongues, and the dead will be raised to receive their reward. The righteous will enjoy all the blessings of the New Age from which the unrighteous will be excluded. This judgment will be the end of the age-long conflict between good and evil and with the destruction of Satan and his hosts the present age will pass away. In a world renewed and purged of evil heaven and earth will become one.

In the reign of Herod the Great belief in the nearness of the kingdom of God had grown to fever-heat in the Jewish mind. Herod was a hated Idumean and reigned in virtue of the goodwill of Rome, an alien power. Surely God could not for long tolerate this state of affairs! He must establish His kingdom. So when John the Baptist suddenly appeared proclaiming the long-looked for kingdom he created a profound impression. John was a Nazirite, dedicated to God's service from infancy, forbidden to cut his hair or to touch intoxicating liquor. He spent much of his time in the wilderness of Judaea in communion with God and in meditation upon the religious life and outlook of his time. That he lived as hermit and ascetic is by no means strange. In that age there were many communities of ascetics who lived in the wilderness. Josephus lived for three years in the desert " and used no other clothing than came from the trees, and had no other food than that which grew of its own accord, and bathed himself in cold water, both day and night, to preserve his purity." John lived on " locusts and wild-honey." Among the Bedouin locusts are thrown into boiling water with salt and after being dried and cleaned are packed in bags, to be fried in butter or honey when used for food. John paid occasional visits to the villages and to Jerusalem, and disgusted with what he saw of gaiety, luxury, poverty and vice, retired to his hermitage. He saw that the Pharisees were zealous for the Law and that the lives of the common people remained unhallowed; that the priests were zealous for the maintenance of the Temple services but had waxed fat on their extortions; that the nation believed in the nearness of the kingdom but showed no evidence of preparation for its coming.

John felt the call of God and like Moses and Elijah left the desert to proclaim the divine message to men. Not for centuries had a prophet appeared in Israel and when this mysterious figure with long flowing locks and clad in a coarse cloak of camel's hair leapt into view men mused in their hearts whether he were the Messiah or not. John insisted that he was the Forerunner. When a king was on a journey the population, without fee, levelled and cut and prepared the road, and on the completion of the highway, forerunners or heralds went in advance proclaiming his coming. In Persia heralds still run in front of a governor's carriage or horse, to clear the road. John insisted that he was the herald of One the latchet of whose sandals he was unworthy to unloose. To refer to the shoes of an ordinary person was " bad form " as the feet were ceremonially unclean, and John, in confessing his unworthiness to carry the shoes of the Coming One, indicated the inferiority of his own work as forerunner, in contrast to that of the coming Messiah.

John's message was a message of repentance. " Repent ye, for the Kingdom of Heaven is at hand." To him the ethical demands of the Law were primary. For all who in the coming kingdom would stand before the judgment-throne of the Messiah and be deemed worthy of eternal life John demanded a moral preparation, a change of heart, the manifestation in their lives of justice, mercy and truth. He asked that tax-gatherers take no more than their due, that soldiers do not rob, that the rich give of their abundance to their less fortunate brethren, and that all who joined his fellowship be honest with one another.

Baptism was the symbol of a changed life and when John was convinced of the repentance of those who came to him he baptised them in the Jordan. His use of the rite followed Jewish usage. Proselytes to Judaism underwent the rite of immersion. According to Old Testament prophecy the rite was to be a sign of the age of the Messiah. " In that day there will be a fountain opened to the house of David and to the inhabitants of Jerusalem, for sin and uncleanness." To John baptism symbolised spiritual regeneration. It was evidence of repentance on the part of those who had received it, a passport to the Kingdom when they came before the Messiah in the Judgment. We tend to underrate the service that John rendered as Forerunner. " Here was a man who stabbed the soul of Israel awake . . . a man who spoke with the old fire and purpose and a bravery that faced kings unafraid. The return of the prophet was as news that the long absent, the long-looked for God had come back at last. . . . He drew the religion of his people from festering insurrection to wholesome regeneration. . . . To pull a people out of the sour brooding and melancholy of generations, to draw their gloating gaze from the expected slaughter of their tyrant oppressors, to stir them to face the leanness of their own souls, and persuade their steps towards the grand and simple landmarks of morality, was to effect a profound revolution. . . . This grand recall of Israel to the moral commandments was to prepare the essential atmosphere in which a Messiah could come with saving power."

The Baptism of Jesus—*Mark* i. 9-11.

The news of John's appearance as a prophet spread like wildfire. The people believed themselves to be down-trodden by Rome and were ready to listen to any message that offered hope of deliverance. John moved up the river from the fords of Jordan followed by large crowds, and when news of his activities reached our Lord it must have been to Him as a summons to His public ministry. He "took His place in the queue of those wanting to see the new teacher and presented Himself as a candidate for baptism." What did His baptism signify to our Lord? John's baptism was not merely a symbol of cleansing from ceremonial and moral impurities. It was a rite of initiation into a fellowship of believers who shared his expectation of the coming kingdom and accepted his demand for righteousness as the condition of initiation. Our Lord also proclaimed that the kingdom of God was at hand. He shared John's faith. So His baptism signified for Him His unity of faith with John and perhaps a sense of indebtedness to John as Forerunner. It symbolised too a break with the past. Our Lord had given up the Nazareth workshop and entered upon His calling as Redeemer. Originally baptism was a death by drowning, "held to be propitiatory for the offerer and meritorious in the victim," and to our Lord baptism symbolised consecration to His redemptive mission, to the sacrificial life even unto death for humanity's sake. St Mark tells us that He had a Vision of a Dove descending upon Him and heard a Voice from Heaven, the expression in symbolical form of a personal experience of the whole power of God at His disposal for His redemptive work, an experience of the divine approval of His self-surrender. His baptism also symbolised His identification with sinful humanity in its desire for new life. The Jewish religious leaders separated themselves from the community and prided themselves on their exclusiveness. The Pharisee pledged himself in the presence of three associates that he would not eat or drink in the presence of an ignorant man, that he would not travel in his company, that he would buy nothing from him, nor sell him any of the products of the soil. The Saviour of the world on the other hand identified Himself with the sinner and the outcast whom He had come to save.

JESUS PREPARING—THE TEMPTATIONS—*Matthew* iv. 1-11.

The first question that our Lord had to answer after His call was what Messiahship involved, what kind of Messiah He was going to be. Only in solitude, alone with His Father, could He solve this problem. And so we read that " He was led up into the wilderness to be tempted of the devil." We must picture Him alone amongst the rocks of the Wilderness of Judaea battling with His spiritual problem, the mental tension such that He was indifferent to the needs of the body. He was an hungered for 40 days. That statement can be accepted literally or the number 40 may be a round number to signify a long period. After the fast there came the first temptation—" Command that these stones be made bread." The temptations must be interpreted in light of the Messianic ideas of the time. In the Messianic kingdom, it was believed, all physical ills would be banished; there would be no more pain, nor sorrow nor crying, for the former things would be done away. That our Lord passionately desired the elimination of pain and suffering and want from God's world is evident from His healing miracles. That He longed for the transformation of human life is abundantly clear. Why not turn stones into bread? Why not come forward as a " bread-and-butter " Messiah and banish hunger and pain and physical suffering? " As He reflected on this prospect of the kingdom—the transformed earth from which the ills of life had been removed—Jesus would discern that this was only a different if higher version of a Canaan flowing with milk and honey. . . . The gift of Canaan had been to a desert people like the turning of stones into bread. But that transformed existence had not brought spiritual health to Israel." Our Lord recognised that the soul of reformation is the reformation of the soul, that the first essential was not the relief of physical suffering but a sure grasp of God and such a self-surrender to God as would lead to the abolition of suffering and to the transformation of human life. He set the temptation aside by an appeal to the Old Testament. " Man shall not live by bread alone, but by every word which proceedeth out of the mouth of God." To-day the spiritual needs of men are greater by far than their physical ones. All thinking people recognise that the self-surrender of the peoples of the world to God would lead at once to a miraculous transformation in the world-situation and in economic conditions.

The second temptation was a temptation to seek personal glory, to take the short road to success, to force recognition of His Messiahship, to gain an unmoral victory, to entice men into the Kingdom of God by miracles and magic rather than to win them by love. The Jews of His age thought of the kingdom as a kingdom descending from God, a kingdom to be set up by divine intervention. God was conceived as a Miracle-worker and many were ready to revolt against Rome, "to make a daring bid for destiny, a blind leap from the pinnacle of the Temple" in the belief that God would send His angel hosts to succour Israel and to bear her up. Our Lord was tempted to court a crisis, to demand from God a sign in vindication of His Chosen before the whole world. He put the temptation aside by an appeal to the Old Testament. "Thou shalt not tempt the Lord, thy God." Religion is not magic. God cannot be put to tests and played with and treated as a fetish. Although the want of religion is the cause of much suffering, mental and physical, religion is not an "escape-mechanism" from life.

In the third temptation "the devil taketh Him up to an exceeding high mountain and sheweth Him all the kingdoms of the world and the glory of them and saith all these things will I give Thee if Thou wilt fall down and worship me." Galilee was Galilee of the Gentiles, a busy commercial centre, permeated by Greek culture. From His home in Nazareth as a boy our Lord "could see all the fullness of the many-coloured life of Galilee spread before Him. The caravans toiling wearily from Egypt, the pilgrims climbing up from the fords of the Jordan, the long train of Arab camels, and the merchants of Damascus, all passed within easy view. Or, if the boy looked northwards, there was the highway between Acre and the Decapolis, with troops and merchantmen coming and going, and princes and noblemen journeying on business of State or pleasure. Now and then the sound of the Roman trumpets would waken the village, and the long, dusty, iron ranks would swing past in the valley under the eagles; while all the stories of Rome and of the subject princes, the Herods and the like, would be common talk around the village doors." How was our Lord to win this Gentile world? Israel, He knew, as the custodian of divine truth, had a sublime mission to the Gentile world. The kingdom of the Messiah must embrace all peoples.

The civilisation of the Gentile world with its culture, its law and its order must have made a powerful appeal to Him. Why not capture it by compromise? Why not come to terms with the world powers? Why confine His mission to His own people? That would have meant the worship of the devil. "It would have been to evade the particular issue He

had raised and the vocation to which He was called. Jesus
had called Israel to repentance, and He stood for certain
truths about God, His forgiving love, the presence of His
kingdom, the spirituality of His ways. He had heard a call
in His soul to witness to the character and purpose of God,
and from that vocation there was no escape. . . . For Jesus
to have failed to take the way of the Cross would be to
have shown that He was not righteous; it would have meant
that He was untrue to His real nature, and over against this,
bodily comfort and all that the non-spiritual world could give
would be no compensation. To have failed would have been
to have lost the objects of His holy and Divine quest, for it
would have meant the failure of love, and that which
was needed to reach the hearts of men would have been
lacking; they would have been left derelict." He set the
temptation aside again by an appeal to the Old Testament.
" Thou shalt worship the Lord thy God, and Him only shalt
thou serve."

CALLING THE DISCIPLES—THE FISHERMEN—*Mark* i. 16-20.

Galilee, unlike dry and sterile Judaea, was well watered
and fertile. It owed its fertility to the streams that coursed
down the snow-clad slopes of Lebanon and Hermon. So
abundant was the olive that it was said : " It is easier to raise
a legion of olives in Galilee than to bring up a child in
Judaea." In the time of our Lord the province was densely
populated. Josephus tells us that there were 240 cities and
villages in Galilee with 3 million inhabitants. The people
were volcanic like their district. They differed from the
Judaeans, says the Talmud, in that they cared for honour
rather than for money, and in their hearts the hope of deliverance from Roman rule burned fierce and intense. They were
despised by the cultured Judaeans who sneered at their uncouth
speech. " Can any good thing come out of Nazareth? " they
asked; " Out of Galilee ariseth no prophet," they said. These
utterances expressed their contempt for a province whose
splendid network of roads kept her in close touch with the
Gentile world and made her inhabitants less bigoted and in-
tolerant than those of the South.

The Sea of Galilee was the centre of Galilean life.
" Imagine that wealth of water, that fertility . . . those great
highways, that numerous population, that commerce and
industry, those strong Greek influences—imagine them all
crowded into a deep valley, under an almost tropical heat,
and round a blue lake, and you have before you the conditions

in which Christianity arose and Christ Himself chiefly laboured." The Lake, called variously the Sea of Galilee, the Sea of Tiberias, the Lake of Gennesaret, measuring 13 miles by 8, provided the main food supply of the poor in the form of fish. The fish were caught with "cast nets" and "drag nets," the former being circular with lead weights around the fringe and cast by the fisherman from the bank or from the water. The net fell like a ring enclosing the fish, the weights were drawn together and the catch pulled ashore. The drag net was similar to that used by salmon-fishers to-day and was used in the same way.

The lakeside was dotted with buildings, the chief "city" being Tiberias, founded by Herod Antipas and therefore anathema to the Jew. Capernaum was the centre of a prosperous fishing trade and of a boat-building industry. It is identified with Tell Hum where the spade of the excavator has unearthed a magnificent synagogue, 78 feet by 59, which may have been the structure in which our Lord delivered some of His discourses. There were other towns, such as Magdala, famous for its purple dyes, Emmaus with its medicinal baths to which people flocked in thousands to be healed of disease, Bethsaida with its perennial green, Gadara, a few miles inland (not in Galilee), with its amphitheatre and acropolis, and Taricheae with its hippodrome and fish-curing yards. Our Lord's Galilean ministry, then, "was cast not in a secluded country district—a backwater of the great world-stream—but in a district far more populous, far more commercial, far more permeated by outside influences than was Judaea. Galilee gave to Jesus a race of men far readier to receive the new truth than the stubborn men of Judaea; but it gave Him and His Apostles also the Open Door, by which the word of truth could go forth, east, west, south and north, to the conquest of all the nations whose representatives thronged the cities of Galilee, and crowded its busy roads."

While recognising that there is a salvation of individuals through the community, our Lord saw clearly that there is a salvation of the community through individuals. Anticipating the findings of modern psychology He recognised that the solution of the problem of the individual is the only sure road to the solution of the problems of society. Therefore He addressed Himself to individuals who would form the nucleus of the kingdom that would save the world. From the throngs that followed Him He selected twelve, "that they might be with Him and that He might send them forth to preach." These were to be the salt of the earth, the light of the world, fishers of men. In them the principles of the Kingdom of God were to be realised. Our Lord summoned them to follow Him, to sublimate those instincts that made them successful fishermen, to consecrate them to the service of God and to embark on a greater quest than the quest for fish.

It is almost certain that Andrew and Simon Peter were acquainted with our Lord before they responded to His call. The Fourth Gospel suggests that they were followers of John the Baptist and they may have been present at our Lord's baptism. Simon was called Peter or Cephas, the Rock, because of his confession of our Lord's Messiahship. A born leader and the spokesman of the disciples he was yet prone to act on the impulse of the moment. That he was a rough, uncultured peasant is incredible in view of the speeches that he made after the Ascension and at Pentecost. After Pentecost he healed a cripple at the Gate Beautiful and such was his power as a healer that " they brought forth the sick into the streets, and laid them on beds and couches, that at the least the shadow of Peter passing by might overshadow some of them." He took part in the evangelisation of Samaria and was responsible for the admission of the first Gentile— Cornelius—to the Christian Church. The tradition is that he died a martyr's death at Rome during the Neronian persecution and there is a beautiful story that as he fled from the city he encountered our Lord, and having asked, " Quo vadis? " (" Whither goest thou? "), he received the answer : " To Rome to be crucified a second time for thee " : whereupon he turned back to meet his death.

Andrew, his brother, a disciple of John the Baptist, appears in the role of evangelist from the first. He brings Peter to Christ and may have had to do with the call of Philip. When our Lord fed the hungry multitude it was Andrew that brought the lad with his loaves and fishes. The Greeks who desired to be presented to our Lord made application to Philip who reported to Andrew. According to tradition Andrew was crucified at Patrae and part of his cross is enclosed in one of the four piers of the dome of St Peter's at Rome.

Zebedee, the father of James and John, was a man of substance, the owner of a boat, with hired servants. His wife, Salome, accompanied our Lord on certain of His missionary journeys and on one occasion requested for her sons posts of honour in the Kingdom of God. James and John were called by our Lord " Sons of Thunder " because of their impetuosity. They asked Him to imitate Elijah and call down divine vengeance upon the Samaritans who had refused Him hospitality. They desired to prohibit an exorcist from exercising his gift because he was not of their company. " Master, we saw one casting out devils in thy name, and we forbade him because he followeth not us." James, probably the elder of the two, was the first of the Twelve to suffer martyrdom, the victim of Herod Agrippa's cruelty. John, although not occupying a prominent place in the Gospel story, is " the Jonathan of the New Testament." He was present at the raising of Jairus' daughter and at the Transfiguration. At the Last Supper John had a special place at the table. Peter, James and John were together in Gethsemane. John was at the foot of the cross and was entrusted by our Lord with the care of His mother. With Peter he visited the tomb and was the first of the two to recognise that the Lord has risen. He was present with Peter at the healing of the lame man at the Gate Beautiful and he accompanied Peter to Samaria in order to bestow the gift of the Holy Ghost on Philip's converts. There is a tradition that he lived till the reign of Trajan (100 A.D.).

LEVI—*Luke* v. 27-28.

The fifth member of the most living and intimate circle is Levi, the publican, who collected taxes at the customhouse on the quays. Rome put up the position of taxcollector to auction and purchase was made by wealthy companies who engaged publicans or taxgatherers to levy on their behalf and as many of these were men of doubtful character there was often cruel extortion. In Judaea the taxes were paid through the procurator but in Galilee payment was made to Herod Antipas, the tetrarch. In the time of our Lord the publican sat at the receipt of custom, at the gate of the town, assessing the dues on exports and levying toll. Capernaum, with its big fishing trade, must have provided large revenues. The only tax recognised by the Jew as legitimate was the Temple-tax for the maintenance of the Temple services. For a Jew to take the oath of allegiance and act as a servant of the Emperor was not only unpatriotic and degrading but was a serious religious offence. He was regarded as a disreputable character, an outcast, and the door of the synagogue was closed against him. But many of these Jewish " publicans," like Levi and Zacchaeus, must have been fine men who appreciated the advantages to their country of Roman administration and were proud to serve under Rome. At the outset of their career they probably exacted no more than their due but in the end repaid hate with hate and waxed rich on wrongful gains. Our Lord recognised that their souls still lived though almost buried within their golden tombs. Had they been no more than publicans He would have left them to their gold-telling but it was " the something more " that aroused His interest and His ministry was peculiarly acceptable to them. St Luke tells us that there " drew near unto Him all the publicans and sinners for to hear Him." One can imagine that the four fishermen disciples would scarcely welcome the presence of Levi in the inner circle and would resent our Lord's extending to him the hand of friendship. But they would soon appreciate the transformation that contact with the personality of our Lord effected not only in themselves but in the wily publican, and they would be knit together in the bond of fellowship. Our Lord was no respecter of persons and recognised no caste barriers or class distinctions.

OUR LORD AS HEALER.

The Gospels in their present form come to us from the hands of editors that have brought together from various sources the oral tradition that came down to them. This Tradition may be divided into Sayings, Parables, Miracles and Passion Narrative. Our Lord gained fame as a healer of mental and physical disease and stories of His mighty deeds were in circulation in His own lifetime. In Palestine in His day disorders of the mind and certain diseases of the body were attributed to the activity of demons. Behind the material world there was supposed to be a whole legion of demons, with Satan or Beelzebub at their head, and it was the common belief that when the Messiah came He would bring these spirits into subjection and set their victims free. Our Lord accepted the psychological ideas of the time and cast out devils—evidence to His contemporaries that the Messianic Age had come. His miracles were an essential part of His revelation of God as Love. In Him men saw God in action, relieving pain and restoring to the demented the kindly light of reason.

The ancient Roman ideal of health was a sound mind in a sound body. Without a sound mind there cannot be a sound body, and without a sound body there cannot be a sound mind. Mental science has for long been alive to the influence of the body upon the mind, but only of recent years has it begun to study the influence of the mind upon the body. Not only are psychological methods of treatment proving a success but they are forcing the medical profession to reconsider many foregone conclusions. "Medical men are seriously considering the question of mental healing, inquisitively searching out the laws which govern the process and endeavouring to correlate the outward manifestations of a psychological phenomenon with their exact clinical knowledge. These psychological phenomena are no longer despised as they were in the nineteenth century; no longer are they looked upon by the learned as trickery, lies and humbug. Unobtrusively there is creeping into the medical man's attitude a desire not merely to know the diseases from which mankind suffers but to know the personality of the patient as well."

Diseases to-day are classified as either functional or organic, those that have their origin in the mind and those that have their origin in the body. Just as the latter—e.g., chronic alcoholism—may produce mental disorder, so the former may manifest themselves in physical symptoms. Certain forms of deafness, blindness, asthma, stammering, paralysis, gastro-intestinal disorder, hysteria, are bodily manifestations of internal mental conflict and dissociation. St Paul's blindness on the Damascus Road may have been functional, a self-punishment for his long unwillingness to see the truth of the Christian Gospel. As before the spiritual experience he had been spiritually blind, so now he is physically blind. Functional disorders are the result of disintegration of personality, and only by the unmasking of motives and restoring wholeness to the personality can a cure be effected.

That many of the sufferers who came to our Lord for healing were functional cases appears evident, but that they were all functional cases cannot be proved. There is a tendency in some quarters to deny the possibility of "organic" disease responding to spiritual treatment. But we can set no limits to the power of mind over body. There is no illness in which the mind does not play its part, there is no organic disease in which the fundamental possibility of mental or spiritual influence can be denied. A man suffering from an apparently incurable "organic" disease may have strong psychological reasons—of which he may not be conscious—for opposing his own recovery, and if his motives for clinging to his illness are exposed, recovery may take place. In our imperfect knowledge we can set no limits to the power of the

mind in maintaining health and aiding recovery from disease.
Masters, in *The Conquest of Disease,* says : " Will-power has
helped many a person to overcome tuberculosis, as is proved
by the case of Dr D. Macdougall King, the brother of Mr
Mackenzie King, the Prime Minister of Canada. Some time
ago Dr Lazarus Barlow, the famous physician, instanced two
cases of women whose will-power enabled them to overcome
that awful disease—cancer. The one case was in hospital for
three years and then recovered. The other was an even more
remarkable case. She had suffered for eighteen years and
had spent fourteen years in hospital. Everybody except
herself looked upon her case as hopeless. In spite of her
sufferings she maintained a cheerful spirit, and the will to
get well was so strong within her that she actually triumphed
over the disease. What enabled her to vanquish the disease? Did she, by exercising her will-power, bring about
some chemical change in her body which affected the disease
and eliminated it? . . . Illness, when it affects the human
organism, brings the defensive forces instinctively into play ;
the effort is unconscious. The mind itself is powerless to
produce antitoxins ; only the germs or their poisons in the
human organism can do that. But can the mind consciously
call certain defensive forces into play, can it set the unseen
forces fighting for health? A man stricken with a slight
illness makes up his mind he is going to die and dies. Another man, whose condition seems desperate, makes up his
mind he is going to live and recovers. What are these
magical forces over which the mind appears to have control,
and how do they operate? "

The methods employed by psychotherapy are three—persuasion, suggestion and analysis. Treatment by persuasion
aims at readjustment by argument, at healing the patient by
showing him the absurdity of his belief in the reality of his
illness. If a man says that he cannot walk and if it can
be proved to him that he can if he will, he may recover the
use of his limbs. The success of persuasion depends upon the
degree of .faith in and love for the person of the healer.
Suggestion is the process by which an idea is accepted without logical grounds for its acceptance. Freud has shown
that the power of the hypnotist depends upon the *suggestibility* of the patient and that this suggestibility depends upon
a love-tie between them. Suggestion implies a personal relationship between two individuals who must be *en rapport* if
suggestions are to be accepted and realised. The child is

D

more suggestible than the adult because it has more faith
and love, and instead of speaking of a " tendency " to accept
suggestions we should rather speak of a " tendency " to trust
and love. If a suggestion is to be realised, faith and love
are necessary. Finally, there are the methods of analysis
employed by the various schools which, instead of disposing
of the symptoms, reach the underlying causes of the symptoms, unmask the motives responsible for the disease, and so
restore the patient to health. It is obvious that, as methods,
persuasion and suggestion are inadequate. They may dispose
of the symptoms and the relief may be permanent, but unless
they touch the moral cause of the ailment they cannot result
in " health."

Of late years there has been a revival of interest in faith-
healing in Church circles as a result of the apparent successes
achieved by faith-healing missions. It is essential that the
same distinction must be made between faith-healing and
spiritual healing, as has just been drawn between healing by
persuasion and suggestion and healing by analysis. Faith
may dispose of the symptom, but unless it leads to a readjustment of the inner life and an outpouring of love there
can be no spiritual health. Let us consider the methods of
Coué. Coué professed to cure people *en masse,* irrespective
of the nature of their disorders. He simply required of them
that they repeat his formula so many times per day in a
certain way. The success of his and of all such methods is
a phenomenon of group psychology. The followers of Coué
formed a group with Coué as leader, the bond between them
being a love-bond. The leader professed to be able to
banish all ills by the formula : " Day by day and in every way
I get better and better." Those who attended his meetings
identified themselves with him, they used the leader's
formula, their faith in their own powers was intensified, there
was a rise in their self-esteem. The words "in every way "
absolved them from thinking of their specific complaints as
they uttered the formula. As members of a group they had
formed a love-tie, they were therefore credulous and suggestible. They realised that others had illnesses and their interest was displaced from illness to the power of self-mastery.
" Where a powerful impetus has been given to group formation," says Freud, " neuroses may diminish and at all events
temporarily disappear."

In all mass movements of this kind cures transient or
lasting are constantly effected. Without minimising the ex-

cellent results that may be achieved in some cases, it cannot be admitted that the patients have been set free from their bondage. There has been no transformation of self-love into object-love, and the diseases of which the physical ailments are but symptoms are the result of self-love. Freud says: " We must love in order that we may not fall ill, and we must fall ill if in consequence of frustration we cannot love." Adler states that " all psychopathology is of the nature of egoism." A patient who believes in his doctor may by rubbing his brow with a piece of camphor be relieved of a nervous headache, and the same result may be achieved by a clergyman anointing him with oil or laying his hands upon him. If these are magical rites they can never lead to spiritual health. The headache may be due to a desire to shirk work or it may be the product of some unholy, repressed wish; and until the motive has been disclosed and the patient made to face and fight out his conflict his last state is no better than his first. He is restored to health only when his self-love has been transformed into object-love.

Our Lord stands apart—apart from all psychotherapists and faith-healers of to-day. He not only healed the sick. He stilled the storm. He raised the dead. As there is no salvation in the narrow sense so there is no health apart from God. Our Lord demanded faith in God, the Father, or in Himself, a faith which implied the outpouring of love, such a faith as alone could effect a cure.

" When an individual is brought into relation with a personality of the moral purity and spiritual power of our Lord," writes Hadfield, " the adjustment of his life is healthy. In true spiritual healing we are brought into personal relation with a God who is as perfect as we can conceive Him. In the Christian religion we discover our ideal in the life and character of our Lord to whom our adjustment is made, and the personal relation between Him and the sufferer, pre-eminently a relation of love, can sweep away the repressing barriers of egotism and liberate the forces lying latent in the soul of the patient, restoring him to life and health. Every neurosis and functional nerve disorder is based on selfishness and a return to infantile egotism. Anything that can awaken the soul to real love will liberate it from its self-centredness and therefore incidentally from its neurotic symptoms. Every mission which seeks to achieve this conversion from selfishness to love will inevitably be a healing mission. The " religious " man who remains a neurotic has not experienced that true miracle of religion."

Two Blind Men Cured—*Matthew ix. 27-31.*

This miracle is recorded only in St Matthew's Gospel. Our Lord demanded faith. "Believe ye that I am able to do this?" And receiving an answer in the affirmative, He touched their eyes. He made use of the conventional form. Just as the bottle of medicine prescribed by the medical practioner to-day is of great importance in the eyes of the patient, so in the time of our Lord to the touch there was attached great significance. It is probable, too, that the touch was a means of conveying power and evoking love. Blindness was prevalent in Palestine owing to the dust and sand and exposure of the eyes to noxious dews on the house roofs, and to the carelessness of mothers in not driving away the flies that settled on their infants' eyes. But possibly the blindness of these two men was functional, due to some emotional disturbance. In this lesson emphasis should be laid on the majesty and mystery of One who could restore sight to the blind. "Who is this," men asked, "who opens the eyes of the blind?"

Draught of Fishes—*Luke v. 1-11.*

The story of the draught of fishes is found only in St Luke's Gospel and probably came from his special source. The fishermen had toiled all night and had caught nothing. Our Lord encountered them at the washing of their nets and requested them to put out a little from the land and let down their nets, and they had a record catch. There are no grounds for doubting the historicity of the story as in the Lake of Galilee fish moved about in dense shoals. How are we to interpret this incident? In the first place we must bear in mind that the New Testament rests upon an Old Testament background and that our Lord regarded Himself and was accepted by His followers as the fulfilment of Old Testament prophecy. Just as the healing of the two blind men was a literal fulfilment of the prophecy of Isaiah concerning the Messianic Age (Isaiah xxxv. 5), so in this incident our Lord fulfilled the words of the psalmist, "Thou hast put all things under His feet . . . the fish of the sea" (Psalm viii.). That a Carpenter should "sense" fish where fishermen failed was "a miracle of discernment" to Peter. He whose eye could pierce through the waters could see through Peter's heart. Was he fit to become a disciple? And so he fell down saying: "Depart from me, for I am a sinful man, O Lord."

In the second place, we must remember that the early Church gave a symbolic interpretation to all our Lord's miracles. In this story the symbolism is clear. As Peter fished all night and caught nothing so later as a fisher of men in Israel his labours were fruitless. Just as he showed reluctance to launch his boat out into the deep so later he was unwilling to go to the larger Gentile world with his message. But when he did put out into the Gentile world he drew a great draught. The two boats symbolised the Jewish and the Gentile sections of the early Church, and the breaking net the threatened disruption between them. "Many are the truths which shine out from the symbolism of this scene," writes Edersheim; "that call itself; the boat; the command of Christ despite the night of vain toil; the unlikely success; the net and its cast at the bidding of Christ, with the absolute certitude of result, where He is and when He bids; the miraculous direction to the spot; the multitude of fishes enclosed; the net about to break, yet not breaking; the surprise . . . and last of all, the lesson of self-knowledge and humiliation : all these and much more has the Church most truly read in this history. And this stands out to us as its final outcome and lesson : 'And when they had brought their ships to land, they forsook all and followed Him.' "

HEALING THE LEPER—*Mark* i. 40-45.

Leprosy was a terrible disease, a living death. The leper was treated as one dead, his rent garments, bare head and uncovered lip being evidence of his contact with the dead. The Jew spoke of leprosy as "the finger of God," the outward sign of sin and spiritual disease, and maintained that the one condition of restoration to health was repentance. The regulations for the treatment of lepers are given in Leviticus xiii. and xiv.

Our Lord in cleansing the leper clearly fulfilled the prophecy of Isaiah and gave further evidence that through Him God was in action for the salvation of man. He commanded the leper to show himself to the priest "as a testimony unto them," a testimony that the Messianic Age had come, that the kingdom of God was present in Him. The leper had to undergo ceremonies of purification and to present the offering required by the Law before he could be declared clean and re-enter the society of his fellows.

In the New Testament there are frequent references to the Law of Moses. What was this Law of Moses?

To begin with it was the Law revealed to Moses by God
at Mount Sinai, the Ten Commandments or the Ten Words.
But this Law naturally underwent expansion to meet the
changing needs of the Hebrew community. After the settlement in Canaan a fresh body of Law, largely ritualistic, came
into existence to meet the needs of an agricultural community.
But as it was but an expansion of the Mosaic Code and
Mosaic in principle it was still called the Law of Moses. The
priests at the local sanctuaries, and the prophets, gave the
people instruction in this Law. During the Exile new laws
came into being to preserve the purity of Hebrew religion
and to save it from extinction in the midst of a heathen environment but these laws were all such as might be deduced
from the original Law of Moses.

With the return from Exile we enter upon a new stage
of development. The Pentateuch—the first 5 books of the
Old Testament—was set apart as the canon of Scripture, the
Law of Moses, the teaching given by and through him, and
Ezra proclaimed this Law which God had given for their
direction. This Law was to be the Jew's authority and guide,
proclaiming, as it was believed, the will of God not only for
the Hebrew race but for each individual in the Hebrew community. From this time forward the religion of the Jew
became the religion of a book and his relationship to God
a legalistic one. Now this Law had to be applied to particular cases. Each individual was held responsible for keeping the Law and there arose in his life situations with which
the Law did not expressly deal. How could he obey the
Law? There must be interpreters—Scribes, they were
called—to explain the Law as occasion required. And so
there gradually accumulated unwritten laws to cover every
possible contingency of life. Laws had to be inferred from
the written Law to meet every possible emergency and to
safeguard the Jew from any possible infringement of the
divine commands. For example, a Jewish shopkeeper who
read in Proverbs that " a false balance is an abomination to
the Lord " and consulted a scribe for a ruling, was informed
that to do the will of God he ought to wipe his measures twice
per week, his weights once, and his scales every time he
used them. The Scribes ordained how many paces a man
might walk from his house on the Sabbath day without
breaking the Law and seriously debated the question as to
whether it was lawful to eat an egg laid on the Sabbath.
Their office became one of great importance and their words
were of more weight than those of the prophets. They even

regulated the ritual and practice of the priests and through their representatives in every village they controlled the life of the religious community. They were held in great respect, receiving a homage greater than that given to parents—and to the Jew the fifth commandment was the weightiest of the weighty commandments—and the authority which they exercised was that of the word of God. According to the light of the age in which they lived they were the best of men, animated by the purest of motives, viz., loyalty to God and to His revealed will for the life of mankind, and their aim was to make that Will effective throughout the whole of life.

But they made no distinction between laws ceremonial and laws moral. How could they? If all the laws were revealed to Moses by God, each must have the same value in the sight of God—a logical inference. The law in Deuteronomy xxii. 11 which says: "Thou shalt not wear a garment of divers sorts, as of woollen and linen together," was just as important as the law forbidding murder. Were they not both divine commands? The scribe held that it was not for man to argue about the relative importance of different laws, as they were all divine commands and therefore to be obeyed. Unfortunately in many cases there was a tendency to substitute external ordinances for the homage of the heart, and our Lord accused certain of those who prided themselves on their observance of the Law, of making clean the outside of the cup and the platter, while within they were full of extortion and excess, of tithing mint and anise and cummin, to the neglect of judgment, mercy and faith. The life of the sincerely religious man was made burdensome because he had to reckon not only with the 613 written precepts but with the unwritten law, the "tradition of the elders" against which our Lord directed His criticism. In contrast to the heavy burden laid upon men's shoulders by the scribes our Lord affirmed that His yoke was easy and His burden light. This "tradition of the elders" consisted of decisions formulated by each successive generation of scribes and handed on to their successors, and was of greater importance than the written Law. It was held that the whole Law, written and unwritten, had been imparted to Moses and that the function of the scribes was to make explicit what had been implicit from the beginning. To our Lord the unwritten Law was secondary. It killed the spirit of the Law by the load of outward observances which it imposed. It made the Law void.

In the healing of the leper, greater than the physical

miracle was the spiritual miracle in our Lord's break with Jewish convention. He touched the leper and that meant in the eyes of the community ceremonial defilement. The scribes ordained that a leper must be kept six feet away and must not be saluted. At the approach of a leper people either pelted him with stones or took to their heels.

Ten Lepers—*Luke* xvii. 11-19.

The teacher might ask : " Seeing that we have just taught a lesson about the cleansing of a leper, how can we be expected to teach another on the subject of leprosy? " The emphasis in the story of the ten lepers is not on the physical but on the spiritual miracle—our Lord's international mind and outlook. Our Lord bore witness not only by His teaching but in His life to the Fatherhood of God and the brotherhood of man, and this story makes clear the spirit that His followers must manifest to other races.

After the fall of Samaria in 722 B.C. the cream of the northern kingdom (Israel) was deported to Assyria and alien colonists were sent to take the place of the dispossessed. These aliens intermarried with the resident population and adopted their religion. Their descendants were the Samaritans, a mixed race. When Jerusalem fell in 586 B.C. there was a large deportation from Judah. In this case the Jewish exiles retained their racial purity and when, on their return from exile, they set about the rebuilding of the Temple they refused recognition to the Samaritans. The latter built a Temple on Mount Gerizim and from that time there was bitter enmity between the two kingdoms. A strict Galilean Jew when he went on a visit to Jerusalem made a long detour over the Jordan and through Peraea. He thus avoided the territory of the despised Samaritans, and saved himself the trouble that they were sure to occasion him. On the borders of Samaria and Galilee, however, Samaritan and Galilean lepers would be united by a common bond. They would band themselves together for mutual help. Our Lord made no distinction between them. His touch cleansed the lepers of Israel and the lepers of Samaria alike. Of the ten, however, who were cleansed but one returned to give expression to his gratitude, and that one a Samaritan. Here was a miracle indeed!

Feeding the Five Thousand—*Mark* vi. 35-46; *John* vi. 1-14.

The story of the feeding of the five thousand is recorded in the four Gospels and the four accounts should be carefully

compared. As God fed the Israelites with manna in the
wilderness so our Lord feeds the hungry multitude. Although
He refused to come forward as a " bread-and-butter " Messiah
our Lord never failed to meet the needs of suffering humanity.
" The touch of Jesus," writes Shafto, " did for the bread what
the touch of the soil does for the seed-corn.   One mystery is
really as great as the other, though we are accustomed to the
one and speak of it as a natural process. . . . To say that this
miracle is a warrantable interference with the laws of nature
is to overlook the very partial state of the knowledge we
possess of those laws; the biologist's experiments with
nitrogen-producing bacteria, reports of the effects of electrical
stimulations of vegetable growth, warn us against too confident
dogmatism."

Some scholars attempt to rationalise the story. They hold
that our Lord delivered a discourse which held the multitude
spell-bound and as it was late afternoon and many of them
had come long distances He commanded His disciples to give
them to eat. A boy was discovered with 5 barley loaves and
two fishes.   Barley loaves and fish were the staple food of
the poor, and our Lord's influence upon the crowd was such
that those who had provisions with them in the baskets in
which Jews carried their food on a journey, handed them
over for distribution and there was enough and to spare.
But it seems necessary to assume that we have here a miracle
of divine providence. " The prophets had promised the people
that when the theocracy was perfected they should receive
the fulness of blessings in all things temporal; Jesus did not
dispute this promise or reduce the blessing. The people were
to see and experience that it was He who would completely
fulfil this promise also. . . . It was a figurative fulfilment of
the Messianic promise and a powerful practical sermon that
He had come to supply their wants and communicate to them
the plenitude of blessings even in regard to temporal things."

Some teachers make the lesson centre round the boy.
They present the boy, not Christ. If the teacher has difficulties in accepting the miracle, the story should be omitted.

THE SYROPHENICIAN WOMAN—*Matthew* xv. 21-28.

This incident belongs to the period when our Lord was
turning His back on His own country. The end, He knew,
was not far away and He took His disciples on a tour through
Gentile territory to commit to them His message, to train
them in the shadow of the Cross. News of His healing

powers had travelled and He was accosted by a Canaanitish woman, *i.e.*, not a Jewess, but a descendant of the early inhabitants of the Phoenician coast-lands (called by St Mark a Syrophenician), on behalf of her child. The woman appealed to Him as Son of David but He answered not a word. Why this apparent harshness and indifference? He was deep in thought about His mission and only when the disciples asked Him to send her away—the importunate Gentile dog!—was our Lord made conscious of her presence. As she looked in His face she felt encouraged to renew her appeal—" Lord, help me." Still thinking of His mission and of His rejection He answered that He was not sent but to the lost sheep of the House of Israel and that it was not meet to give the children's bread to the little house-dogs that sat at the table waiting for crumbs. She caught His spirit and replied that although the Gentiles were to the Jews as house-dogs to the children, yet the house-dogs were the master's and received the crumbs. So saying, she made the confession that He was Messiah not only of the Jew but of the Gentile, that in Him all nations would be blessed. " O woman," He replied, " great is thy faith : be it done unto thee even as thou wilt." Through His conversation with the woman He had an eye to the instruction of His disciples.

The point of the story is that our Lord recognised no national barriers and taught the disciples an unforgettable lesson about responsibility to alien races.

THE BLIND AND DUMB MAN—*Matthew* xii. 22-30.

We have here obviously a case of psychogenic or functional blindness and dumbness as the sufferer is said to have been possessed of a devil. With the spread of our Lord's fame as Healer the Pharisees were stirred to active opposition and endeavoured to discredit Him by saying that His goodness was devil-born. He was devil-possessed and worked His cures through Beelzebub, the Prince of devils. Our Lord exposed their inconsistency by pointing out that their condemnation of Him was a condemnation of their own professional exorcists. If their inferior cures were due to the operation of the Spirit of God, then His expulsion of demons must be accepted as evidence of the presence of the kingdom of God. Our Lord here expressly claims that in Him a new era has begun, that the kingdom of heaven is come upon them, that in Him the Living God has intervened to save men from the powers of evil. Playing upon the word

Beelzebub (Lord of the House), He says: "No man can enter into a strong man's house, and spoil his goods, except he will first bind the strong man; and then he will spoil his house." In other words, He affirms that His miracles are a binding of the strong man of evil and a snatching away of his vessels. Only the Messiah can be stronger than the Prince of evil.

THE TRANSFIGURATION—*Matthew* xvii. 1-13.

The story of the Transfiguration can be understood only in the light of the events that preceded it. Our Lord after His rejection by His own people had taken the disciples on a tour through Gentile territory to train them through fellowship with Him. Their ideas of the Messiah were the ideas of their time, of a triumphant Messiah who would set up a new temporal kingdom and restore the glory that was Israel's. The conception of a suffering, humiliated Messiah was one with which they were unfamiliar and because of their false ideas of Messiahship our Lord could not claim to be Messiah. The recognition of His Messiahship must be made by themselves. And so at the heathen village of Caesarea Philippi at the foot of the Lebanons He put the momentous question: "Whom say ye that I am?" Peter as spokesman of the party replied: "Thou art the Christ, the Son of the Living God." But neither Peter nor the rest of the company fully understood what Messiahship involved. They still believed that our Lord would introduce the kingdom in some spectacular way. So He made intimation of His approaching death. "He began to teach them that the Son of Man must be delivered into the hands of men and they shall kill Him."

Our Lord, in times of crisis, ascended a mountain with His three favourite disciples. In this case the mountain may well have been Mount Hermon. In the peace and solitude of a slope of that great eminence, the highest in Syria, He could commune with His Father and so fit Himself to go down into the valley of humiliation and death with fresh courage. Younghusband in his preface to *The Living Universe* writes: "Every mountaineer knows how when he has climbed into a clearer atmosphere and risen physically above the scenes of ordinary life, he seems to have risen spiritually too. And in a sense he is right. Having risen above the turmoil, and the rough and tumble of life, he has placed himself in a position where he can see things in their due proportion. He is not unmindful of the pains and evils, the

cares and worries, and sorrows and disappointments of life.
But, for the time, he ceases to be obsessed by them. . . . The
mountaineer knows that he will have to return to the city
and face hard facts.   But he will face them with all the
better heart for having enjoyed a whiff of fresh air from the
heights."

On the Mount our Lord consecrated Himself to the service of death.   He withdrew from His disciples and prayed
to His Father to give Him strength to continue steadfast
unto the end.   And His whole being was transfigured with
the vision of coming victory.   His exhausted disciples,
weighted with sleep, saw His Figure bathed in light, His
garments glittering like the snows of Hermon.   They saw
Him communing with Moses and Elijah and knew that the
Father approved of the Son.   In later life they testified that
they had heard a Voice out of the cloud, saying : " This is
My Beloved Son : hear Him."   That the disciples recognised
the two figures as those of Moses and Elijah indicates that
they had a visionary experience.   If we believe in a divine
revelation, if we believe that our Lord is rather a divine gift
than a human achievement, we cannot doubt the reality of the
vision.   What was the purpose of it?   To give the disciples
divine assurance that the Messiah who was taking the way
of the Cross was the fulfilment of the Law and the prophets.
Malachi (iii. 22) prophesied the appearance of Elijah before
the coming of the Messiah, and only such an experience could
convince the disciples that the Son of Man in His humiliation
was the Son of God.   Our Lord enjoined them to keep silence
as to what they had seen because, before His Resurrection,
any account of their experience would have been meaningless
to others.   Our Lord was the Messiah, the disciples knew.
Yet Elijah who was to precede the Messiah had just appeared
to them.   What was the explanation?   So they asked Him :
" Why then say the scribes that Elias must first come? "   Our
Lord interpreted the prophecy as bearing on John the Baptist.
The purpose of the Baptist as Forerunner was to effect a
moral reformation but like Elijah he had been rejected, and
the Son of Man must also be set at naught (Mark ix. 12, 13).
According to the Old Testament the Messiah who was to
come would suffer and die.

To talk to a class of juniors about visionary experiences
would be foolish.   The teacher should draw a mental picture
of snow-capped Hermon, that great and wonderful commanding mountain, and simply tell the scholars what happened there without attempting any explanation.

The Epileptic Boy—*Mark* ix. 14-29.

During our Lord's absence with the three on the Mount a large crowd had gathered, among them scribes who had tracked Him down and were pestering the nine disciples with questions. A man had arrived with an epileptic boy. Epilepsy was regarded as due to devil-possession, a diagnosis not so far out, as the treatment of epilepsy to-day falls within the domain of the neurologist and the psychotherapist. "Its attacks differ so in intensity that possibly the involuntary giggling of a class of school girls and the violent mania of the dangerously insane are simply degrees of one disease, arising from the same fundamental cause—a weakness of self-control."

The disciples to whom our Lord had given authority to heal tried to cure the boy but failed. The father was despondent, the disciples were discomfited, the scribes jubilant, when our Lord arrived upon the scene. While He was questioning the father about the duration of the illness the boy had a seizure, falling down shrieking and foaming at the mouth. The father, after his experience of the failure of the disciples, was naturally somewhat sceptical about our Lord's power. He said: "If thou canst." Our Lord demanded his active co-operation. "If thou canst believe, all things are possible to him that believeth." Our Lord demands an answering faith in the power of God. The father recognised that our Lord could help because of His strong faith, and replied: "Lord, I believe, help thou mine un-belief," i.e., "Let thy strong faith support my weak faith." Our Lord exorcised the deaf and dumb spirit, and after another paroxysm the boy lay motionless, in the eyes of the bystanders dead. He took him by the hand, and at His touch he was restored whole to his father.

The disciples, perplexed by their failure, asked Him: "Why could not we cast him out?" "This kind," came the reply, "can come forth by nothing but by prayer." In these words our Lord rebuked them for the weakness of their spiritual life. Their powerlessness was due to their failure to keep in constant touch with God and to lack of confidence in God's power to use them as His instruments of healing. "Nothing can be impossible to any man in whom there is the slightest glimmer of unconditional trust in God's power and willingness to work by Him; for such assurance is only produced by Him who will also justify it. The fact remains that Jesus is represented by Mark as saying: "It must be prayed for." The lesson is one of contrast, contrast between the power of our Lord and the powerlessness of His disciples.

Stilling the Storm—*Mark* iv. 35-41.

The Lake of Galilee, surrounded by hills and lying 700 feet below the level of the Mediterranean, is subject to local storms which arise suddenly and as quickly subside. Our Lord, after a tiring day, put out on the Lake with His disciples with the intention of crossing to the other side and fell asleep on the steersman's cushion. A sudden squall arose and the boat was in danger of being swamped. The disciples, terror-stricken, aroused their Master. He rebuked them for their lack of faith and reminded them that those who had committed themselves to God knew no fear. Professor MacMurray divides humanity into two classes, the fear-determined and the love-determined, the former standing for death against life, the latter for life against death. The fear-determined demand protection and salvation from the hostile forces of the world. The fear principle is central in religion because fear lies at the root of most of our troubles, individual, social, economic and international. Perfect faith, like perfect love, casteth out fear. How often our Lord rebuked men for lack of faith! "Why take ye thought for raiment?" "Be not anxious about the morrow." Our Lord did not promise salvation from suffering, loss, death, but He did offer men deliverance from the fear of these. He said, in effect, "if you have faith, you will meet suffering, disaster, death without fear, with serene calm." Professor MacMurray writes: "Real religion will save us from our fear but not from the things we are afraid of. . . . Any form of Christianity which offers us protection from life, defence against the consequences of our ignorance and folly and escape from the natural demands of our human existence is spurious. To demand security is the expression of fear, and the religion that offers us security is a false religion, fear-determined and death-determined. And such a religion is the greatest destructive force known to human life. . . . I do not think that Christianity will save us from the things we are afraid of. I think it would save us from the fear of them which paralyses us. . . . I see the history of our civilisation as a struggle against Christianity, as an effort to turn the one real religion, the religion of love and abundant life, into a fear-religion which would minister to our desire to be secured against the forces of life."

St Matthew's Gospel relates that after our Lord's rebuke of His disciples for their lack of faith He rebuked the winds, and the storm subsided, i.e., the disciples when asked why they were fearful had no assurance that they would be saved. Mark and Luke, on the other hand, represent our Lord as calming the sea before addressing the terrified disciples. Some interpreters think that our Lord's arousal from sleep coincided with the lull in the storm, but the impression left upon us by the Gospel narrative is that our Lord cast a spell upon the waters when He said " Peace," or " Be thou muzzled," and the miracle supplies an answer to the question : " Who is this that the winds and the waves obey Him? "

WALKING ON THE SEA—*Matthew* xiv. 22-33.

This incident follows on the feeding of the 5000. The multitude wanted to make our Lord a king, and as the disciples were infected by the passions and ideals of the crowd He had to constrain them to go away while He Himself sought the solitude. At second evening—from 6 p.m. to dark, the first evening corresponding to our afternoon—He sent the disciples away by boat with orders to wait for Him. They had to struggle against a head-wind, and by the fourth watch—between 3 and 6 a.m.—they had not touched land. All at once they saw a Form passing by the boat, and imagining it to be a ghost, a portent of evil, they were terror-stricken. Their alarm can be understood as they were not expecting their Master. Our Lord rebuked their fear. " Be of good cheer; it is I; be not afraid." St Matthew's Gospel tells us that Peter offered to come out to Him and our Lord said " Come." The issue depended upon Peter himself. Had he sufficient faith? He believed that he had, but his faith failed him. When he saw the storm he began to sink, and appealed to our Lord. " Immediately Jesus stretched forth His hand and caught him " and gently chided him for his lack of faith.

Did our Lord actually walk upon the water? The possibility of levitation cannot be ruled out. What would be out of place in another is quite in keeping with His personality. The accounts given in the Gospels are probably reports of actual occurrences, but more important for us than literal fact is the symbolism of the story. "As fared that bark

upon those stormy billows, so fares it oftentimes with the
Church. . . . It seems as though its Lord had forgotten it,
so little is the way it makes; so baffled is it and tormented
by hostile forces on every side. . . . But His eye is on it still.
. . . and when at length the extremity of the need has
arrived, He is suddenly with it, in marvellous ways past
finding out; and then all that before was so laborious is easy,
and the toiling rowers are anon at the haven where they
would be. . . . Peter represents to us here the faithful of all
times, in the seasons of their unfaithfulness and fear. So
long as they are strong in faith, they are able to tread under
foot the most turbulent agitations of an unquiet world; but
when they are afraid, when, instead of " looking unto Jesus,"
they look at the stormy winds and waters, anon these prevail
against them, and they begin to sink; and were it not for
their Lord's sustaining hand, stretched out in answer to their
cry, they would be wholly overwhelmed and swallowed up."

JUNIOR (First Year).

B.—STORIES TOLD BY JESUS.

THE PARABLES.

IT has been already stated that critics to-day analyse the
tradition that came down to the editors of the Gospels into
Sayings, Parables, Miracles and Passion Narrative. There is
general agreement that one of our Lord's methods of teaching was by parable and that He was the Master of the art.
Jewish teachers made use of the parabolic method—e.g., the
parable of Nathan in 2 Samuel xii. 1-7—but our Lord made
it peculiarly His own. " Nowhere else are there attributed
to anyone parables that in number and beauty can be compared with those of the first three Gospels." The question
of His motives for making use of this method is more easily
asked than answered. David, ignorant of the application to
himself, impersonally and impartially pronounced judgment
when Nathan had spoken his parable and then to his horror
realised that he was the man. Our Lord's motive, in some
of His parables, may have been to get from the Pharisees

a similar judgment and then to point out the application to themselves. St Mark tells us that our Lord spoke in parables "that seeing they may see, and not perceive; and hearing they may hear, and not understand." Some scholars urge that as He always spoke so as to be understood, and taught in parables, these words came not from Him but from the evangelist to whom the parables were an enigma. But St Mark, the disciple and interpreter of Peter, had a more profound insight into the mind of our Lord than we can have to-day, and there are good reasons for holding that our Lord made use of the parable not only to reveal but to conceal truth. The Hebrew word translated as parable means not only a proverb but an enigma, and certain of our Lord's parables were not concrete illustrations of spiritual and moral truth, but "enigmas" by which He made known to His inner circle "the mystery of the Kingdom," the mystery of His own personality, a mystery which the outsiders could not perceive.

The fact that there are different versions of the same parable in the Gospels suggests that our Lord repeated the parables on different occasions, and one of the problems to which an answer must be found in order to obtain a satisfactory explanation of a parable, is the situation which called it forth. Many attempts have been made at classification of our Lord's parables. Cadoux divides them into parables (1) of Israel and the nations, (2) of conflict, (3) of vindication, (4) of crisis and opportunity, (5) of the future, (6) of duty and personality, (7) of God and man. Jordan's classification is as follows: (1) to the multitudes, (2) to the scribes, Pharisees, chief priests, lawyers, (3) to the disciples; and Jordan calls attention to the fact that more parables were spoken to the disciples than to the other groups combined— a fact not without significance.

The Foolish Virgins—*Matthew* xxv. 1-13.

This parable, recorded only by St Matthew, was spoken to the disciples. Weddings in Galilee were celebrated at night. The bridegroom, in this case, came from a distance, and young women, friends of the bride, made preparations, according to custom, to go a short distance to meet the bridegroom and turn back with him as he was on his way to fetch his bride from her father's house. As soon as he made his appearance with his torch-bearers the bride's companions, carefully selected for the occasion, began to

E

chant his praises, and their torches had to be lighted to light
the way for him and his party. Five of them had lit their
torches before receiving the signal of the bridegroom's
approach, and all of them fell asleep. When at last the
lights of the bridegroom's procession were seen in the distance the five found to their dismay that their lamps had
burned dry and that they had not provided an extra supply
of oil. Their five companions to whom they made appeal
refused to part with any of their oil, and while they
were away purchasing oil at the town the bridegroom arrived
at the bride's house, the feast began and the doors were shut.

How is the parable to be interpreted? It is clear that
our Lord is the Bridegroom and that the virgins symbolise
His followers, who must live continually on the spiritual
heights in a state of preparedness and expectancy. The oil
is divine grace, which alone can produce the bright light of
Christian character in the lamp of human personality. As our
Lord called Himself the Light of the world, so He said of His
disciples that they were the light of the world. His light
must shine in them. They must attempt to reproduce His
character. The Christian character cannot be hid. "The
halo round the head of the saint in Christian art is something
more than an imaginative symbol; it is the pictorial representation of a reality. The saint manifests his saintliness by
the mystic translucence, the light that never was on sea or
land, by which he is always surrounded. It clings about
him like a golden mist, and it is this which gives him his
real influence and value in the world, for it lights up with
the glow of tenderness and beauty the darkness of life's
journey." Unless the lamp of human personality is kindled
by the Spirit of Christ and burns with a steady flame, it
fails of the purpose for which God created us. Our Lord
offers Himself to us through the indwelling of His Holy
Spirit, and if our personality is to be Christian in any real
sense our lamps must be constantly replenished with the oil
that He supplies. This oil cannot be borrowed from another,
nor is there any substitute for divine power. "There can
be no loan or gift," writes Hoskyns, "of that which secures
salvation."

During the absence of the five foolish virgins to procure
oil, the Bridegroom came. There is continually in the life
of the nation and of the individual a catastrophic coming of
Christ. To the nations in the trough of depression, facing
problems of unemployment, social unrest and militarism,
trying to save themselves by refusing to trust and to co-

operate with one another, Christ comes and passes judgment. Daily to the individual in every situation that calls for decision—the *sine qua non* of Christian personality—He comes and divides the wise from the foolish. " Our temptations and opportunities may seem to us to be trifling, but we do not thereby escape the tremendous issue of our decisions. . . . It is not only the martyr as he goes forth to meet the Bridegroom, on the scaffold or through the fire, who needs the supernatural strength of God, and who exhibits it in the lustrous flame of Christian character shining in his soul. We need the strength as much, and can exhibit it as truly, as we try to bear bravely and with unembittered hearts, the constant grind of commonplace routine, and trudge to meet the Bridegroom along life's common highway."

THE FRIEND AT MIDNIGHT—*Luke* xi. 5-8.

In this parable there is presented to us the picture of a poor man's house with a single room in which the whole household eats and sleeps, a household living a hand-to-mouth existence, with only enough bread to serve for the day. A guest arrives about midnight, and as hospitality is a sacred duty in the East, the householder gets up and importunes a neighbour until he responds to his appeal. There is fairly general agreement that our Lord's purpose in telling this parable was to impress upon His disciples the need for praying with their whole heart and soul, with all the powers of their being, and to give them the assurance that to such prayers God would not prove unresponsive. The psychologist to-day affirms that according to our faith so is it done unto us, that God's response is proportionate to our faith and love. The individual in prayer is at one with God and enriches his life from a divine source. He has meat that the world knows not of. There is at his disposal divine power for the healing of disease, and for the transformation of fear into courage and of despair into hope. " Ask and it shall be given you; seek and ye shall find; knock and it shall be opened unto you."

THE HIDDEN TREASURE—*Matthew* xiii. 44.

It must have been a not uncommon experience in Galilee for a ploughman to come upon hidden treasure. In times of social upheaval and war the only safe place for valuables was the ground, and the average man who stumbled upon a hidden hoard would cover it up and dispose of all his possessions in order to acquire the field. The parable emphasises that the spiritual riches to be found in our Lord are hidden. By many in Palestine He was regarded as no more than a prophet. To many in Nazareth He was but the carpenter. To the inner circle He was the Messiah. Our Lord in expounding the mystery of the kingdom to His disciples by this parable may have had in mind men like Levi and Zacchaeus, who had unexpectedly made a tremendous spiritual discovery and surrendered all for the kingdom's sake.

The parable teaches too that the riches of Christ are always to hand. The boy who trudged across the valley and up the hill to see the house with the golden windows discovered, as he looked back, that his own house in the rays of the setting sun had golden windows too. The shepherds abiding in the fields heard the angelic song. The fishermen toiling at their nets and the publicans sitting on the quays heard the call of Christ. " We journey far in the search for fulness of life, and when at last we stoop to pick our treasure up, we find it shining close by the footprint we left when we set out to travel in a circle." For the treasure when found, no price is too high to pay for possession. There are scales of value, and our Lord emphasises the incomparable value of the new life in Him and the necessity of giving up everything to obtain the one thing needful. In every walk of life men continually surrender wealth and comfort and ease for what to them is the pearl of great price. Wilberforce, when he took up arms on behalf of the slaves, left the House of Commons a pariah, with the doors of most of the respectable members of the community shut in his face. By many Schweitzer was regarded as at least not quite in his senses when he resigned a professor's chair and went to Africa as a missionary. The parable is a commentary on our Lord's words, that he who is not prepared to give up father and mother and home and friends for His sake is not fit to be a disciple.

LOST AND FOUND.

A SHEEP AND THE GOOD SHEPHERD—*Luke* xv. 1-7.

St Luke tells us that " both the Pharisees and the scribes murmured . . . and He spake unto them this parable." In the New Testament the scribes and the Pharisees generally

appear in company. The former held an office, the latter
represented a religious party, but they formed practically
one body. Josephus says that in his time the Pharisees
numbered only 6000. But they controlled the life of the
community, their authority being that of the Law of God.
The word Pharisee means " separatist," the ideal of holiness
being separateness. The Pharisee separated himself from
the rest of the community and set the example of punctilious
observance of the minutiae of the Law, making no distinction
between ceremonial and ethical commands. Not only was
there a displacement of values, but the Pharisee's besetting
sin was self-righteousness. He prided himself on his superiority and thanked God that he was not as other men. He
wrapped himself in his praying-shawl and engaged in long
prayers at the corners of the street to let men see how
pious he was. He had his reward in the reputation for piety
which he acquired. For the mass of the people who had to
toil for daily bread the keeping of the Law as interpreted
by the scribes and Pharisees was an impossibility, and there
was a clear-cut distinction between them and the fellowship
of the learned. " This multitude that knoweth not the Law is
accursed," said the Pharisee, but our Lord admitted them to
His fellowship. " Pharisaism suddenly found itself confronted by Jesus. . . . There had been nothing in the past
history of Judaism to prepare men for the appearance of
one such as He. It is true that John the Baptist had come
and gone, and Jesus at the outset took up his message. But
Jesus was far other than a second John; and it may be truly
said that He took the Pharisees entirely by surprise, when
they began to be aware of His presence in their midst. And
not the Pharisees alone. Until Jesus actually appeared, the
like of Him had never been known. . . . When the first
attempts were made to write down the earliest recollections
of what He had said and done, the ancient prophecies were
quoted in order to show that this and that was fulfilled in
Jesus. . . . But the prophecies had been read for centuries;
and, in spite of them no one was prepared for Jesus. The
effect of His coming into the world has been greater than
that made by anyone else in history; and since it was the
effect produced by one who, at the outset, was entirely
unknown and unexpected, it can only be understood as due to
the impression made by a personality of tremendous force
and intensity. . . . That Jesus was a teacher is certainly true;
that He taught many things which the Pharisees taught is
also true; but the vast difference in the effect produced in

each case must have been due to a difference in the personality of those who gave the teaching. The teaching itself was, by comparison, of hardly any importance. . . . One in whom there was so vivid a consciousness of God would neither seek nor recognise any human authority for what He said or thought or believed in regard to religion. The ultimate authority is that of God Himself. It was so for the Pharisees no less than for Jesus; but while for them it was apprehended through the Law, by Him the authority of God was owned and felt in immediate experience. . . This is the point of collision between Him and Pharisaism, the irreconcilable difference that admitted of no compromise. . . . He found His first call to service in the needs of the uncared-for masses. . . . They were outside the Pharisaic circle, and so also was He. He gave them out of the abundance of His heart such good treasure as is contained in the Sermon on the Mount and the Parables, and it is not wonderful that they ' heard Him gladly ' and that ' the people all hung upon Him, listening.' . . . People were more impressed and over-awed by Him than by any definite message which He proclaimed. . . His concern was to speak out of Himself what He had it in Him to say, and not to ask what others might think of it. . . . The Pharisees saw Him do things which were not in accordance with the Tradition, simply on His own authority. Religion for them was unimaginable without the Tradition, as the main and dominating element in the Law. They believed in it and taught their followers to believe in it as ' the Way, the Truth and the Life,' as for them it really was. Necessarily, therefore, they looked upon Jesus as a source of serious danger, a revolutionary teacher whose influence threatened to destroy what to them was of life and death importance. They must resist Him or be false to their own convictions. The alternative was to capitulate and own that they and their forerunners had all been mistaken."

The parable of the lost sheep is one of vindication of our Lord's attitude to the outcasts. " I am come," He said, " to seek and to save the lost." Emphasis should be laid not upon the lost sheep but upon the seeking shepherd, upon the unwearying search of God and of Christ for the sinner. Our Lord called Himself the Good Shepherd. In Him we see God searching for the sinner, making no distinction between the self-righteous Pharisees and the outcast publicans and sinners.

A Coin—*Luke* xv. 8-10.

In this parable, directed to the interests of women, emphasis is also upon the Seeker, to whom the sinner is of infinite value. A woman has lost a drachma (value about 7½d.), one of the coins of the frontlet worn across the forehead under the veil. The frontlet was worn on all public occasions and jealously guarded, as it was the bridegroom's gift at marriage. In the story of the woman's anxious search for the lost coin our Lord proclaims the value of man to God.

The recent discoveries of astronomy have tended to emphasise the idea of man's insignificance in the Universe and the world-situation has bred in many hopelessness and despair. Our greatest need is the conviction that man is precious to the Creator. Our Lord, who was not so much a human achievement as a divine gift, gave us the assurance that the loss of a human soul is a loss to Him, and that as the woman summoned her friends to rejoice with her over the recovery of the lost piece of silver, so there is joy among the angels in Heaven when one sinner repenteth.

The teacher should show that as the purpose of a coin is to be used, so we are put in the world to spend ourselves in the service of Christ. However difficult it may be for many to find any true satisfaction in their work, work in which they feel that they are but cogs in a machine, yet every occupation can be consecrated by a sense of divine vocation. As the coin was valueless until replaced in the frontlet, so we are useless apart from God, unless we are spending ourselves in His service. "When at last, beaten, worn and battered with constant service, we are withdrawn awhile from circulation, we shall be purified from dross and re-minted, to be re-issued with enhanced value and sparkling lustre as standard currency in the shining coinage of the New Jerusalem."

A Son—*Luke* xv. 11-32.

This is a parable of vindication, "the crown of Christ's defence of His friendship with the religious outcasts." The three figures in the parable are the Father who represents our Lord, the prodigal who symbolises the outcasts, and the elder brother who stands for the Pharisee. The father says to the elder brother: "Son, thou art ever with me and all that I have is thine." This saying suggests that the parable was spoken by our Lord early in His ministry when He still had hopes of opening the eyes of the religious leaders, and shows His tenderness towards those who could not understand His attitude to the publicans and sinners.

The father, according to custom, divided his estate between his two sons, the elder receiving two-thirds (Deuteronomy xxi. 13), the younger the remaining third, which he at once proceeded to squander. The younger son wanted to live his life in his own way. Man is a divine being with animal instincts. He may transmute his instincts and respond to God and to all that is highest and best, or he may gratify his instincts in crude ways. "He has the power of choosing between the pull-back of his racial origin and the pull-forward of his spiritual destiny." As the father allowed the boy to go his own way, so God is no despot. Man is morally free to choose good or evil, and God will have us surrender ourselves to Him of our own choice or not at all.

The prodigal went to a far country. Away from the old environment, away from those amongst whom his life had been cast, he believed that he would find happiness. His hopes were doomed to disappointment. He forgot that only in God's service could perfect freedom be found. He lived for himself, a dissolute life of pleasure and was soon reduced to beggary. He wasted his substance—the first result of his separation from God—and became the wreck of his former self. "When he had spent all, there arose a mighty famine in that land, and he began to be in want." There comes a time when the man who has been living apart from God realises that he is spiritually bankrupt, and he touches the depths of human degradation. The Prodigal turned swineherd, a detestable occupation in the eyes of the Jew, and would fain have filled his belly with unclean food.

But he came to himself and said : " I will arise and go to my father." He had been obsessed with the mania for self-expression, and the pleasures purchased by emancipation from home ties were as Dead Sea fruit. Having experienced the futility of self-expression he attained to self-realisation, and his fundamental need was for the restraints of his former life. He arose and came to his father, made confession of his sin and was received with open arms. There is a tendency to-day to speak of "bad taste" or of "moral evil" rather than of "sin." While the sense of guilt is, as the psychologists tell us. almost universal, there is a surprising lack of a sense of individual responsibility to God. We all need to be convicted of sin. "It is not what we have done, it is what we have left undone. It does not depend merely on what stands in the foreground, but on what lies in the background. The conviction we have resisted, the still, small voices we have refused to hear, the opportunities we have neglected, the profession we have disgraced, the hedges we have thrown down around us, the barriers we have over-leapt, above all the love we have put away from us, and the grace we have quenched; these are the things that, when once we realise them, make us say with the prodigal : "Father, I have sinned against Heaven and before thee, and am no more worthy to be called thy son." God's love is equal to man's need. The father had compassion, and ran and fell on the prodigal's neck and kissed him.

Our Lord does not condemn the elder brother, whose steady virtue is too real for condemnation. His words are tender and affectionate. The man has plodded home from his day's darg in the fields to find in progress a celebration of the return of the young " scallywag " who had shaken off the domestic discipline so scornfully and light-heartedly and had " wasted " so much of the product of industry. In these circumstances some touch of rueful indignation on the elder brother's part was natural. " All these years " he had served with dogged, dependable faithfulness. No doubt in the heat of the moment he failed to realise that there are moments when the homelier virtues are irrelevant, but his possession of these virtues would prevent him from " keeping his anger still," and he would soon recognise that he " did not well to be angry."

(1) CHRISTMAS.

STORY OF THE SHEPHERDS—*Luke* ii., 1-20.

There are two stories here.

(1) *The Story of the Birth of Jesus.*—This is contained in verses 1-7. The teacher will confine attention to its essential points, his main purpose being to tell the second story, that of the Bethlehem Shepherds.

Luke is alone among the Evangelists in seeking to relate the life of Jesus to contemporary history. Here he records that His Birth took place at the time of a world-wide enrol-ment ordered by the Emperor Augustus. In Palestine everyone went to be enrolled to his own city. Joseph, therefore, went up from Nazareth to Bethlehem taking with him Mary his wife. Finding every lodgment in the city occupied they betook themselves to a caravanserai—a rude structure such as is common in the East erected for the shelter of travellers and their beasts—and it was there that Jesus was born.

Certain statements in these seven verses have been the occasion of much difficulty.

(*a*) There is no direct evidence that Augustus ordered such a world-wide enrolment as is mentioned here. Yet that he did give instructions that an estimate should be made of the population and resources of his far-flung empire is by no means improbable. Discoveries of household enrolment papers made in Egypt show that in that land in the time of the Roman emperors enrolments were made at intervals of fourteen years. The same practice may have obtained in the neighbouring land of Palestine. Since one Egyptian enrolment is known to have been made in A.D. 20, it may be inferred that earlier ones were made in A.D. 6 and B.C. 8.

(*b*) A Roman enrolment did not necessitate a man's journeying to his native place. It is possible, however, that the Roman authorities considered it well to follow in Palestine the usual Jewish way.

(*c*) This enrolment is described as "the first enrolment made when Quirinius was governor of Syria" (Revised Version). Now Quirinius did not become governor of Syria until A.D. 6, whereas it is generally agreed that the Birth of Jesus took place before the death of Herod the Great in B.C. 4. Considerable evidence has, however, been produced by Sir William Ramsay that Quirinius held, between 8 and 6 B.C., a military appointment of a kind that may have been loosely described as a governorship. It is suggested that an enrolment throughout Palestine was ordered then and that responsibility for making it was committed to Quirinius. On the other hand, it is certain that an enrolment was made in A.D. 6 when Quirinius was governor of Syria in the ordinary sense. The possibility thus remains that Luke has confused that enrolment with an earlier and less known one made at the time of the Birth of Jesus. While right in his statement that there was an enrolment at that time, he may be wrong in the name he gives of the governor of Syria under whom it was made. In recent years some have suggested that no such justification of Luke as Ramsay has attempted is really necessary. The enrolment of Luke ii., it is urged, was the well known census of A.D. 6, and the Crucifixion must be dated not earlier than A.D. 35 and not later than A.D. 36. This chronology, while it solves certain difficulties, raises others.

(2) *The Story of the Bethlehem Shepherds* (verses 8-20).—
Concerning this a recent commentator has said with a peculiar
happiness, " Critical discussion of this perfect story is idle."
The older rationalism sought to relate the angelic vision to
the " ignis fatuus " forgetting that of all men shepherds were
among the most familiar with that phenomenon. The mythical
school found in this story but another of those legends of
the ancient world in which divine apparitions are frequently
ascribed to country-folks and notably to shepherds. Some
will find more satisfaction in the view that, while the revealing
Spirit of God wrought in the minds of these Bethlehem
shepherds, it is no dry, prosaic account of their experience
that has come down to us but one clothed in poetic form.
Others will see no reason why they should not believe that,
while the entry upon the stage of human life of the Son of
God remained unnoticed by the great ones of the world, a
company of the heaven-host, rejoicing in the stupendous
event, " burst the bounds of their invisibility " in order to
proclaim it to such humble, pious men as it is not unlikely
these Bethlehem shepherds were. But, however that may be,
this is a story not to be explained away or even to be
explained but simply to be told.

The traditional Field of the Shepherds lies at the distance
of an easy walk East from Bethlehem. On the spot where the
angels were believed to have appeared to the shepherds there
stood for centuries a church and a monastery. Of these there
are now but ruins.

That Palestinian shepherds can have been watching their
flocks by night in the month of December is not impossible.
While ordinarily sheep were folded by the towns and villages
in the winter the season may have been a mild one. It has
been suggested that the sheep the Bethlehem shepherds were
tending were intended for Temple sacrifices. From a passage
in the Talmud it has been inferred that such sheep were
kept out all the year round. It needs to be noted, however,
that the tradition that our Lord was born on 25th December
appears to be Western and cannot with any certainty be
traced back beyond the 4th century.

While the Revised Version rendering of the Gloria in
Excelsis Deo is preferred by many scholars, much can be said
in support of that of the Authorised Version. Christ came
that God might be glorified, that there might be peace on
earth, that men might experience the divine grace.

(2) EASTER.

CHILDREN'S PRAISES—*Matthew* xxi. 1-11, 14-16.

(*a*) Matthew xxi. 1-11; see below, Junior (Second Year), Jesus' Triumphal Entry. Mark xi. 1-11.

(*b*) Matthew xxi. 14-16.

Our Lord was a lover of children. In the words of Irenaeus, He became a child for the sake of children. Then in the days of His flesh His love for them was shown in His attitude towards them as seen, e.g., in the account of the raising of Jairus' daughter, and in the emphasis which in His teaching He laid upon their value and importance. Moreover this supreme lover of children had Himself a peculiar attraction for children. That is what is revealed here.

Children are great imitators. Ordinarily parents who glorify God will have children who will do likewise. The acclaim of the children of this episode, " Hosanna to the Son of David " they had learned of their seniors upon the way between Bethany and Jerusalem (*see* verse 9). They had come in the adoring multitude that had accompanied our Lord into the Temple area, had seen His majesty as He swept the sanctuary of its unholy traffic and then, the same or the following day, His graciousness as He healed blind and lame : and the more they had kept observing Him the more had admiration and love for Him been quickened in their young hearts. From being a mere repetition of what others were saying their acclaim changed into an expression of what they themselves felt. Their praise now was " perfected praise "—praise that came not merely, as the indignant Pharisees suggested, from their lips but, as our Lord affirmed, from their hearts.

This episode is peculiar to Matthew, for which reason apparently some have doubted its historicity. A somewhat similar story occurs in Luke xix., 39 f. There our Lord's reply to those who bade Him rebuke His disciples was, " If these should hold their peace, the stones would immediately cry out." Now in Aramaic the words " stones " and " children " closely resemble one another. It is suggested that in the Lucan story as it reached Matthew our Lord was reported to have said, " The children would immediately cry out " and that the story that has been before us is the result. On such slender grounds does criticism seek to rob us of one of the most pleasing incidents of the last days of our Lord's earthly life.

JUNIOR (Second Year)—NEW TESTAMENT.

A.—STORIES OF JESUS.

THE BAPTISM OF JESUS—*Matthew* iii. 13-17.

John baptised unto repentance and remission of sin. Matthew is the only Gospel that meets the objection to a sinless Jesus seeking a baptism associated with repentance. As our Lord approached, the Baptist had a presentiment that He was the Messiah and was reluctant to baptise Him. " Suffer it to be so now ": said our Lord; " for thus it becometh us to fulfil all righteousness." As Messiah He felt that He must fulfil all the ordinances of the old covenant which included the baptism by John.

JESUS IN NAZARETH—*Luke* iv. 16-32.

The village of Nazareth where our Lord spent His boy-hood lay in a hollow among the hills some 1,600 feet above sea-level. Yet, although secluded, it was in touch with the commercial and political life of the times, as two of the great Roman roads passed within sight of its walls. " Across Esdraelon there emerged from Samaria the Jerusalem road, thronged at festival seasons with thousands of pilgrims. From the fords of Jordan came the Midianite bands of traders taking their commodities to Egypt as they did in Joseph's day. The caravan from Damascus wound round the foot of the hill on which Nazareth stood. Visible from another point was the highway between Acre and Decapolis, along which marched the Roman Soldiery."

St Luke has brought this visit to Nazereth forward to the beginning of the Galilean ministry. He introduces our Lord's ministry as the fulfilment of the Isaianic prophecy, " as the incursion of the salvation of God into human life." There is no doubt that in His native village our Lord claimed to be the Messiah. He read the words of Isaiah lxi. 1, 2. Then, when He had closed the book, " To-day," said He, " hath this scripture been fulfilled in your ears." But the people of Nazareth were not prepared to accept Him without a sign. Let Him as a physician, they said, heal and help Himself in the first instance; let Him produce His credentials by giving evidence of His power. There was annoyance because Capernaum, not Nazareth, had been the first village in Galilee to benefit by His ministry. " Whatever we have heard done in Capernaum, do also here in thine own country." But our Lord refused to give a sign. He declined to come forward merely as a miracle-worker. He reminded them that the mighty works done by the heroes of faith in the past had been limited to a few, and not within the confines of their own land. In a time of famine it was a widow in a heathen city of Sidon whom Elijah helped, and it was a Syrian captain, one of their hated enemies, whom Elisha cured of leprosy. Why did our Lord choose these examples? Surely to show that God's grace was not confined to Israel, and that He, the Messiah, had a mission not only to Nazareth and to the Hebrew race but to the whole of humanity. Our Lord told them bluntly and courageously that Elijah, rejected by Israel, found acceptance with the heathen, and hinted that although rejected as Messiah by His own people, the Gentile world would find salvation in Him. In a fury of rage His townsfolk hustled Him out of the city, with the intention of casting Him over the summit of a cliff. But overawed by the majesty of His personality they fell back and He passed calmly through their midst—rejected by His own. Throughout the lesson stress should be laid on the majesty and fearlessness of our Lord. It required great courage to launch His campaign in the territory of Herod, who had put John the Baptist to death; it required greater courage still to proclaim in His native village that He, as Messiah, recognised no racial distinctions.

JAIRUS' DAUGHTER—*Luke* viii. 41, 42, 49-56.

Jairus, ruler of the synagogue, had an only daughter, 12 years of age, at the point of death. The ruler of the synagogue was responsible for maintaining order and deciding who was to conduct public worship. He was not a scribe, but stood in rank immediately after the scribes. Our Lord, followed by the curious crowd, accompanied Jairus to his house but delayed on the way to heal a woman of a hemmorhage. While He was engaged in conversation with the woman there came news of the death of the girl. Why, therefore, trouble Him to come? " If you have faith," said He, " she will recover." On arrival at the house they found that the hired mourners were already present. At death the hired mourners gathered about the bier, beating their breasts, tearing their hair and flesh, shrieking and waving their arms, and throwing dust upon their heads. Our Lord put them all out saying " She is not dead, but sleepeth," but He was laughed at because they knew that she was dead. Taking her by the hand He said : " Maid, arise," and she got up at once. To give her parents the assurance of her recovery He ordered that she be given food.

Healing a Woman—*Luke* viii. 43-48.

As our Lord was on the way to Jairus' house, a woman who had been suffering from menorrhagia for 12 years joined the crowd and surreptitiously touched the sacred tassel of His garment. Magical virtue was supposed to reside even in the clothes of the great and her touch testified to her faith in the Person of Christ. Our Lord was " psychically sensitive," He perceived that virtue had gone out of Him, He knew at once that although many thronged there was but one who had touched. When the woman saw that she was detected she came forward in fear and made confession—an act of tremendous courage, as she was unclean according to the Jewish Law and might not come into contact with others. Our Lord acknowledged her touch and thereby set that Law at naught. It may seem that in insisting on a confession before all the people our Lord was unnecessarily harsh towards this woman. But if she had been allowed to steal away unnoticed she would have lost much of what that day's experience was destined to give her. Our Lord sent her away with words of wonderful kindness. " Daughter," he said, " thy faith hath made thee whole. Go in peace."

The Man with Four Friends—*Mark* ii. 1-12.

Two issues are raised in this story, that of the connection between sin and suffering and that of our Lord's claim to forgive sin. There is an intimate connection between sin and suffering. Psychology speaks of guilt-complexes with physical symptoms, of buried memories that produce paralysis and kindred troubles. This paralytic brought to our Lord was probably a functional case. In accordance with the thought of his time he traced his suffering to sin and had been brooding upon his past. Our Lord was a perfect diagnostician. He read the man's heart and knew that He must minister to a mind diseased before strength could be restored to the

limbs. " Son," he said, " thy sins be forgiven thee." The
paralytic, forgiven by the Messiah, could forgive himself, and
at our Lord's command took up his bed and walked.
" Medical science has never gauged . . . the intimate connection between moral fault and disease. To what extent or in
how many cases what is called illness is due to moral springs
having been used amiss . . . we hardly at all know. . . . Certainly it is due to this very much more than we commonly
think; and the more it is due to this, the more do moral
therapeutics rise in possibility and importance. The bringer
of light and happiness, the calmer and pacifier, the invigorator
and stimulator, is one of the chiefest of doctors. Such a
doctor was Jesus, such an operator, by an efficacious and real,
though little observed and little employed agency." But
although we can understand the rationale of our Lord's procedure, He is not in the same category as mental and spiritual
healers to-day. He whose suffering is due to sin needs to be
saved from sin; and Christ is Saviour. He alone " breaks
the power of cancelled sin." What caused astonishment and
indignation was His claim to forgive sin. Our Lord did not
deny that it would be blasphemy for a man to forgive sins.
What he did say was that God had given to Him, as Messiah,
the power to forgive sins, and as proof of His divine
authority He commanded the paralytic to walk.

THE MAN WITH THE WITHERED HAND—*Matthew* xii. 9-13.

In this story the interest is in the Sabbath controversy.
Our Lord regarded the fourth commandment as fundamental
but He refused to be bound by the literality of His time.
The purpose of the Sabbath Law was beneficent, to give
every member of the community a day of rest, and our Lord
endeavoured to show that His interpretation was in agreement with the intention of the Law. His contemporaries,
however, held that man was made for the Sabbath.

Healing on the Sabbath was forbidden by the Law unless
life were in danger. To force the issue our Lord raised the
question and presented the case of a sheep fallen into a pit
on the Sabbath. The owner, He said, would have no hesitation in going to the rescue. Our Lord then called attention
to the value of a man in contrast to the value of a sheep and
claimed the right to heal, at the same time compromising
" the guardians of the law in the eyes of the people by condemning them to shame-faced silence." As the man stood
in the synagogue listening to the burning words that fell from

the lips of the Messiah, there was wrought in him the conviction that to Him nothing was impossible, and when the
command came he stretched forth his hand, and it was
restored whole—like as the other.

HEALING A NOBLEMAN'S SON—*John* iv. 46-54.

In St John this is the first miracle wrought by our Lord
after His return to Galilee. The nobleman was an officer of
high rank in the service of Herod Antipas, tetrarch of Galilee.
He came from Capernaum to Cana to intercede for his son.
Our Lord at first was reluctant to heal on the ground that
He was not to be regarded as a mere wonder-worker. But
the officer repeated his request with importunity and was told
to go his way as his son would live. In faith he set out for
home and was met by some of his servants with the news of
the boy's recovery. Enquiry showed that recovery had set
in at the very hour in which our Lord had spoken. The
healing differs from most of the miracles in that it took place
at a distance through a third party. Another miracle followed
—the father, a Gentile, became a believer with all his house.
So our Lord was not only a Deliverer from physical death
but also the Giver of spiritual life.

HEALING OF BARTIMAEUS—*Mark* x. 46-52.

This incident took place on our Lord's departure from
Jericho. Bartimaeus' blindness may have been psychical as
he asked for the recovery of his sight, implying that he had
not always been blind. Our Lord informed him that his faith
had made him whole, but as the Gospels inform us that
Bartimaeus became a follower of our Lord, here we have
clear proof of the fact that our Lord effected a spiritual cure
by calling forth his love.

The blind beggar was a familiar figure owing to the
prevalence of eye-trouble. Beggars congregated on the
pilgrim-routes, outside the gates of the wealthy and the
Temple-gate. As a rule they claimed alms on religious
grounds, a propitiatory virtue being ascribed to alms in
Judaism. Through alms, it was said, a man partakes of
eternal life, and alms-deeds were reckoned as more meritorious than all sacrifices. Our Lord purified almsgiving of
much of the ostentation with which it was associated.

F

ZACCHAEUS—*Luke* xix. 1-10.

Zacchaeus may have become a tax-gatherer through force of circumstances or because of his appreciation of the value of Roman administration, but latterly lived up to the evil name with which he was credited. He returned hate for hate. From the fact that he was seated on the branch of a tree to see the Messiah passing by, our Lord knew that his soul still lived and He decided to save that soul. He went to be the guest of a publican and shared with Zacchaeus the enmity of the crowd that followed with hisses. His friendship marked the turning-point in the life of the tax-gatherer. Zacchaeus offered to pay back four times over the money of which he had defrauded the people. He lost his worldly wealth but entered upon a new way of life. Salvation had come to his house. Contact with the personality of our Lord had made him a new creature.

MARTHA AND MARY—*Luke* x. 38-42.

Martha and Mary lived in Bethany, some distance from Jerusalem. The impression given by St Luke's narrative, due to his literary method, is that at the time of this visit the sisters were living somewhere in Galilee. St Luke suggests that the two women had previously come under the spell of our Lord and that He was with them on this occasion for the express purpose of accepting their hospitality. Our Lord knew loneliness as did no other, and He must have valued the friendly atmosphere of the Bethany home. A striking point in the story is the gentleness of our Lord's rebuke, expressed in the repetition of Martha's name. Rebuking there must be, but there are ways of doing it. The two sisters are distinct types. Martha was practical and our Lord's rebuke of her is not to be taken as indicating disapproval on His part of practical people. Mary differed in this, that she realised that there are other things than the things that are seen and temporal, and our Lord commended her for choosing the good part—the spiritual nourishment that He provided.

THE ALABASTER BOX—*John* xii. 1-9.

The teacher might note the different setting in time of this incident in the Synoptic Gospels. According to the Fourth Gospel, six days before the Passover our Lord came to spend His last Sabbath upon earth with the family at Bethany. A supper was given in His honour and Mary took an alabastron—a flask with a narrow neck, full of costly perfume—broke it and poured its contents on our Lord. This flask of perfume may have been reserved for the embalming of her body at death. Judas, the utilitarian, blind to the value of the things of the spirit, made remonstrance. Our Lord, whose thoughts were of His coming Passion, divined Mary's motive and appreciated the love that prompted her deed. She had rendered Him the last service of love and the house was filled—as His House has ever since been filled—with the odour of the ointment. The teacher should stress our Lord's appreciation of the beautiful and the symbolic.

NICODEMUS—*John* iii. 1-13; vii. 50-52.

From a spectacular point of view our Lord's ministry had been a great success. He taught with authority and worked miracles, and while there were many who accepted Him as the Messiah, there were others who, though regarding His signs as evidence that He was a Teacher from God, were not prepared to surrender their hearts to Him. Nicodemus, a Pharisee and member of the Sanhedrin, like others of his class had been impressed by the work of this Teacher from Galilee. He was desirous of obtaining first-hand knowledge, but because of his position and the criticism to which he might be exposed, he paid his first visit in secret. Coming by night when few were abroad and the chances of detection almost nil he climbed up the outside stair to the guest-chamber for his interview. He came, proud of his birth and his traditions, and with the conception of the Kingdom held by his class. Our Lord cut him short and replied to the question underlying his remark. Except a man be born from above, He said, he cannot see the kingdom of God. But the legalism in which Nicodemus had been trained placed the demands of our Lord beyond his mental grasp. Judaism was spiritually dead and had no conception of spiritual birth as the condition of entrance into the kingdom. Nicodemus " could understand how a man might become other and so ultimately be other, but how a man should first be other in order to become other . . . passed alike his experience and his Jewish comprehension." Consequently he gave a literal interpretation to our Lord's words. Our Lord tried to show him that only by living personal experience could he enter into the kingdom. As the wind came sweeping round the house He said : " You hear its sound, but you do not know where it has come from or where it goes. It is the same with everyone who is born of the Spirit." But Nicodemus wanted to know the how, and the why, and the wherefore. "You are a teacher in Israel!" said our Lord, "Your religion was designed to set you trembling with expectancy for Me and for My kingdom, but hardened by legalism you do not even understand My analogies from birth and from the wind to the processes of that kingdom you were meant to herald. If you cannot take the first step it is useless for Me to try to take you further." And so the interview closed.

Although not a word is said about the impression made upon Nicodemus it would appear as if the interview had left him with a vague uneasiness, as he later put in a plea before the Sanhedrin that our Lord might be heard. But he was still a night-disciple. He spoke as a righteous Pharisee and his plea deceived nobody. The story throws a revealing light upon the ferment caused among the best of the Jewish legalists by our Lord's advent and upon their anxiety to use and control His power within the bounds of the old faith. But the new wine of Christianity could not be put in the old bottle of Judaism. Christianity is a new faith, a new life, and demands a complete inward change.

The Pool of Bethesda—*John* v. 1-9.

At the time of a festival of which, curiously enough, the name is not given, our Lord went up to Jerusalem and made His way one Sabbath to the sheep-pool with its five porches, the local "hospital," where the invalids lay in crowds, waiting for the water to bubble. Remains of the excavated arches may be seen to-day. In the time of Eusebius the pool, probably an intermittent chalybeate spring, was referred to as being marvellously red, and it is probable that the waters did have a therapeutic value. Because of its strengthening properties a large concourse of sufferers gathered around the mineral spring, the popular idea being that an angel caused the waters to bubble up and that only the first to enter would be cured.

(Some scholars regard the last clause of verse 3 and verse 4 as an interpolation.) That such healing took place no one to-day would deny. "Bethesda had its legitimate place and value, because suggestion and mineral water are both gifts of God."

Among the crowd of expectant sufferers lay one who was indifferent, a man who had been impotent for 38 years, who gave to our Lord the excuse that he had no helper when the water was disturbed. Having been unsuccessful for so long he had given up hope. Our Lord began by quickening his hope. "Do you *want* your health restored?" He asked. The invalid responded to His threefold command and the paralysis of will and of limbs departed. "This scene stands in the Fourth Gospel as expressing what most bewildered the Church at Ephesus. Mankind so helpless, so suffering, so indifferent to its state. The world's remedies, at Ephesus illustrated by the shrine of Artemis with its treasures, its powers, its miracles. . . . And the Christ—patiently standing— standing under the dark shadow of Artemis, attracting indeed His responsive souls but getting no notice from the crowd."

The Pool of Siloam—*John* ix. 1-11.

The entrance to the Temple was a place where beggars were much given to sitting, soliciting alms. Amongst them those who were blind were looked upon by the Jews as specially entitled to charity. As our Lord and His disciples passed by, the sight of a blind beggar, instead of proving a stimulus to action, prompted the question—a favourite subject for speculation— as to whether he or his parents were responsible. Certain diseases in children, blindness in particular, were ascribed to the sins of the parents. Our Lord brushed aside the question of the disciples by asking them to consider the purpose now served by the man's affliction, *viz.*, that the work of God through the Saviour might be illustrated in him.

For eye troubles saliva was supposed to have therapeutic properties, and our Lord moistened a lump of clay with His spittle, sealed the patient's eyes, and commanded him to wash them in the pool of Siloam. He went and washed them, and according to his faith so was it done unto him. Both the cure and the means are symbolical. Before a man can see he must know that he is blind. In the Fourth Gospel the discourses of our Lord are related to the miracles that either precede or follow them, and St John invariably brings out the inner meaning of the miracle. Our Lord said : "I am the Light of the world," but the eyes of the Pharisees were holden and they did not know it; and He could not enlighten the unreceptive. In the case of the responsive, however, He removes the veil that is upon their eyes, and makes them a new creation.

Jesus' Triumphal Entry—*Mark* xi. 1-11.

Our Lord's hour had come. While the great hosts of Jewish exiles were assembling for the Passover He set out to die. In the multitude accompanying Him were those really devoted to Him, constituting the main part of it. Through their enthusiasm our Lord sought to impress the Capital. If, as Windisch, Goguel, and other scholars suppose, He had been working in Jerusalem and neighbourhood since the Feast of Tabernacles, He would have a large band of disciples.

While the multitudes were streaming from Jerusalem to the Mount of Olives He made His departure from Bethany. He came as the Messiah who fulfilled Old Testament prophecy. Zechariah had prophesied that the King would come, not as a revolutionary war-like Messiah, but as the Prince of Peace, meek, and riding upon a colt, the foal of an ass. Our Lord proclaimed in deed that He was the Christ of prophecy. As the red heifer upon which never came yoke (Numbers xix.) and the two milch kine (I. Samuel vi. 7) were consecrated to the service of God, so an ass whereon never man sat was consecrated to the service of the Messiah, and, as the Israelites placed their garments under Jehu on his anointing as king (II. Kings ix. 13), so the disciples spread their garments upon the ass and set our Lord thereon. When the two streams of people from Jerusalem and Bethany met there were great scenes of enthusiasm. The multitudes tore down branches from the trees by the wayside and strewed them on the road as a carpet, and hailed Him as Messiah. Our Lord's triumphal entry was an acted parable. For the first time He made open and public acknowledgment of His Messiahship and the divine decree was verified when His people accepted Him as their king. This entry made a deep impression on Jerusalem, and explains in part the resolution of the Sanhedrin to put Him to death. The Triumphal Entry in the Synoptics takes the place of the raising of Lazarus in the Fourth Gospel. (For this lesson the teacher might refer to Chesterton's *Donkey*.)

CLEANSING THE TEMPLE—*Mark* xi. 15-18.

According to the Fourth Gospel the cleansing of the Temple took place at the commencement of our Lord's ministry, according to the Synoptics at the end. It is possible that there may have been two cleansings. According to the Synoptics the cleansing was the Messianic act that aroused the enmity of the priesthood.

The Jew, with all his scrupulosity about ritual and ceremonial, was in bondage to the letter of the Law. There was no prohibition in the Law against holding a market in the Temple, as such a contingency had never been anticipated.

The priesthood took advantage of the omission, and as they had the right to rent out the ground they exercised that right to their own advantage. A Temple-tax of about 1s. 2d. had to be paid by every Jewish pilgrim and as only Temple coins —shekels and half-shekels—were accepted, those who had foreign coinage, debased by images, had to have recourse to the money-changers who made a minimum profit of 12 per cent. on the transaction. No pilgrim could present himself before God in the Temple without a sacrifice and as the animal victims had to be bought on the spot and pass official scrutiny they were sold at exorbitant prices. It is said that one morning pigeons were on sale at 15s. 3d. per pair but there was such an outcry that by evening the price was reduced to a penny. In addition to these abuses the Temple Court was used as a short-cut by people laden with household utensils (Mark xi. 16).

Our Lord, in righteous indignation, cleared the House of God of the unholy traffic. Making a quotation from Jeremiah (vii. 11) He accused the priesthood of turning the Temple into a thieves' den to which they carried their spoils, and quoting again from Isaiah (lvi. 7) He pointed to its real destiny—" My house shall be called a house of prayer for all nations." Our Lord's indignation was most deeply stirred by the fact that the traffic in sacrifices was carried on in the Court of the Gentiles who came thither to worship Israel's God. As the Messiah He had a mission not only to the outcasts of Jewry but to the despised Gentiles.

ENMITY OF THE PRIESTS—*John* xi. 47-57.

The priests were Sadducees. The name Sadducee comes from Zadok, whom Solomon installed as High Priest, and means a follower of Zadok, an adherent of the priestly aristocracy. The Sadducees held all the high offices and stood for practical politics in contradistinction to the religious life of the Pharisees. They held only to the written Law, rejecting the tradition of the elders. They rejected the Pharisaic belief in the survival of personality, future judgment and a life to come, as they could find in the Old Testament no grounds for such beliefs. They were the party of vested interests and as they thought that these interests were threatened by our Lord therefore they proved to be His deadliest foes. In His time they were the predominant party in the Sanhedrin and on them rested the chief responsibility for our Lord's crucifixion. The Sanhedrin—the Council of Seventy, the Supreme

Jewish Court—came into being about the time of Hyrcanus and the Romans found in it an excellent intermediary between them and the Jews. Rome permitted the Sanhedrin to adjudicate in all ordinary cases between Jew and Jew, reserving to herself the power to decide on matters of supreme importance. A man deemed worthy of death by the Sanhedrin had to appear for a final trial before the Roman authorities. In criminal cases the High Priest, the official head of the Jews in the eyes of Rome, acted as president.

The signs wrought by our Lord, in particular the raising of Lazarus, stirred the Sadducees to action, and a meeting of the Sanhedrin was called. About our Lord's power there could be no doubt, but there was doubt as to how He might use that power. Caiaphas, the High Priest, argued that if He were let alone all men would believe on Him and He might head the Messianic movement against Rome, in which case Israel as a nation would almost surely perish. He reminded them of the Jewish adage that it was in their interests that one man should die for the people, instead of the whole nation being destroyed. His words were an unconscious prophecy that our Lord should die for the nation and not merely for the nation, but to gather into one fold the scattered children of God. " This was the last prophecy in Israel; with the sentence of death on Israel's true High-Priest died prophecy in Israel, died Israel's High-Priesthood. It had spoken sentence upon itself."

CRUCIFIXION AND RESURRECTION—

John xix. 16-18, 23-30, 38-42; xx. 1-18.

The Passion Story was the first part of the primitive Tradition to attain the form of a continuous narrative and was current in different forms in the different Christian communities. The Tradition dwelt in minute detail upon every episode of our Lord's Passion because there God was seen in all the fulness of His love for man, and because the Christian Church had to show that a crucified One on whom the Law pronounced a curse was the Messiah of prophecy and the Saviour of the world.

Pilate, the Roman governor, who alone could sign the death-warrant, delivered our Lord up to be crucified. According to custom our Lord carried His own cross to the place of execution—Golgotha, a rocky, skull-like eminence, it being the Roman practice to make the place of execution visible to all. Crucifixion, a pagan mode of punishment, was a refined invention for the prolongation of the death agony. The Greeks and the Romans inherited it from the Phoenicians. Alexander the Great on one occasion crucified 2,000 Syrians and at the siege of Jerusalem in 70 A.D. Titus erected so many crosses that the supply of timber ran out. In Judaea Roman rule began and ended with crosses. The condemned man was stripped naked and his hands attached to the transverse beam with cords. Sharp-pointed nails were then driven into his hands. Finally he was hoisted into position and sat upon a peg, the " sedile."

With our Lord were crucified two thieves, and so the Isaianic prophecy that He should be numbered with the transgressors was fulfilled. The garments of the crucified were the soldiers' perquisites, and, in the case of our Lord, the soldiers, the unconscious instruments of God, drew lots for His raiment, so fulfilling the prophecy contained in Isaiah xxii. 18. By the Cross stood Mary, His mother, and His mother's sister, Mary the wife of Cleophas, and Mary Magdalene. Even on the Cross His care was for others. He entrusted His mother to the guardianship of the Beloved Disciple. " Woman, there is your son! Son, there is your mother! " Even on the Cross He was calm and possessed but when the climax of suffering had been reached, knowing that He had accomplished all that God had given Him to do, He yielded Himself to the needs of the body. He said : " I thirst," and a compassionate soldier filled a sponge from a jar of sour wine, placed it on a spear and held it up to His parched lips. At last, with the word, " It is finished," He bowed His head and gave up His spirit. He faced death not as conquered but as conqueror. It was not the manner of His death that impressed men but the spirit in which He met death. He voluntarily gave up His life that men might live. He endured the agony of the Cross because of His desire to redeem. Many Jews had died on a cross in silence but He, on the Cross, was without parallel in word and deed.

Joseph of Arimathaea, a man of wealth and standing and a member of the Sanhedrin, went to Pilate and asked for His body. Pilate granted the request, and, accompanied by Nicodemus, Joseph removed the body, embalmed it with myrrh and aloes, wrapped it in a clean linen cloth, and laid it in his own rock-hewn new tomb. The well-to-do had their own tombs in caves, usually in gardens, in which their dead were laid. The tombs were either rock-hewn or natural caves with niches for eight bodies hollowed out in the walls. At the entrance to the vault was a court 9 feet square for the bier and the bearers, and it was probably in the court that the embalming of our Lord's body took place. The doorway of the tomb was small and was protected by a round stone like a grindstone which ran in a groove. It was an act of great magnanimity to bury a stranger in the family tomb but with the approach of sunset and the Sabbath Joseph realised the difficulty that our Lord's friends would have in arranging for internment. "The spectacle of the crucified Saviour had quickened his faith and love, and combined, doubtless, with his shame for past faintheartedness, to raise him above the fear of man. His boldness is the more notable, because, to all human appearance, he was showing sympathy with a ruined cause, at the risk of persecution to death."

A satisfactory reconciliation of the Resurrection stories given in the Gospels is very difficult. To give assurance that Christ had risen single stories were enough and different cycles of stories were current at different centres. But of the fact of the Resurrection there can be no doubt. It is the only fact that can account for the transformation that took place in the disciples and for the rise and growth of the Christian Church. The Tradition testified that our Lord's body saw no corruption but was changed into a spiritual incorruptible body. The physical miracle was the natural correlative of our Lord's moral uniqueness.

The Fourth Gospel takes for granted the fact of the Resurrection. On the first day of the week—the third from our Lord's death—Mary Magdalene went to the sepulchre while it was yet dark, i.e., before the darkness of night had been fully dispelled by the rising sun, and found the stone rolled away. Sensing that Christ was not there, she ran to the lodging of Peter and of John, the Beloved Disciple. Both men started to run but John, the younger, outran Peter. Reverence and awe kept him from entering but the impulsive Peter went in to clear up the mystery. The Beloved Disciple followed and saw and believed. The word " believed " points to the calm, patient acceptance of a mystery as yet in part inexplicable, with full confidence in the divine love.

John, accompanied by Peter, went home without communicating his thoughts to Mary. Mary returned to the tomb, and knowing only of its emptiness, lingered outside, wailing in her grief. There came to her a vision of angels asking the cause of her sobbing, and turning round, she encountered the Risen Lord whom she took to be the gardener. " If thou hast borne Him hence tell me where thou hast laid Him, and I will take Him away." Our Lord spoke but one word,

" Mary," and she responded with one word, " Teacher." It was as another unbinding, another call into a new life, but she did not realise the meaning of the Resurrection. She would have clung to Him but Christ commanded her to go to His brethren with the message of His Ascension and of His coming to them again in spirit. " Thus, the fullest teaching of the past, the clearest manifestation of the present, and the brightest teaching of the future, came to the Apostles through the mouth of love of her out of whom He had cast seven devils."

ASCENSION—*Luke* xxiv. 36-53.

The impression given by St Luke's Gospel is that the Ascension followed immediately upon the Resurrection. What St Luke writes in the concluding verses of his Gospel is given at greater length in the Book of Acts.

Our Lord had promised His disciples that He would be with them alway, even unto the end of the world, and had commanded them to tarry in Jerusalem for the fulfilment of His promise. As the Jewish feast of Pentecost approached He made His last appearance and led them forth to Bethany. The disciples could not rid their minds of the Jewish conception of a temporal kingdom and probably enquired of Him about the restoration of the kingdom to Israel. He reminded them that the Scripture predictions about Him must be fulfilled, and added that the Gospel of repentance and remission of sins must be preached to all nations. He summoned them to service and gave them the promise of spiritual power from on high. So speaking He lifted His hands and blessed them, and as He blessed them He parted from them. Satisfied that He had sat down at the right hand of God, they returned to Jerusalem with great joy and spent all their time in the Temple, blessing God.

JUNIOR (Second Year).

B.—STORIES TOLD BY JESUS.

THE GRAIN OF MUSTARD SEED—*Matthew* xiii. 31-32.

THE mustard-seed is one of the smallest of seeds, but endowed with such an innate vitality that in a short time the plant grows to a height of some 12 feet. In our Lord's time the popular idea of the kingdom, as we have seen, was that it was a kingdom that would be introduced suddenly and catastrophically. In this parable emphasis is laid on the fact that the kingdom, though insignificant in its beginnings, will have a unique growth, because it is of God's planting and therefore endowed with vitality. History bears witness to the fulfilment of this prophecy in the ever-growing influence of our Lord and the extension of His sway over men's hearts and their social life. In the Old Testament the tree giving shelter to the birds is a recognised figure for a great empire giving protection to the subject nations (Ezekiel xvii. 22, xxxi. 3). Our Lord as Sower planted a seed that rapidly became a great tree under whose branches the peoples of the world find shelter. Christ Himself is the seed and the Christian Church is the plant that was grown out of that seed, embracing men of every race and class. Christianity makes a universal appeal, and in this respect differs from all other religions. In the world to-day no religion is aiming at the conquest of the whole earth as is Christianity. Judaism prides itself on its exclusiveness; Mohammedanism insists on the inferiority of woman in the sight of God; Buddhism demands monastic self-withdrawal from the world; Hinduism is a religion of caste; Confucianism is confined to the soil of its founder. In the Christian Church alone is there no trace of national narrowness or religious exclusiveness.

The Leaven—*Matthew* xiii. 33.

In the parable of the mustard-seed our Lord proclaimed to His disciples that He would draw all men unto Him. In this parable He explains the method by which this result will be achieved. "The parable of the mustard-seed has to do with the outward organisation of the kingdom," says Findlay, "that of the fermenting yeast with its unseen permeating influence." The kingdom will not come from without as the result of a miraculous intervention of God or of any political or social upheaval. It will come from within. His Spirit implanted in the hearts of the disciples will slowly but surely, like the leaven, permeate and vitalise the lives and institutions of men. He will effect His purposes through human agents who through contact with their fellows will impart to them new life. "History again comes to our aid," says Levison, "in proving how very true the parable has been to life, and contemporary literature proves how the leaven is working. . . . We find in Judaism men like Professor Abrahams and Dr C. G. Montefiore permeated with the leaven of the kingdom. In India Rabindranath Tagore, as representative of Hinduism, shows in every page of his writings the transformation which Christianity is effecting in the world. The great prophet of Arabia himself shows it and bears manly testimony to it. The monks of Syria, with whom he seems to have come in contact, had introduced the leaven, and I make bold to say that, with a reign of reason and goodwill, the two monotheistic communities of Islam and Israel will come to rest on the tree of God's planting."

The teacher might introduce the lesson by a talk about leaven and how it works. The opportunity should not be missed of pointing out to the pupils how important company is and how much good or ill a single individual can work in a group.

The Pearl of Great Price—*Matthew* xiii. 45-46.

The hid treasure was discovered by accident. The perfect pearl is discovered after a long and deliberate quest. But the hid treasure is no less perfect than the perfect pearl when discovered. Some are born into the sunshine. Some, born in darkness, pass, it may be easily and quickly, it may be slowly and laboriously, into light. The pearl merchant having found the flawless gem sells out his stock to acquire it. Like the tiller of the soil, he abandons everything to possess his find. The man whose life's purpose is the quest for God can find the satisfaction of his spiritual aspirations only in our Lord, and when he has discovered the pearl he knows its value. Of the parable another interpretation can be given. The pearl merchant may symbolise our Lord Himself, who gave up all, even His own life, to possess Himself of those who had come into believing fellowship with Him.

The Labourers in the Vineyard—*Matthew* xx. 1-16.

This story deals with the grape-growing season in Palestine. Casual labourers congregated in the market-place for hire, and because the wage was needed to keep them in life, they were paid by the day (*cf.* Deuteronomy xxiv. 15). It seems unnatural that men should be engaged at a late hour, although some scholars think that this was customary. It

is possible that the story is in more than one respect unnatural. When one bears in mind how differently many
behave in things spiritual and in things material, we see that
a parable story may actually need to be unnatural. What
occasions surprise is the owner's generosity in commanding
his overseer to pay all hands the same wage. What is the
explanation of his generosity? He recognised that the late-
comers were not idlers. Men in dire need, they had been
unemployed through no fault of their own. When found,
they had come to work without any definite bargain being
struck. For that reason the owner felt that they were
entitled to full pay. The early comers felt aggrieved, but
had no grievance. They made their bargain and received
payment.

What did our Lord mean by the parable? Some think
that He was defending His attitude to the social outcasts
and to the Gentile world. Many sections of the Jewish
nation which had served God at the cost of much suffering
resented the idea of the inclusion of the Gentiles in the kingdom of God and asked why they should have equality of
privilege. The reply of the parable so interpreted would
be that this leaves out of account "the Gentile's lack of
opportunity, the goodness of God, and the fact that religious
truth is not an honorary privilege but a necessity of life."

But it seems clear that the parable should be related to
Peter's question: "Behold we have forsaken all and followed thee: what shall we have therefore?"

The parable teaches that our human estimates will be sur-
prisingly upset on the day of judgment. The Jew engaged
in good works to obtain a reward, and the reward corres-
ponded strictly to merit. To our Lord the reward of
righteousness is spiritual, and He upset the Jews' standard
of values. "Many that are first shall be last," He said, "and
the last shall be first."

The parable also shows our Lord's attitude towards the
unemployed. It has been said that "Christianity is the
religion of all poor devils." Our Lord's compassion went out
to the broken men and women, to the demoralised multitudes
reckoned as the failures of life, and surely He indicates in the
parable what our attitude should be to the problem of unemployment. However justified the demand may be for
maintenance where work cannot be obtained, it can never
be a satisfactory substitute for work. It is not beyond the
power of an enlightened civilisation to deal with this urgent
problem; and it is particularly the business of a nation which

still claims to be directed by Christian principles to say to its citizens first: " Go ye into the vineyard "; and secondly, " Whatsoever is right," that is to say, whatsoever is necessary for adequate and honourable maintenance, " that shall ye receive."

THE HIDDEN POUND—*Luke* xix. 12-26.

This parable may be based on an incident in the life of Archelaus, one of the sons of Herod the Great, appointed by Augustus, ethnarch of Judaea. Archelaus made the journey to Rome to press his claims in person, and on his return rewarded his supporters with cities and avenged himself on his enemies.

What did our Lord mean to teach? St Luke informs us that the parable was spoken while our Lord was on His way to Jerusalem to suffer and die, "and because they thought that the kingdom of God should immediately appear." That suggests the following interpretation. Our Lord is about to take His journey into a far country and entrusts His followers with the privilege and responsibility of establishing His kingdom. He knows that after His death some will prove faithful to their trust and some will fail Him, and gives them the assurance that when He comes again—in the life to come—those who have made use of their opportunities shall be given further opportunity, while those who have proved unfaithful stewards will continue their spiritual development at a lower level as a result of spiritual failure here.

On the other hand, the parable may have been directed against the Judaism of our Lord's day. The Jew drew a hedge about the Law and declined to carry God's revealed truth to the Gentile world. He refused even to come into contact with the publicans and sinners of his own race lest he should infringe the Law, for God was strict and exacting in His legal demands. Yet he held that God demanded righteousness of the Gentile.

Our Lord accuses him of insincerity, of not lifting a finger within the limits of the Law to win the Gentiles and the outcasts to righteousness.

THE SAMARITAN TRAVELLER—*Luke* x. 25-37.

This is, perhaps, the most beautiful of all the parables. In it our Lord shows Himself a Master of teaching-method.

The scribe's question He answers by another. "What is written in the Law?" Let the professional exponent of the Law answer his own question. The scribe quotes Deuteronomy vi. 4, part of the most important prayer of the Jew, recited twice daily, and adds: "and thy neighbour as thyself," a saying made popular in Judaism since the time of Hillel, the founder of one of the two great Jewish schools of interpretation. Our Lord agreed with the reply. "Thou hast answered right; this do and thou shalt live." But the scribe was anxious to parade his knowledge of the Law. "Who is my neighbour?" he asked. He knew the answer: "All Israel are neighbours." "Thou shalt love thy fellow-Jew but thou shalt hate thine enemy, the Samaritan and the Gentile."

Our Lord told him a parable by which He taught him the meaning of neighbourliness. He makes the despised Samaritan His hero. Neighbourliness recognises no distinction of race or caste. "Know that the law of mercy is wide as humanity itself, and racial pride or religious strife may not interfere with it. Go thou therefore and, wherever there is opportunity, show mercy if thou wouldst enter into eternal life." In contrast to the exclusiveness of Judaism, He proclaimed the gospel of universal brotherhood. A love that is universal, a love that reveals itself in thoughtfulness, said our Lord, manifests the spirit of neighbourliness. Our Lord at the same time passed a sweeping condemnation on the official religion of His time. The priest and the Levite passed their dying fellow-countryman not because they were devoid of the milk of human kindness but because they were religious! The man might die on their hands, and thus through contact with his dead body render them ceremonially unclean and unfit to serve God in the Temple!

M'Fadyen suggests that in the parable our Lord portrays four attitudes to our fellows. The robber symbolises the commercial spirit that creates the social problem, the priest and the Levite symbolise the conventional Churchmen who see the problem with their eyes but get rid of it by failing to see it with their hearts, the innkeeper symbolises the professional worker who gives his time, skill and apparatus to the "cases" as a business proposition, the Samaritan symbolises the true Christian who seeks out the needy, supplies the finances for treatment, calls again to see that the necessary asistance has been given, and "ensures that the task of the professionals from beginning to end is carried out in a Christian spirit."

THE REFUSED INVITATION—*Luke* xiv. 15-24.

It is suggested by some commentators that the parable in Matthew is a version of the parable in Luke. But there is no reason why our Lord should not have used His illustrations on more than one occasion. Findlay says: " Like all good preachers, He never merely repeated Himself."

A great supper, as depicted here, was a common event in the life of the Jew. Not only did the host invite his friends, but he sent a servant to call them when the meal was ready. The friends who had accepted the invitation insulted their host if they made polite excuses on receipt of the second summons. Amongst Arab tribes the refusal of the second invitation sometimes led to war.

In the present case one man asked to be excused on the ground that having recently acquired some land he wished to go to see it. A second man had bought five yoke of oxen. He asked to be excused on the ground that he was anxious to try them. A third man asked to be excused, as he had recently married. The first man's interests were in his material possessions. The second was so engrossed in making a living that he neglected his promise. The third put his enjoyment before his obligations. The excuses they made were different, but behind all three of them there lies the same spirit of indifference to the host.

The indignant host sent his servants into the streets and lanes to bring in the poor, the maimed, the lame, the blind. On being informed that there was still room, he ordered his servants to search the countryside for the poor and the needy until the guest-room was filled.

Some, e.g. Cadoux, are of the opinion that the invited guests apply to the Jewish nation as a whole. " It was in the Jews' pride of national privilege that Jesus found an obstacle to that repentance which would bring them to their highest privilege in the kingdom of God. And the filling of the supper with the unprivileged, the outsiders from the highways beyond the city bounds, hinted that what Israel might miss through its arrogance as a privileged nation, would be welcomed by the large world without." But the Jewish people as a whole did not refuse our Lord's invitation, and the invited guests represent those who, while outwardly and officially religious, put secondary things first and were not prepared to seek first the kingdom of God and His righteousness. To certain of such our Lord said on another occasion: " The publicans and harlots enter the kingdom before you."

G

When He realised that many of the outwardly religious and respectable had no heart-hunger for Him and no insight into His heart-hunger for them, He took to Himself those who were conscious of their need, the social outcasts.

JUNIOR (Second Year)—INTERLUDES.

------

(1) CHRISTMAS.

THE COMING OF JESUS—*Matthew* i. 18-25.

THE passage in Luke corresponding to this is i., verses 26-38. There we have the account of the annunciation to Mary of the immaculate conception : here we have the account of the same to Joseph. Whether it be believed that actually the intimation was made to Mary by the angel Gabriel and to Joseph by a messenger of the Lord who appeared to him in a dream or whether it be believed that the form of the two accounts is to be put down to the narrators, the essential truth is that in its nature each annunciation was a divine revelation. The annunciation to Mary did not make a subsequent annunciation to Joseph unnecessary. He required more than assurances on her part that an angel had appeared to her to be satisfied that he ought to take her home to be his wife. That such needed further assurance was given him from on high is the message of the passage before us.

Among the Jews betrothal was a much more solemn engagement than it was among the Romans or is amongst ourselves. After it and before marriage the man was legally " husband " (verse 19), the woman legally " wife " (verse 20). A man desiring to be loosed from a woman to whom he was betrothed had to give her a writ and pay a fine. This was indeed done before witnesses, yet not in a public court but privily (verse 19). When a man found that the woman to whom he was betrothed had proved faithless, it was in his power to visit her with severe penalties (Deuteronomy xxii. 23-27). Joseph was a just man, a man, i.e., who was conscientious in his observance of the Law ; but he preferred the kindlier way and was minded to take it.

The words to him of the messenger of the Lord, " That

which is conceived in her is of the Holy Ghost," are parallel
to those of Gabriel to Mary, "The Holy Ghost shall come
upon thee, and the power of the Highest shall overshadow
thee." In the words of Sanday, " the same two Gospels,
though differing widely in the details of the narrative, assert
unequivocally that Joseph had no share in the parentage of
Jesus, and that the place of a human father was taken by
the direct action of the Spirit of God. The differences show
that the two traditions are independent of each other; yet
both converge upon this one point."

The messenger said to Joseph: "Thou shalt call his
name Jesus." Essentially that means that Joseph came to
know that it was God's will that he should assume the part
of a father towards the child that was to be born. In the
name Jesus (= he will save), which according to our narratives both Mary and Joseph were divinely instructed to give
their child, we ought perhaps to see an expression of the
Messianic hopes centred in Him which the revelations made
to them kindled in them.

Verses 22f. doubtless come from the Evangelist. It is
one of his characteristics to quote Old Testament prophecies that he believed had been fulfilled in the life of Jesus.
Here the quotation is from Isaiah vii. 14. In it the Hebrew
word translated " virgin," and so understood by Matthew,
in this place did not necessarily mean that. It was applicable
to any young woman, married or unmarried, fit to be a
mother.

THE VISIT OF THE MAGI—*Matthew* ii. 1-12.

Three questions here present themselves.

There is first the question, Who were the Magi of this
narrative? From Herodotus it is known that the Magi
formed one of six tribes of the Medes. In the days of the
Persian Empire they appear to have occupied a position
which some have compared to that of the Levites in ancient
Israel and others to that of the Brahmins in India. Strictly
the Magi were priests. The word, however, was used in a
wider sense, being applied to astrologers, to interpreters of
dreams, and to such as dabbled in the occult. That the Magi
of this narrative were magicians was a common view in
earlier times. This view, and with it the interpretation of
this narrative which discerns in it the downfall of the black
arts occasioned by the advent of Christ, are now abandoned.
There can be little doubt that the Magi of this story were

principally devoted to the study of the stars : it is possible
also (verse 12) that to a less extent they were interested in
dreams. Matthew describes them as Oriental Magi. Nothing
is known as to the country whence they came or as to their
number. Definite statements in regard to these matters
either come from later legendary additions to the present
story or are the doubtful inferences of commentators.

There is secondly the question that presents itself concerning the star that the Magi saw at its rising (verse 2),
and which afterwards, as they proceeded from Jerusalem to
Bethlehem, went before them, till it came and stood over
where the young child was (verse 9). Many have regarded
it as a star specially prepared by God to serve a special
end, a star that was not subject to astronomical law but
appeared and disappeared, moved and stopped according to
the divine will. Others have regarded it as a real star and
have sought to identify it. Of such attempts one of the
most notable is that of Kepler. That great astronomer noted
the appearance in the autumn of 1604 of a star of great
brilliance which soon began to fade and disappeared by the
end of 1605. At the same time there was a conjunction of
Saturn, Jupiter and Mars in the sign Pisces. Kepler associated the two phenomena and, since there had been a like
conjunction of the planets in 7 B.C., inferred that then there
had shone a temporary star which was that of the Magi.
Astronomers, however, have now abandoned the idea of any
relation between the two phenomena which Kepler observed.
His theory as to the time of the visit of the Magi is in part
retained by those who urge that what occasioned that visit
was not some temporary star but the conjunction of the three
planets. The Magi, however, did not speak of a conjunction :
they spoke of a single star. " We have seen his star," they
said. Altogether the data are so indefinite and there are so
many possibilities, no certain identification of this star seems
possible.

The third question is that as to the historicity of this
narrative. That the events which are here reported to have
taken place actually did so has been denied and the story
has been accounted for in various ways. Some hold that it
was formed under the influence of heathen ideas. One
theory is that it originated in a story told by Dio Cassius and
by Pliny of a journey made by the Parthian king Tiridates
with a company of Magi to Rome, where they worshipped
Nero and presented him with gifts. It was felt—so runs
the argument—that, if Nero the Antichrist received such

homage, Christ himself could not have received less. The present story, however, is throughout intensely Jewish in language and character. It cannot have come from pagan sources but must have originated on Palestinian soil. Others have regarded this story of the Magi as a legend formed on the basis of the prophecy of Balaam of a star to come out of Jacob (Numbers xxiv. 17) and on prophecies, such as those contained in Isaiah lx., Psalm lxviii., and Psalm lxxii., of Gentile pilgrimages to the light that was to arise in Zion. It is clear, however, from the parallelism that the " star " of Numbers xxiv. 17 refers to the Messiah himself, not to a heavenly body the appearance of which is to announce His advent. Moreover, it is noticeable that none of the above-mentioned Old Testament passages are quoted. That none of them are cited by Matthew, who delights in noting Old Testament predictions believed to have been fulfilled in the life of Jesus, is significant. In view of these considerations this explanation of the present story does not appear tenable. Yet another view of it—one that has been advocated and received with some favour by a number of scholars in this land—is that it is a Christian midrash on the story of Moses. It may be objected, however, that the present story is too simple to be so understood.

Considerations of a general nature have been urged against the historicity of this story. Thus it has been said that this visit of the Magi must have made a big impression and that it is surprising that no secular historian of the time has made any allusion to it. It is possible, however, since the mind of Herod was known, that it was thought well to keep any report of this visit from getting abroad. Again it has been urged that to find a place for this visit in the narrative of Luke is not easy. That difficulty needs to be acknowledged; but what able scholars have made of it shows that it need not be put down as an impossibility. It is thought that certain details in the story itself tell against its historicity. On these, however, some would appear to lay overmuch stress.

In seeking to come to a decision on this question two matters need to be borne in mind. In the first place, there is good reason to believe that through the Jews of the Disperson, Gentiles in Eastern lands had become acquainted with, and in some measure had begun to share, the expectation of God's ancient people of the coming of a King who was to be born in Judaea. In the second place, the coming of great ones into the world was in those lands associated with

the appearance of stars.   One doctrine of the Magi was that
of the " fravashi," or double, according to which, while part
of a man's personality dwelt on the earth, the other part was
in heaven.   When, therefore, a star of unusual brilliance
appeared the inference made was that some great man had
been born.   Though we may be quite unable to determine
what star it was that they saw at its rising, there is no good
reason why it should not be believed that the rising of some
star was taken by the Magi as proof that the King of the
Jews whom they themselves, though Gentiles, had learned
to expect, was now born.   The statement of verse 9b that
the star went before them and stood over where the young
child was, need not be reckoned a serious difficulty.   Any
star on which a traveller fixes his eyes seems to him to move
as he moves and to stop when he stops.   In proceeding from
Jerusalem to Bethlehem the Magi did not need the leading
of a star; but the sight of this one at this particular juncture
was to them a peculiar joy.   The story is told by Matthew
alone.   It is unconfirmed.   It has a certain vagueness.
Nevertheless, it appears to rest on a historical basis and to
involve at least a substratum of fact.

Matthew's account of the visit of the Magi is the counter-
part of Luke's story of the Bethlehem shepherds.   The Magi
were Gentiles : the shepherds were Jews.   Christ is the desire
of all nations.   The Magi were scholars : the shepherds were
working men.   The Christ around whose cradle there was
room for sage and shepherd is Lord of learned and simple.
The story of the Magi presents a series of questions; but it
is rich in spiritual meaning.

(2) EASTER.

The Easter Garden—*John* xix. 38-42; xx. 1-18.

See above, Stories of Jesus, Crucifixion and Resurrection.

Breakfast on Shore—*John* xxi. 1-14.

The last chapter of the Fourth Gospel is clearly an
appendix.   Its concluding two verses are from a hand other
than that of the Evangelist.   Whether the same is true of the
rest of the chapter is disputed.   Some think that the story
before us was told in the lost ending of Mark.   While that is
possible, it is a matter about which there is no certainty.

In the earliest days of the Church one story of an appearance of the risen Christ was sufficient to establish the fact

of His Resurrection. It was, therefore, for the most part in isolation that such stories were in circulation. Later, when the Gospels were written, different collections of them were made. It is this that accounts in large measure for the difficulty experienced in setting all the stories of the kind preserved to us in their chronological order and in bringing them into harmony in matters of detail. It would appear that the present story was current in a part of the Church where it was told as the first appearance of Jesus after His Resurrection to His disciples. The author of the appendix to the Fourth Gospel had, however, to take note of the fact that already in that Gospel two appearances of the risen Christ to the disciples had been reported: consequently he is at pains to correct the current tradition and writes: " This is now the third time that Jesus was manifested to the disciples, after that He was risen from the dead " (verse 14).

That there is some connection between this story and that of the call of Peter as recorded in Luke v. 1-11 is clear. In both, Peter plays an important part. In both there is the same kind of unusual happening. On the other hand, the differences between the two stories are of little importance. The conclusion can scarcely be avoided that both proceed from a common source. But in that source was this story a story of the first call of Peter or a story of an appearance to Peter and other disciples of the risen Christ? Each of these two views has its advocates. A strong argument in favour of the second is to be found in the words of Peter: " Depart from me for I am a sinful man " (Luke v. 8). That is precisely what we may well believe that Peter, who had denied Christ, said to Him on the first occasion of his seeing Him after His Resurrection.

The incident took place at the Sea of Galilee, here called the Sea of Tiberias, from Tiberias, a magnificient town built by Herod Antipas on its western shore. The seven disciples who figure here all belonged to the neighbourhood of this sea and had apparently resumed their calling as fishermen. That, it is difficult to understand if, before they left Jerusalem, Christ had appeared to them and had instructed them to be His witnesses. The difficulty, however, disappears if it be assumed that this story as originally told was that of the first appearance of the risen Christ to His disciples. Making the same assumption, we are able to understand the failure of these disciples to recognise Christ standing on the shore. Otherwise, that failure may be put down to the distance or the darkness or to their preoccupation with their work. But it has been well said that explanations here are vain. " After the Resurrection Christ was known as He pleased and not necessarily at once." When to Christ's inquiry whether they had any catch these disciples answered, " No," He, perhaps seeing from where He stood a big shoal of fish, instructed them to cast their net on the right side of the ship, and assured them that they would have a take. As it turned out the take was more than they could draw. Straightway, the disciple whom Jesus loved, who is almost certainly to be identified with John, the son of Zebedee, discerned that the Figure on the shore was the Lord. He said so to Peter, who at once put on his fisherman's coat, which he had cast off while working, and jumped into the water. The other disciples also desired to join Christ. Accordingly, they took to the dinghy and, having fastened the ropes of the net to it, came ashore in it, towing their catch after them. Coming to land they saw a fire of coals there and fish laid thereon and bread. The Lord had a meal prepared for His disciples. But first it was needful that what He had in readiness for them should be completed by the product of their own toil. Hence His instruction to them to bring of the fish they had caught. Peter, always first in action, drew the net to land, took out the fishes from it and, counting them as he did so, found that there were 153. That was a big number, for which reason and not because a mystical meaning was discerned in it, it was remembered.

The breakfast to which Christ then invited His disciples had much of the character of a Sacramental Meal. Christ was Host. The disciples were filled with awe and reverence. Their words were few. These conditions obtain where the Sacrament of the Lord's Supper is dispensed.

SENIOR (First Year)—NEW TESTAMENT.

A.—JESUS THE HERO.

Birth and Childhood.

ANNA AND SIMEON—*Luke* ii. 22-39.

TAKING with them the Infant Jesus, Joseph and Mary went up to the Temple in Jerusalem for a twofold purpose, to present there an offering for the mother's purification and, having there presented the child to the Lord, to redeem him according to the Law (Exodus. xiii.). It was on this occasion that they met the two saintly persons Simeon and Anna.

Even in the most decadent days there is a godly remnant. In Palestine, at the time when our Lord was born, there was more religiosity than religion; there were many also who had no connection with religion—publicans, harlots and sinners. But there were also those who were keeping the lamp of true religion burning in the land, people who read the Old Testament and understood it, who were waiting for the consolation of Israel. Simeon and Anna belonged to that class.

Simeon was an aged saint. God had wrought in him the assurance that before he died he would see the Messiah for whom he was waiting. Coming into the Temple under the guidance of the Spirit and seeing the Infant Jesus, at once he was certain that this was He, took Him in his arms and, blessing God, uttered his Nunc Dimittis.

His hymn—one of singular sweetness and solemnity—may be divided into two parts. In the first Simeon speaks of what the advent of Christ means to himself. Comparing himself to a sentinel now released from a long watch, he praises God that he can now depart in peace since his eyes have seen what he has waited to see. In the second he speaks of what the advent of Christ is to mean for the world. In Him God has set salvation before all nations,

" A light for revelation to the Gentiles,
    And the glory of thy people Israel."—*Revised Version.*

The universalism of this song, while distinguishing it from Jewish writings of the time, shows how deeply Simeon was imbued with the spirit of the greatest of the Old Testament prophets.

Surprise has been expressed at the statement that Joseph and Mary, who were aware of the destiny of their child, were amazed at Simeon's words regarding Him. It may be, however, that what amazed them was to find that precisely the secret which they had been guarding in their own hearts was known to another.

Simeon, who saw with prophetic glance the blessing that the advent of Christ would bring to the nations, saw also that by His life other lives would be tested (verse 34); he saw, moreover, that He would be rejected of men and that this rejection would occasion sorrow to His mother (verse 35). Simeon's words of prophecy should be read thus broadly: to particularise, e.g., to see in them a prediction of the experiences of Mary as she stood near the Cross, is to put more into them than may have been in Simeon's own mind.

The prophetess Anna is described as a daughter of Phanuel and as belonging to the ancient tribe of Asher. That she was advanced in years is plainly stated, but it is not clear whether the narrative intends to give her age as 84 or, affirming that after seven years of married life she had been a widow for 84 years, leaves it to be inferred that she was now over 100. She was a woman of great saintliness and spent most of her time in the Temple. Coming up at the time Simeon was uttering his song, she took up the same note of praise and afterwords spoke of the Holy Child to those of her circle in Jerusalem.

It is an interesting question, which we cannot answer, whether Luke obtained the substance of this pleasing portion of his nativity narrative directly from Anna or from a Christian circle who had it from her or from Mary, the mother of our Lord.

THE FLIGHT INTO EGYPT—*Matthew* ii. 13-15, 19-23.

This has been a favourite theme with Christian artists. We may, however, rest assured that the conditions of the actual Flight were in general quite different from and much more difficult than those that they have depicted.

But was there an actual Flight? We answer that question in the affirmative and we do so for the following two reasons :—

(1) The story as told by Matthew is characterised by an absolute simplicity. It has none of those embellishments that

are so abundant in the same story as told in the apocryphal gospels (see, e.g., " The Gospel of the Infancy "). This indicates either that Matthew sifted the information that came to him concerning this Flight and recorded only what seemed to him trustworthy or else that his form of the story reaches back to a time before it had begun to receive legendary accretions.

(2) Egypt was a likely place for a Jewish family, seeking refuge from the evil designs of Herod the Great, to betake itself. In that land there was at the time a large Jewish settlement. There Joseph would not be among strangers and there he could stay until such time as he thought it safe to return. The journey to Egypt—by the coast road one of at least three days—must have been exceedingly tedious; but it was the life of their child that was in danger, and we cannot say what trials Joseph and Mary may not have been willing to endure in order to bear Him to a land where they knew that He would be in safety. According to tradition they settled in Heliopolis near Cairo. That is not unlikely, but Matthew neither names the locality where they settled in Egypt nor does he state the duration of their sojourn there. In all probability the latter was quite brief. The secrecy of their flight to Egypt and the brevity of their stay there doubtless in part explain the omission of this story from the nativity narrative of Luke and the fact that no reference to it is found elsewhere in the Gospels.

In the course of the story we read that on three occasions Joseph was directed by an angel in a dream. We may believe that actually an angel appeared to him, or we may believe that the form of the story is due to the narrator. The essential truth is that in all his movements at this time Joseph was divinely guided. Matthew, who delights in quoting Old Testament prophecies believed to have been fulfilled in the life of Jesus, here quotes Hosea xi. 1 : " Out of Egypt have I called my son " (verse 15). There is no good reason to suppose that these words gave rise to the story of the Flight into Egypt. Strictly they are not a prophecy—a fact of which we need not suppose that Matthew was ignorant. What he noted as remarkable was the comparison possible between the experience of Israel and that of the Holy Child. The history of the former was a typical foreshadowing of that of the latter. As the one had been "called out of Egypt," so also had the other.

The concluding verses of the present section contain Matthew's statement of the settlement in Nazareth. This brings us to a matter about which there seems to be a serious disagreement between Matthew and Luke. The impression made by Matthew is that Joseph and Mary originally dwelt in Bethlehem. When after the return from Egypt they removed to Nazareth they did so because they feared that Archelaus would pursue his father's murderous designs. The impression made by Luke is that they belonged to Nazareth. The enrolment necessitated a visit to Bethlehem; but they returned from there to Nazareth as soon as circumstances made that possible. In dealing with this difficulty it is important to note that Matthew's cycle of birth stories is quite distinct from that of Luke. If Matthew learned nothing of an earlier residence of Joseph and Mary in Nazareth, it was natural for him to write of them as though they belonged to Bethlehem. If Luke learned nothing of the Flight into Egypt it was natural for him to infer and write that Joseph and Mary returned directly from Bethlehem to Nazareth. Luke's omission of any reference to the Flight into Egypt does not tell against its historicity any more than his omission of any reference to St Paul's journey into Arabia (Galatians i. 17) proves that the apostle did not go there.

Brave Deeds of Jesus.

FACING A MADMAN—*Mark* v. 1-20.

The accounts given in the first three Gospels should be carefully compared. Our Lord and His disciples landed at Gerasa or Gadara, generally identified with Khersa, on the eastern shore of the Lake. Khersa lay in a district with numerous limestone caves and rockhewn tombs, and with a predominantly Gentile population. The pig, to the Jew, was an unclean animal as the abode of an evil spirit, and in the tombs the spirits of the dead were supposed to lurk. As our Lord and His companions passed along the road that led to the city they were confronted by a man who showed all the symptoms of mania. When the frenzy came upon him he had been bound with chains and fetters, but these he had torn asunder. He had either fled or been driven to the cliffs, where he roamed about naked, shrieking and howling, venting his hate upon his fellows by inflicting pain upon himself. Believing himself to be possessed by a demon, he was beside himself with fear. Recognising in our Lord the Chosen of God and the Conqueror of evil, he felt drawn to Him, but at the same time anticipated judgment and further torture. Our Lord entered into conversation with him and asked him his name. In the thought of the age the knowledge of the name of a demon gave the mastery over it. The lunatic replied: "My name is Legion, for we are many." He was suffering from dissociation of personality, and he felt that he was possessed by a Legion—the Roman Legion numbered 6000 men—of demons. It may be that he was a victim of Roman rule, "a bit of human wreckage left by some act of ruthless quieting of a disturbed district," and that the Roman domination had become an obsession.

As demons must have an abode, the demoniac besought our Lord not to send them out of the country but into a herd of swine feeding not far away. Our Lord agreed, and the herd ran down the precipice into the sea and were drowned. Perhaps the maniac in his last paroxysm flung himself into the herd to which he communicated the spirit of fear. The onlookers would be convinced that the spirits had gone out of the man into the swine. As demons were supposed to have a dread of water, with the drowning of the pigs the unfortunate man would know that there was no possibility of the recurrence of his malady.

The inhabitants of the city on hearing of the cure were concerned about the damage to their property. Fearing further loss, they besought our Lord to depart from their borders. They repaid His love with hate. The healed man asked permission to join His band of disciples, but our Lord commanded him to remain amongst his own people as a missionary, to bear witness to that transformation of personality that He had effected. In this lesson emphasis should be laid on the fearlessness and love of Christ and the need for being a home-missionary.

Jesus the Bringer of Joy.

To Many in Capernaum—*Mark* i. 21-28, 29-38.

In the Capernaum synagogue there was a large and expectant congregation as the news of the arrival of the new Teacher had spread. When our Lord read the passage for the day and sat down to expound it, He held the people spell-bound. "He taught them as one that had authority, and not as the scribes." A man with an unclean spirit, recognising in our Lord the Holy One of God who had come to deliver men from the bondage of evil, began to scream. Our Lord commanded the evil spirit to depart, and quietness was restored. With the dispersal of the congregation, accounts of His unique teaching and of His power to heal would be in circulation all over the town.

When our Lord reached the house of Simon, with whom it is possible that He was staying, he was met with the news that Simon's mother-in-law lay sick of fever. Entering into the house, our Lord took her by the hand and raised her up, with the result that the fever left her and she ministered unto Him and His disciples. The suddenness and completeness of her cure, says Shafto, are not so inexplicable as they appear. " Malaria, in its commonest form of " country fever " or ague, may come on in the midst of good health : a feeling of chill and violent cold-sensations—teeth chattering, fingers dead white, pinched features, a rise of five or six degrees above normal in the body temperature—are the first stage. Dry heat, burning thirst, the usual intellectual unfitness or confusion of the feverish state, mark the second stage, and are followed by the perspiration stage, with a return to normal temperature. The paroxysm may complete this cycle in three or four hours, but it is usually longer in temperate climates. When it has passed there is a fair degree of bodily comfort and fitness." But, as St Luke tells us that Simon's mother-in-law " was holden with a great fever," there are no grounds for holding that she was suffering merely from ague.

When the Sabbath came to an end at 6 p.m. the people brought all manner of sick and suffering to Simon's house, and soon the whole town was gathered at the door. Our Lord, moved with compassion, healed many that were sick, and cast out many devils. The teacher should indicate the importance of Capernaum as a centre for teaching and healing.

To a Desolate Widow—*Luke* vii. 11-16.

This incident is recorded only by St Luke, who may have heard it from the lips of the widow herself. Nain lay some seven miles from Nazareth. Ramsay suggests that in the time of our Lord it lay on the top of a hill above the modern village, and was actually the " city set on an hill " of the Sermon on the Mount. At the gate of the town our Lord met a funeral procession on its way to the tombs outside the city walls where the dead were laid. The body of the dead, embalmed and swathed in linen, was carried on a bier or wickerwork shell with staves for the bearers. In the East a

widow bereft of her children had no claim upon her husband's family and must depend on her own people for
support, or starve. Our Lord, moved with compassion, commanded the bearers to stand still, and touched the bier. He
ordered the young man to arise, and he sat up and began to
speak. There was restored to the widow the support of her
old age. The proof of the power of Christ evidenced by the
raising of the widow's son from the dead thrilled the bystanders, and they glorified God.

To a Cripple Woman—*Luke* xiii. 10-17.

In one of the synagogues where our Lord taught was a
woman who for eighteen years " suffered weakness from an
evil spirit." She suffered from paralysis of the muscles and,
bent double, could not lift herself up. Her nerves refused
to do their work. When our Lord noticed her, He called
her to Him and gave her deliverance. " Woman," He said,
" thou art loosed from thine infirmity." " And He laid His
hands on her : and immediately she was made straight and
glorified God." This miracle led to controversy between
our Lord and the synagogue authorities about the observance
of the Sabbath. Our Lord argues that if it is permissable
to lead an animal to drink on the Sabbath without breach of
the Law, surely it is permissable to set free a descendant of
Abraham, the founder of the Jewish race, from bondage to
the power of evil. This story, like the preceding, belongs to
Proto-Luke. Both stories show Luke's sympathy with
women.

Fearless Friendships.

Jesus makes Friends with a Roman Centurion —*Matthew* viii. 5-13.

In Capernaum, in the service of Herod Antipas, were
Roman soldiers under a centurion, a Gentile. This Gentile,
a man well-disposed to Judaism, had in his service a slave
as personal attendant. The slave became paralysed, and the
centurion, who had heard of our Lord and His healing
power, went to Him with a request for help. Our Lord
showed Himself ready and willing to aid, because of the
centurion's obvious faith in His power and his desire to
help his slave. The centurion knew that our Lord as a Jew
would incur ceremonial defilement by coming under the roof

of a Gentile and, assuming that our Lord exercised control over
the powers of evil, as he controlled the men under him, he
said: "But speak the word only, and my servant shall be
healed."

The Gospel records that our Lord marvelled at his faith,
a faith such as He had never experienced among the Jews.
He assured him that his request was granted, and in that self-
same hour the servant was healed. "Such a healing is
without any authentic parallel in modern medicine."

The Jews prided themselves on their exclusiveness and
maintained that descent from Abraham guaranteed them a
place in the kingdom of God. At the Messianic banquet—a
feature of the kingdom—they held that they, and they only,
would sit down. Our Lord, on the other hand, not only
maintained that descent from Abraham provided no title for
admission, but that Gentiles who, like the centurion, showed
their spiritual fitness, could enter the kingdom. The children
of the kingdom, He said, whose membership of Judaism was
but a birthright membership devoid of living spiritual experience, would be cast into the outer darkness, the antithesis of
the banquet-hall, and to the Jewish mind the symbol of divine
punishment.

FRIENDSHIP FLOUTED BY A PHARISEE—*Luke* vii. 36-50.

Simon, the complacent Pharisee, out of sheer curiosity
or as an act of condescension, invited our Lord to his house.
But he violated all the rules of eastern hospitality. He did
not, as was the custom, receive his guest with a kiss nor did
he see to the washing of His hot and dusty feet, nor did he
pour oil on His head in token of friendship. As the company
reclined on the floor around the low table in the guest-
chamber, a woman that was a sinner—an outcast because of
her notorious trade—entered. Because of the freeness of
social life, any passerby had the right of entry, but it is unlikely that one of her class would have crossed the threshold
of a Pharisee unless for a special purpose. It seems clear
that she knew of our Lord's presence, had heard of His out-
flowing love and forgiveness, and hoped for the touch of
healing. She washed His feet with her tears, wiped them
with her hair, and anointed them with ointment.

Simon meantime was thinking his own thoughts. If our
Lord were a prophet, as he had been led to believe, surely
He would have recognised in this woman one of the un-
touchables. A prophet would never suffer her touch! Our

Lord divined his thoughts. " Simon," He said, " what needs
explanation is your want of love in contrast to this woman's
depth of love. To whom little is forgiven, the same loveth
little."

Our Lord said : " for she loved much." There are two
possible interpretations :—

1. For = because; i.e., love preceded forgiveness and led
up to it. Faith, the condition of forgiveness, involves love.
Though the woman was a sinner, deep down in her heart she
loved Christ and the things He stood for. Her love made her
bold to come into Simon's house, and because of that love she
was forgiven.

2. For = for, in our saying, " the weather will improve, for
the glass has risen." That is to say, forgiveness preceded
love. Our Lord inferred from the woman's tone that she
was already a forgiven woman. This means that she had
been forgiven before she came to Simon's house. The
message is that there is a correspondence between the tone
we show and what experience of forgiveness we have had.
Simon flouted our Lord's friendship because he was not a
forgiven man. He did not know Christ as Saviour. That is
what is wrong with men and women to-day. Many there be
who have no living, moving experience of the forgiveness of
their sins through Christ. Hence their indifference to the
criminal and the prostitute and the conditions that create
these classes.

Facing Death.

SETTING HIS FACE TO JERUSALEM—*Mark* x. 32-34.

One of the features of the Second Gospel is the place
given in it to the thought of suffering. The shadow of the
Cross reaches as far back as the words, " But the days will
come when the bridegroom shall be taken away from them,
and then shall they fast in those days," in the second chapter,
while the story of the Passion occupies almost a third of
the entire Gospel. It is usual now to regard the words before
us as introducing that story. They contain (1) an impressive
reference to the bearing of Jesus and its effects upon His
disciples, and (2) a third announcement of His Passion and
Resurrection.

(1) Of Jesus Himself, now on the road leading to Jerusalem and the Cross, but one thing is said. It was He who
led the way. Behind Him there followed the disciples not
merely amazed but " lost in awed wonder," and then further

H

in the rear came adherents of our Lord moved by a vague fear. Usually it is said that what troubled these followers was a dim foreboding of impending disaster. That, however, does not do full justice to the language in which Mark refers to them. The awe and the fear that possessed them were occasioned not by what they anticipated but by the impression made upon them issuing from our Lord. It was "the immediate impression of the numinous" (Otto). In touch with Christ men felt and knew themselves to be in touch not with a mere man but with one who belonged to a higher order of being. That impression issued from Him at other times; it did so especially on this occasion when He was seen resolutely setting His face towards Calvary and the Cross, and nowhere is it more clearly characterised than in the words before us.

(2) Taking again the twelve, our Lord spoke to them words that reveal to us the matter with which He Himself was preoccupied. For the third time (see viii. 31 and ix. 31) He told them what was to befall Him in Jerusalem. It is likely that certain details in these prophecies are *ex eventu*, particularly in this, the most precise and circumstantial of them. All three, however, testify how completely during the last portion of His earthly life the thought of approaching death to be followed by resurrection possessed His mind. He knew what His vocation involved. He knew that for Him death was divinely necessary. He knew that to bring the salvation of God to men He must needs suffer and die and rise again. The disciples did not understand that. They did not understand it, Luke (xviii. 34) reports, even on being told it this third time. Not until the Resurrection had actually taken place were their minds opened to it.

The Arrest of Jesus—*Mark* xiv. 43-50.

Outside the gate of the Latin Gethsemane there stands the fragment of a column. It marks the spot where, according to tradition, Judas betrayed his Master with a kiss. From the Upper Room in Jerusalem our Lord and the Eleven had come down to this garden beyond the Kidron in the night time. Earlier in the evening Judas had left that same room that he might be about his work of direst treachery. He now appears at the garden gate leading a company of men whose purpose is the arrest of our Lord and to whom, to prevent any mistake, he has given a token that will point out their victim. "Whomsover I shall kiss," he has said to them, "that same is he."

As to the character of the company to which Judas acted as guide, two views are entertained. According to the one it was a rabble that had been hastily gathered together and hastily armed. According to the other it was a detachment of Temple police acting under definite instructions from the Sanhedrin. While the jurisdiction of the Sanhedrin was certainly limited by Roman authority, it seems clear that it had power to make arrests and in doing so to employ its own officers. Our Lord's protest (verse 48), was made not on the ground that those arresting Him were acting *ultra vires* but that they were proceeding against Him as though He were a bandit and not a teacher whom they might have arrested while discoursing in the Temple. While the description of the company as " a multitude " and the fact that its members were armed with cudgels and short swords such as were carried by ordinary persons may seem to support the first view, the second consists better with Mark's statement that it was " from the chief priests and the scribes and the elders." This second view also consists with John's statement that this company comprised a band of soldiers. Their services can have been obtained only as the result of negotiations between the Sanhedrin and Pilate. It may also be that it was the delay which these negotiations occasioned that explains why the arrest of our Lord was made not in the Upper Room but in Gethsemane. In all probability, Pilate's main object in granting the soldiers was not that they might assist in the arresting of Jesus but that they might be at hand in case the arrest should lead to a tumult.

If the officers of the Sanhedrin had come unaccompanied by the Roman soldiers it is conceivable that the disciples of our Lord would have offered resistance. In the circumstances only one blow was struck in His defence. Even if John had not told us (xviii. 10) we should have guessed that it was Peter who struck that blow. Due, no doubt, to the indignation he felt when he saw the multitude beginning to lay violent hands upon his Master, Peter's act was rash and added to the danger in which the disciples stood. If not at once, very soon afterwards they all, not excluding Peter himself, turned their backs and sought safety in flight. The incident of the young man which follows in Mark may be taken as indicating that they did so just in time. As it was, having now arrested Him whom they wanted, the officers did not follow in pursuit of His disciples. The flight of the latter was not, as some have supposed, back to Galilee, but from Gethsemane and its immediate neighbourhood.

Older writers insisted that the arrest of our Lord was "itself an essential element of the Passion." Whatever may be thought of certain arguments they adduced in support of it, the contention is sound. Here we see wicked men, through their servants, binding hands that were never lifted save to bless. Here we see them leading away captive Him who came for the deliverance of man from his bondage. The arrest is an exposition of sin—a revelation of what sin does with goodness.

His Trial and Death—*Mark* xv.

(*a*) Verses 1-20. See Senior (3rd Year), At Jerusalem, The Trial (*b*).

(*b*) Verse 21. See Senior (2nd Year), Friends of Jesus, Simon of Cyrene.

(*c*) Verses 22-41.

These verses contain an account of the crucifixion and death of our Lord.

1. The *place* where the crucifixion took place bore the name Golgotha (in the Aramaic, golgolta, goulgoulta). The interpretation of this is "the place of a skull," in the Latin *Caluariae locus,* whence Calvary (Luke xxiii. 33). The name has been variously explained. Jerome mentions, but himself rejects, a view current in early Christian times that the name was due to a tradition according to which the skull of Adam was buried in this place by Noah after the Flood. According to another explanation, the place was one of public execution where skulls lay about. But the view generally accepted is that the place was a rocky protrusion, a knoll or mound not necessarily of any great eminence, resembling a skull in shape. From the New Testament we learn that this place was outside the walls of the city yet nigh to it, that it was near to a high-road and near also to a garden where there was a tomb cut in the rock. These particulars, however, are insufficient to determine the site; and the problem is much aggravated through the demolition of the city first by Titus and then by Hadrian and the many alterations subsequently made in its aspect. The traditional Golgotha is beneath the roof of the Church of the Holy Sepulchre. It stands within the present city. Whether the spot it marks was within or without the north wall of the city as it was in our Lord's time is a crucial question to which so far the majority of investigators find

themselves unable to give any certain answer. So recently as 1849, it was suggested that Golgotha is the skull-shaped knoll above Jeremiah's Grotto outside the present north wall of the city and not far from the Damascus Gate. In the same neighbourhood a tomb, the so-called Gordon's tomb, is pointed to as that wherein Joseph of Arimathea and Nicodemus laid the body of the Lord. For a time and in certain quarters these modern identifications were in considerable favour. To-day many call them in question, while some competent authorities unhesitatingly dismiss them as fantastic and describe the arguments advanced in support of them as fatuous.

2. At two points in this passage reference is made to *the hour of the day*. In verse 25 it is recorded that the crucifixion took place at the third hour, in verse 33 that there was darkness over the whole land from the sixth hour until the ninth hour. The Jews followed the ancient mode of reckoning the hours of the day from sunrise. According to Mark, therefore, the crucifixion took place at 9 a.m. From John xix. 14, however, it appears that the trial of our Lord before Pilate was in progress " about the sixth hour," i.e., according to the same mode of reckoning, about mid-day. By some it has been supposed that John, writing in Ephesus, followed the modern method of reckoning the hours from midnight. That certainly secures harmony, for it puts the Roman trial at 6 a.m., i.e., three hours before the time to which Mark refers the crucifixion. The view, however, that in Asia Minor the old method of reckoning the hours of the day did not obtain has been stoutly challenged by Sir William Ramsay, and the attempt has been made in other ways to bring Mark and John into harmony. Some have suspected corruption in the letters used as numerals. Some suppose that Mark has identified Pilate's delivering of our Lord to be scourged with his pronouncement of the death sentence. Yet others, emphasising the vagueness of ancient notes of time and understanding alike by Mark's third hour and by John's sixth hour the second quarter of the day, maintain that both the Roman trial and the crucifixion took place within that period and that greater precision is not possible. This last, while only a partial, seems on the whole the happiest solution.

3. As our Lord hung upon the Cross He uttered seven sentences, sometimes called " the seven last words of Jesus," but more accurately, " the seven words from the Cross." In the Second Gospel only one of these is recorded, *the cry*,

" My God, my God, why hast thou forsaken me?" These
are the opening words of Psalm xxii. Mark gives them in
Aramaic and adds a translation for the benefit of his non-
Jewish readers. From the fact that some of those that stood
by thought that our Lord had called Elijah, it is inferred
that He must have said " Eli," which is Hebrew, and not
" Eloi," which is Aramaic, and hence that He uttered this
cry not in His mother tongue but in the original language of
the Old Testament in which it was ordinarily read in the
synagogue service.

The seven words from the Cross fall into two groups
between which there elapsed an interval of some three hours.
It was by the present word, the fourth in order of the seven,
that our Lord broke that long silence. It is a strange cry, a
cry of seeming abandonment and desolation, the very sound
of which upon the ear occasions a cold shuddering within.
It has been variously explained. On the one hand extreme
criticism finds in it but an utterance of despair, a confession
on our Lord's part that God had failed Him and that His
cause is lost. On the other hand, there is the meaning given
it by the older orthodoxy as expressed, e.g., in these words
from Dale, " What is it? He has never sinned. He is the
Son of God, and inherits the infinite love of the Father. In
the hour of His anguish He is consummating the work which
is dearest to the Father's heart; but He endures that loss of
fellowship with the Divine blessedness, that exile from the
joys of God's presence, which is the effect of the Divine
wrath in the case of the impenitent." The former of these
explanations forgets that our Lord had long foreseen the
Cross, that especially in the last period of His earthly life the
thought of the necessity of His death had often been in His
mind. The latter, with its reference to exile from God's
presence and to the wrath of God, is not easily harmonised
with our Lord's own word, " Behold the hour cometh, yea
is now come, that ye . . . shall leave me alone : and yet I
am not alone, because the Father is with me," or with that
of the Father, " This is my beloved son in whom I am well
pleased." All this, however, but shows what difficulty there
is in understanding this word. In modern times considerable
use has been made of the fact that it is a quotation from
Psalm xxii. It has been supposed that our Lord, seeking
relief from his physical agony, began to recite to Himself
this favourite psalm, intending to go on to the splendid confession of faith and to the note of thankfulness for divine
deliverance in which it culminates. Of that, however, there

is not, nor can there be, any certainty. Only this we know, and we have it on the authority of the oldest tradition, that our Lord cried, " My God, my God, why hast thou forsaken me? "—these words of Psalm xxii. and no more. Whilst it becomes us to seek to know their meaning so far as we may, it becomes us also to recognise that here we are face to face with an impenetrable mystery.

4. The central figure in this passage is Christ upon the Cross. It is instructive to glance at *those who stood by* and beheld Him in His agony. We take them in the order in which they appear in the narrative :—

Those who offered our Lord wine mingled with myrrh.

These unnamed persons acted out of a feeling of humanity. " According to an ancient Baraita," writes Klausner, " when a man is going out to be killed they suffer him to drink a grain of frankincense in a cup of wine to deaden his senses . . . wealthy women of Jerusalem used to contribute these things and bring them." It was because He was resolved to meet death with His senses undulled that our Lord refused this draught. The vinegar offered Him later, which must be distinguished from this drugged wine, was possibly the sour wine or posca with which the soldiers refreshed themselves when on duty. It was in all likelihood a Roman soldier who out of pity pressed a sponge that had been dipped in it to our Lord's parched lips.

The Roman soldiers.

The carrying out of the crucifixion of Christ was committed to four Roman soldiers. After they had stripped Him and nailed Him to the Cross and hoisted and fixed in its place that cruel tree with its living burden, their remaining duty was to abide by it until death ensued. The garments of the crucified were regarded as the rightful perquisites of those who had crucified Him. Among the Roman soldiers gambling was a favourite pastime. These four, bringing out some dice, sought amusement in casting lots for our Lord's garments. That, bent as they were on their own profit and their own pleasure, and to all seeming in no wise impressed by the spectacle of the dying Saviour, they were yet capable of an act of kindness follows if the supposition made above be sound that it was one of them

who filled a sponge with vinegar and putting it upon a
reed brought it to our Lord's mouth.

The chief priests and scribes.

That chief priests and scribes should have forgotten
their dignity and come to the place of crucifixion is surprising.   Their presence there we can put down only to
their exultation in the success that so far had attended
their schemes against our Lord and to a thirst for yet
further revenge.   They did not indeed address Christ
directly : they derided Him among themselves (verse 31).
But ordinary folks who stood beside them, and not they
only, but those also who passed by leaving the city or
entering it by the gate near by, and even the two robbers
who were crucified with Him learning of them, taking
up their gibes and calling to mind the charges they had
so recently brought against Him hurled them at the
Sufferer.

The centurion.

The centurion (verse 39) was the officer in charge of
the four soldiers whose duty it had been to carry through
the crucifixion.   He was a man who had doubtless seen
many die upon the cross.   But the death of our Lord
stood apart from all other deaths he had witnessed : it
made upon him an impression such as no other had ever
made.   It was an impression made upon him partly, as
Mark indicates, by the amazing energy of our Lord's
last cry, partly by the circumstances attending His death,
but partly also and, we may well assure ourselves,
especially by the words he had heard Him utter and by
His whole bearing during the hours He had been upon
the cross.   What the centurion had seen and heard constrained him not perhaps to make a full confession of
the Christian faith (as the rendering of the Authorised
Version may suggest) but assuredly to declare that
Jesus had been more than a man.

The women.

On the outskirts of the multitude about the Cross
stood a band of women.   They had come up from Galilee.
With surpassing loyalty they had followed our Lord
to the place of crucifixion and standing there suffered
with Him in His suffering.   Mark gives the names of
three of them.   The first is Mary Magdalene, doubtless
so called as belonging to Magdala, a village on the west

shore of the Sea of Galilee. The second is Mary, the
mother of James the less and of Joses. Whether she is
to be identified with Mary, the wife of Cleophas (John
xix. 25) is uncertain. The third is Salome, almost
certainly the wife of Zebedee and so the mother of James
and John.

5. Mark records that *two extraordinary events* accompanied the crucifixion and death of our Lord.

In verse 33 he mentions a darkness which was over the
whole land from the sixth to the ninth hour. Certain scholars
in early Christian times, and a few also in later times, sought
to explain this darkness as due to an eclipse. While the
work, *Annals of the Olympiads,* by Phlegon of Tralles, is
now lost, the following passage of it, through its having been
transcribed by other writers, has come down to us :—" In
the 4th year of the 102nd Olympiad, an eclipse of the sun
took place, greater than all that had been previously known.
It became dark at the 6th hour of the day, so that the stars
appeared in the sky. There was a great earthquake also in
Bithynia, doing much damage in Nicaea." That the date
that Phlegon here gives for this eclipse and the date of the
Crucifixion cannot be far removed from one another is
certainly true. It was also held by those who sought to
associate the darkness mentioned by Mark with this eclipse
that the language of Luke in the place (xxiii. 45) where he
speaks of this darkness, suggests an eclipse. Nevertheless,
the idea that this darkness at the time of Crucifixion was
due to an eclipse of sun must be, as indeed it has been,
abandoned. In the first place, according to the best text,
Luke merely says that the sun's light failed—which does not
necessarily mean that there was an eclipse of that luminary.
In the second place, and this is decisive, our Lord was
crucified at the time of a Jewish Passover, and the Passover
took place at the time of the full moon of spring-time.
There cannot be an eclipse of the sun when the moon is full.

Mark reports that the darkness was over the whole land.
The word translated "land" can also mean the earth in the
sense of the whole world. Here, however, it is not necessary
to give it its larger meaning. Justice is done to what the
Evangelist says concerning this darkness if we assume that
it was a gloom due to natural causes but of extraordinary
intensity which was experienced throughout the land of
Judaea during part of the time our Lord was upon the Cross.

By some this darkness has been interpreted poetically. They have seen in it an expression of nature's sympathy with her Lord in His Passion. So Milton says that at the time of the Birth in Bethlehem all nature, moved by the spectacle of her Lord's condescension and lowliness,

> "doff'd her gaudy trim
> With her great Master so to sympathize."

Others have understood this darkness symbolically. It was a darkness that enshrouded all those who had any part in crucifying our Lord. In one of His last public utterances He had said to them: "Yet a little while is the light with you. Walk while ye have the light lest darkness come upon you." The warning which these words contain they disregarded; and the prophecy they contain was fulfilled upon them. When, laying violent hands upon our Lord, they crucified Him they put out the light that had been with them and with this result that darkness became their dwelling. Of that spiritual darkness that then enshrouded them this physical darkness was a symbol. Again, this darkness of which Mark speaks enshrouded our Lord's agonizing body. Through it, it is held, the Father spoke to the world of the deeper darkness that then enshrouded His Son's agonizing spirit.

The second extraordinary happening recorded by Mark is the rending of the veil of the Temple. This he puts at the time of our Lord's death. In the Temple there were two veils, one before the Holy Place, the other before the Holy of Holies. The latter is generally supposed to be that to which the Evangelist refers. How this veil came to be rent is not known. That it was rent at the moment when Jesus gave up the ghost cannot be proved but hardly needs to be assumed. It is sufficient to suppose that somehow the inner veil of the Temple came to be rent, that in the evening of the day of the Crucifixion its rent condition was observed, that this unusual happening was noised abroad, and that the disciples of our Lord, at once associating it with what was to them the supreme happening of the self-same day—the death of their Lord—sought its significance in connection therewith. Mark simply records the event; he does not say what meaning was given to it. The early Christians may have regarded it as a symbol of the approaching destruction of the Temple. Again, they may have taken it as symbolizing the truth that through the death of Christ they had gained free access to God. The second of these interpretations is found in Hebrews (vi. 19 and x. 20). The author of that epistle does not indeed refer to the event, but he may have known of it, and in consequence of that have written as he has done in the two places indicated.

(*d*) Verses 42-47.

It has been asserted that after our Lord died upon the Cross, had His body been taken away by the Jews, it would have been cast where either a heap of stones would have been raised upon it or carrion birds and pariah dogs would have devoured it. Whether or not that is true we cannot say. Happily there came forward two secret disciples who secured His body an honourable burial.

Of these one was Joseph of Arimathaea. Arimathaea is believed to be Ramathaim-zophim, Samuel's native place, identified with the hill-village of Beit-Rima, 13 miles from Lydda. Joseph, who belonged to the place, appears to have been resident in Jerusalem. A rich man and a member of the Sanhedrin, he was also a pious man who had been drawn to Christ, yet hitherto had lacked courage to make an open confession of his discipleship. Hard by Calvary he had a tomb hewn out of the rock and doubtless intended for his own last resting-place. Presumably the garden in which this was situated was his property. To-day the traditional sites of Joseph's tomb and of Calvary are beneath the roof of the Church of the Holy Sepulchre. The other secret disciple is mentioned only by the Fourth Evangelist. He was also a member of the Sanhedrin, a Pharisee named Nicodemus. On the two earlier occasions in the Fourth Gospel in which he is mentioned (iii. 1-21 and vii. 45-52) he appears as one upon whom our Lord had made a deep impression but who was afraid to avow his faith. Because it was only after our Lord had died that these two openly declared that they were on His side they have not infrequently been compared to those who seek to atone for their neglect of the living by a profusion of flowers and eulogies in the churchyard. But undoubtedly it was the spectacle of Christ dying on the cross that wrought in them the change manifested, so far as concerns Joseph, in the present narrative. It is the testimony of Christian workers in widely different fields that the account of the Passion more than any other part of the Gospel story touches men's hearts and wins them for Christ.

It was Joseph who went to Pilate and asked leave to remove the body of our Lord. That was an act of considerable daring. But Joseph, as Mark indicates, set aside his timidity and interviewed the Roman governor. Having satisfied himself that our Lord was dead, Pilate granted the permission asked. Thereupon Joseph either himself removed the body from the cross or superintended its being taken down. The Jewish custom was not to burn but to embalm and bury the body of the dead. Joseph and Nicodemus bound the face of our Lord about with a napkin. His body they wrapped in linen cloth into the folds of which they laid a mixture of myrrh and aloes, of which a liberal supply was provided by Nicodemus (John xix. 39). They then carried it to Joseph's tomb, where it remained over the Sabbath. Joseph and Nicodemus had to act in haste. The day was far spent and the Sabbath began at 6 p.m. the same evening. Want of time prevented any anointing of the body : and it is implied in John xix. 42 that Joseph's tomb was intended to serve merely as a temporary resting-place for the Lord's body.

This story of the burial recalls the words of Isaiah liii. 9, but is not to be regarded as a myth based thereupon. By it we are reminded that our Lord was true man, that He really died, that He had part in the sad accompaniments of the grave. It was fitting that the body of Him who is the only true King of men's hearts should have been laid in a new tomb (Matthew xxvii. 60, John xix. 41). As the Swiss commentator Godet says : " When a king is received the objects devoted to his service are such as have never yet been used."

THE VICTORY—*John* xx.

(*a*) Verses 1-18. See Junior (2nd Year), Stories of Jesus.

(*b*) Verses 19-29; 30-31.

It was the evening of the day of the Resurrection. Rumours that our Lord was risen had spread through Jerusalem. His disciples, uncertain what the authorities would now do and filled with fears, had assembled themselves in one place, perhaps in the Upper Room where their Lord had instituted His Supper. Suddenly He appeared in their midst and said unto them : " Peace be unto you."

John expressly mentions that the doors were shut. The doors were shut, he wishes the reader to observe, yet Christ came and stood in the midst. His body had become a spiritual body, a vehicle of self-expression that was no longer subject to ordinary physical law.

The risen Christ said : " Peace be unto you." He said

that twice to the assembled disciples, first on His appearing in their midst and again before He parted from them. The usual Jewish greeting, it was also our Lord's accustomed salutation. With Him, however, it was never conventional. On the present occasion, when on His appearing He said, "Peace be unto you," His purpose was not merely to greet the disciples but also to dispel their doubts and fears : and to do this the more effectively He showed them His hands and His side. Then, writes the Evangelist, were the disciples glad when they saw the Lord. Again, when on taking leave of these disciples our Lord said, "Peace be unto you," He did more than bid them farewell : He left peace with them as an equipment for the work He set them, saying : "As my father hath sent me even so send I you." To equip them still further for that work He breathed on them in symbolic fashion and said, "Receive ye the Holy Ghost."

The words following (verse 23) have been the occasion of much controversy. There is a difference of opinion as to what was the nature of the power that our Lord communicated, some holding that it was merely external and judicial —a power to exercise ecclesiastical discipline, others holding that it was moral—a power to deal with men's sins. There is a difference of opinion again as to who they were to whom this power was committed. From Luke xxiv. 36-43, where the same appearance of the risen Christ appears to be described, many have inferred that the assembled company comprised others besides members of the inner circle of the disciples. The two disciples who had returned from Emmaus were of it, and possibly others. There being, moreover, no indication that Christ addressed the words before us to any one section of the company, it is held that this power He communicated He gave to all present and not merely to those of the Twelve who were of it. Others, emphasising the fact that in this passage John speaks only of disciples and contending that whether others were present or not what John concentrates upon is the appearance of Christ to His disciples, maintain that it was to them alone that He gave alike the commission of verse 21 and the power spoken of in verse 23. On one matter, however, there is general agreement. The words, "Receive ye the Holy Ghost," govern the words following in which authority is given to forgive and to retain sins. Whatever the power communicated may have been and whatever the body to which it was committed, the power was one which that body was to be capable of exercising only as Christ by His Spirit became incarnate in it.

Thomas, also called Didymus or the Twin, was not with the rest of the disciples when the Lord appeared to them on the evening of the first Easter day. A man by no means lacking in courge, he had yet an eye for the dark side of things, and it has been supposed, not unreasonably, that he was absent because buried in the despair which the crucifixion and death of his Master had occasioned him. That supposition is borne out by the fact that when the disciples told him that they had seen the Lord he would not believe it, and still further by the thorough-going conditions on which alone he said that he would believe. He did not, however, separate himself entirely from the company of the disciples. He was with them eight days later when in very similar circumstances and in the same way Christ came and stood in their midst. Turning to Thomas, He gave him opportunity to satisfy himself in the way in which alone he had said that he would be satisfied. Of that opportunity Thomas did not avail himself. He saw Christ, and, seeing Him, did not need to reach forth his finger to behold His hands or to thrust his hand into His side. He saw Christ and that sufficed. Satisfied on less exacting conditions than those he had prescribed, he said : " My Lord and my God."

The beatitude of verse 29 has been fittingly described as "the peculiar heritage of the later Church." Christ we cannot see with the natural eye nor can we hear Him with the natural ear. But, experiencing His love and His power, we too can say : " My Lord and My God."

It is now widely held that the text of the Fourth Gospel has in places suffered dislocation. Not a little can be urged in favour of the transference of verses 21-23 of the present passage to follow verse 29. The confession of Thomas, however, forms a splendid climax to the Gospel and leads naturally to the two verses following with which the author manifestly intended to complete his work and in which he states what has been his great purpose in writing it.

SENIOR (Second Year)—NEW TESTAMENT.

A.—JESUS THE FRIEND.

1.—*Friends of Jesus.*

LITTLE CHILDREN—*Luke* xviii. 15-17; *Matthew* xxi. 15-16.

THIS is the age of the Child. There never has been a period in history in which such care has been devoted to the child as in our own time. All this fresh interest in child-life, child-psychology, child-welfare is the direct result of the operation of the Spirit of Christ. Although the child had a distinct place in the life of the Jews it was the maxim that children should be seen and not heard. Borchert says that our Lord was the first to love children—not His own, but strange children. St Mark (ix. 36; x. 16) tells us that He welcomed children for their own sake and kissed them. At the Triumphal Entry He accepted the acclamations of the boys who accompanied Him. He used the child to illustrate His teaching. He took a child and set him in the midst of the disciples, the child being the symbol of their status. In insisting on the sacredness of personality our Lord gave the child an entirely new value. "As Jesus was the first to look on children with love, so His keen eyes discovered new things about them. We may say that He discovered the soul of the child. He knew that these little ones can put us to shame (Matthew xviii. 3). . . . It was from the Nazarene the world learned that the child is something sacred and inviolable, protected by divine love, and very near to the divine nature (Matthew xviii. 10). We know now that there is a greatness in the child that older men may well envy (Matthew xviii. 3).

"Jesus perceived so much in children that others do not see. . . . The apostle Paul often noticed their immaturity and imperfection and he frequently entreated his hearers not to be as children. The wealth of Jesus' love made Him see beyond their imperfections, and their helplessness made Him feel doubly responsible for these despised little ones."

What did our Lord mean by saying that only those who received the kingdom as a little child could enter therein?

Nothing in the present passages provides an answer but a study of all the relevant passages suggests that the qualification for entrance is not humility nor innocence but the weakness of utter dependence. Unless a man in his weakness has a sense of utter dependence upon God, as a child naturally has upon its parents he cannot enter into the kingdom of God.

SIMON—*Mark* xiv. 3-9.

Simon is not otherwise known. He could have entertained guests only if cured of his leprosy, and it is a justifiable inference that our Lord had healed him. Luke (vii. 36) records a parallel incident where the name of the host is Simon, the Pharisee. In spite of certain similarities the two incidents can scarcely be identified.

TWO UNKNOWN FRIENDS—*Luke* xix. 28-38; xxii. 7-13.

The name of the owner of the colt is unknown but in all likelihood he was a disciple of our Lord (in the wider sense), certainly a man to whom He was known and with whom He may have arranged beforehand for the use of the colt. The carrying of a pitcher of water by the other unknown man may have been a sign previously agreed upon. Water-carrying in Palestine was done by women. It has been conjectured that the young man bearing the pitcher of water was John Mark, the writer of the second Gospel, and that he led the disciples to the upper room of his father's house.

SIMON OF CYRENE—*Matthew* xxvii. 32.

According to Roman rule our Lord had to carry the transverse beam of His Cross to the place of execution. As His scourging had been severe, He collapsed under the weight of the beam. It would have been beneath the dignity of a Roman soldier to relieve Him of His burden, but as the soldiers were put to inconvenience they compelled Simon, a Cyrenian, to bear His Cross. St Mark tells us that Simon was the father of Alexander and Rufus, names well known in the early Christian Church.

TWO MEN OF EMMAUS—*Luke* xxiv. 13-35

The appearance of the Risen Lord recorded here took place late in the afternoon of Easter-day. It was given to two disciples on the way to Emmaus. The site of the village is uncertain. According to some MSS. the village lay not 60 but 160 furlongs from Jerusalem. Of one of the two disciples only, Cleopas, is the name given. The other disciple may have been the wife of Cleopas or, as some think, St Luke. The Stranger made as though He would go further. "The Christ will only abide with us if our longing and loving constrain Him." The two disciples constrained Him and at supper when He gave thanks and broke bread in a familiar way, their eyes were opened and they knew Him. They knew now why His words had so powerfully affected them. Forgetful of hunger and fatigue, they hurried back to the city with the glad tidings.

2.—*The Friend in Need.*
CANA OF GALILEE—*John* ii. 1-11.

The story of the Marriage Feast at Cana is recorded only in the Fourth Gospel. The site of Cana is unknown but the village lay on higher ground than Capernaum, probably a few miles north-east of Nazareth. It was the home-town of Nathaniel. At a Jewish marriage supper the water-pots were set out for purification of the hands before and after eating and of the vessels used, purification being one of the main points in Jewish sanctity. The water-pots were stone vessels, each with a capacity of from 17-25 gallons, and water was drawn from them with a special measure holding " one and a half egg-shells." The water thus drawn was poured over the hands as they were held over a basin. The ruler of the feast was the chief servant, in charge of the supply of food and drink.

We do not know how the water was transformed into wine. St John tells us that by the miracle our Lord manifested His glory, and because of the miracle His disciples believed on Him. The miracle is a revelation of the Person of our Lord. It shows His courtesy in coming to the help of His host in his embarrassment. It shows His wide humanity and His ability to meet all human needs.

3.—*Stories told by Jesus to his Friends.*
THE SOWER—*Matthew* xiii. 1-23.

Matthew, Mark and Luke all tell us that this parable was spoken by our Lord from a boat by the shore of the

I

Sea of Galilee. The soil round the Lake is rich and fertile in parts, barren and rocky in parts, with occasional prickly shrubs growing in the midst of the wheat. The fate of the scattered seed depends upon the quality of the soil.

The parable is a parable of the growth of the kingdom of God. Our Lord expounds to His disciples the mystery of the kingdom. He will not force men into the kingdom. He will sow the seed. Some will refuse to make any response to Him, some will lack the grace of continuance, some will be preoccupied with the things of the world, but there will be an abundant harvest. The parable " celebrates the abundant productiveness of successful growth as far outweighing the worst that all causes of failure can do." Our Lord as Son had faith in the Father. On the Cross it appeared as if His enemies had triumphed. On the Cross their cause was lost. During the past 2000 years there has been a rich and abundant harvest.

M'Fadyen points out that as the farmer's ground by cultivation can be made productive, so men's spiritual and social environment can be changed so as to render the Word fruitful. "For multitudes preaching does not by itself provide a pathway to the kingdom. Our Lord's healing ministry to the distressed in body or in mind, His invitation to the rich to help the poor, His attempts to free the people from the intolerable burdens imposed on them by the religious lawyers, His efforts to open the eyes of the Pharisees to the true nature of their religious code, were all by way of preparation, of ploughing and removing stones and weeds. . . . The varieties of social and educational activities that now accompany our evangelistic efforts are a recognition of the fact that the soil counts for something as well as the seed. But the Church alone can never plough up all the hard ground, can never root out all the thorns that choke the growth of all good. It needs the Church and the State and the School all working together; and perhaps God alone, through the experience of life, can give depth to the shallow soul."

THE TALENTS—*Matthew* xxv. 14-30.

This parable follows and is closely associated with the parable of the Ten Virgins and was told by our Lord shortly before His death. The three servants get different sums but each has the same opportunity and judgment is pronounced in accordance with the use made of the talents given. Our Lord proclaims that although there are diversities of gifts and therefore of responsibilities, each is responsible for the employment of his spiritual gifts and those who approve themselves as His faithful stewards will receive from Him a spiritual reward. Behind the parable "lies the great law of Spiritual Capital. . . . It is in reality the application in the spiritual realm of what is known in the physical realm as the Law of the Conversion of Energy. Life is not something to be hoarded and cherished but to be put to the Great Exchange. . . . Life so invested for Another's service grows and is enriched."

4.—*Friends of Jesus help Him.*

AT THE GATE BEAUTIFUL—*Acts* iii. 1-20.

The writer of the Book of Acts, commonly believed to be St Luke, informs us that the Christian Church founded by our Lord received the gift of the Holy Spirit at the Jewish festival of Pentecost. The Feast of Pentecost, held at Jerusalem on the fiftieth day after the Feast of Unleavened Bread, both marked the close of the Corn Harvest and commemorated the giving of the Law at the "Holy Mount." Jews from all parts assembled then in such numbers that many of them failed to find accommodation within the city walls.

The leaders of the new society were the eleven with Matthias who having been acquainted with our Lord and having seen Him after His Resurrection, had been appointed in the place of Judas Iscariot. Amongst their followers the pre-eminence of these twelve was undisputed. The first believers consisted of orthodox Jews and proselytes to Judaism, the latter being referred to in the New Testament as "God-fearers." They regarded the Jewish Law as binding. They took part in the Temple worship and attended the synagogues. They may even have formed a synagogue of their own. They conceived of their mission as being exclusively to those of their own race and religious persuasion, and had no idea of carrying the Christian Gospel to the Gentile world. They expected the immediate return of Christ to set up the new kingdom, and endeavoured to carry out His counsels. They differed from the rest of the Jews only in their acceptance of Jesus as the Messiah, in living in His Spirit, and in using the power conferred upon them by Him for the service of others.

Outside the "Gate Beautiful," made of beaten brass wonderfully wrought, sat crowds of beggars, many of them the halt and the lame who might not enter the sacred building. As Peter and John were going up to the Temple at the time of the evening prayer a man of forty who had been a cripple since birth made an appeal for alms. In the name or by the authority of Christ Peter exercised His power and bestowed upon the man the use of his limbs.

Peter and John then conducted a mission in favour of the new movement in Solomon's Porch, which lay outside the Temple proper but within the Temple area on the west side of its east wall. Peter explained that the miracle had been performed through the power of Jesus who had been put to death and had been raised from the dead; and ended with an appeal for repentance.

At Lydda and Joppa—*Acts* ix. 32-43.

As a result of persecution and the murder of Stephen, the members of the Christian Church at Jerusalem were scattered. As they felt called to preach the Gospel until the return of Christ they carried their message to the synagogues outside Judaea. Philip, one of the so-called deacons, not the apostle, made his way to Sebaste (Samaria) where he made many converts. Later he conducted a mission along the coast, and, as a result of his activities and those of other refugees, large numbers in Samaria and Galilee accepted Christ. The new converts stood in need of supervision. They could not be regarded as full members of the Church without the gift of the Holy Spirit which could be conferred only by the twelve apostles. To the latter also the power to heal sickness, part of the new faith, was almost wholly confined.

The twelve, therefore, from time to time, left Jerusalem for the purpose of supervising the new communities, appointing local rulers, baptising and instructing converts. Peter visited the districts evangelised by Philip between Azotus and Caesarea. At Lydda (Lod), a village in the Plain of Sharon, on the great caravan route between Babylon and Egypt, he healed a paralytic, Aeneas by name, and received a request to go to Joppa. The importance of Joppa was due to the fact that it was the only seaport of note between Mount Carmel and Egypt. At Joppa the timber from Lebanon was landed (2 Chronicles ii. 16) and there Jonah took ship for Tarshish. About the time of

Peter's visit there was constant friction between the Jews and the Gentiles for possession of the town.

At Joppa there had died a woman named Dorcas (gazelle) who had carried on her activities among the poor. She had been a " disciple " and a woman of considerable substance. Garments shown to Peter by the widows were doubtless presents from her. As our Lord raised the daughter of Jairus from the dead, so Peter by His power restored Dorcas to life and there was a large accession of Jewish converts. Hitherto Gentile converts had entered the Christian Church as proselytes to Judaism, but on the outskirts of Palestine where feeling between Jew and Gentile ran high, Peter realised the impossibility of winning the Gentiles if they had to accept the obligations of the Jewish Law. The fact that he went to stay in the house of Simon, a tanner, indicates that he was contemplating the admission of Gentiles without demanding of them adherence to the Jewish Law. The tanner's trade was held in detestation by orthodox Jews, as it involved the handling of the skins of unclean animals; and the tannery, as a rule, lay outside the city walls.

SENIOR (Third Year) — NEW TESTAMENT.

A.—THE STORY OF JESUS ACCORDING TO MARK.

Beginning of the Gospel.

THE CALL OF THE TWELVE—iii. 7-19.

Our Lord called twelve that they might be with Him. At the outset the twelve joined His fellowship in the conviction that as Messiah He would fulfil the national and political hopes. Slowly they came to see that He was the Son of God. What they recognised Him to be is written in the Prologue to the Fourth Gospel.

Philip belonged to Bethsaida of Galilee, and, as his call probably took place near " Bethany beyond Jordan, where John was baptising," it is surmised that he was a disciple of the Baptist. After the choosing of the twelve, Philip became one of the second quartet, his name standing at the head in each list. His Greek name led the Greeks who came up to the feast to approach him for an introduction to our Lord. Polycrates states that after the Ascension he lived as one of the great lights of Asia, and was buried at Hierapolis. Philip must not be confused with Philip, the evangelist, one of the Seven, who evangelised Samaria.

Bartholomew is generally identified with Nathaniel of the Fourth Gospel. If this identification is correct we can understand the power exercised by our Lord over this disciple. " Before that Philip called thee, when thou wast under the fig tree, I saw thee " (John i. 48). Who could have known of that hour in which, perhaps, Nathaniel had been praying for the coming of the Messiah, save God and the Messiah Himself?

Matthew is given seventh place in the apostolic circle in the first three Gospels. In the first Gospel he is identified with Levi (Matthew ix. 9; x. 3). Matthew, the name given him after his call, means " gift of God."

Thomas volunteered to accompany our Lord to Bethany when the rest of the disciples held back (John xi. 16). He could not bear the thought of separation from the Master (John xiv. 5). He played a large part in the questionings after the Resurrection. He refused to believe that the Lord had risen until satisfied by sight, but, when convinced, addressed Him as " My Lord and my God "—the greatest confession of faith in the New Testament.

Of James, the son of Alphaeus, nothing is recorded in the Gospels. It has been thought by some that he was a brother of Matthew who is also called son of Alphaeus. He is usually identified with James the Little, the brother of Joses and son of Mary (Mark xv. 40; Matthew xxvii. 56).

Simon, the Canaanite or Cananaean, was a Zealot. The Zealots were patriotic Pharisees, discontented with the Pharisaic ideal of waiting for the kingdom. They were anxious to introduce the kingdom by the sword and their watchword was to call no man lord. Their extreme section were the Sicarii, so-called because of the effective use that they made of the dagger. The activities of this section led to the revolt against Rome and the fall of Jerusalem in 70 A.D. Simon after he became a disciple was no longer a zealot in the old sense. It is possible that the term zealot as applied to him was descriptive of his zeal and that he had no connection with any political party. St Paul in his early days was a zealot in that sense, zealous, as he writes, of the traditions of his fathers.

Judas Iscariot is named in the four Gospels as the betrayer. Iscariot means " man of Kerioth," a village south of Hebron. Judas was covetous. He enriched himself from the bag or common purse with which he was entrusted. He was present at the Last Supper and after the betrayal committed suicide in a fit of remorse. Lust of money, the motive suggested in the New Testament, may not have been the determining motive in the betrayal. He *may* have wished to force our Lord's hand. Believing him to be the Messiah he *may* have thought that He would never submit to arrest, but, with His enemies upon Him, would introduce the Messianic kingdom.

Growth of the Kingdom.

THE SEED GROWING SECRETLY—iv. 26-29.

The title given to this parable, recorded only by St Mark, is misleading, emphasis being not on the gradual character of growth but on the fact that when man has done his part, the issue lies with God. Loisy gives this interpretation: " The kingdom of God is also a sowing whose inevitable growth is independent of men's will and even of the will of the sower. Like the labourer, Jesus sows the kingdom by preaching the Gospel: it is not His work to bring the harvest, i.e., the complete coming of the kingdom, and one must not grow impatient if its coming does not follow at once: that is God's business. . . . It is none the less certain that the harvest will come without delay." This does not imply that men are to slack in their efforts. If the members of the whole Church throughout the world consecrated themselves to the service of Christ, the coming of the kingdom would be immeasurably hastened.

Happenings on the Way

THE RICH YOUNG RULER—x. 17-27.

This young man whose name is unknown had been rendered uneasy in mind by the spiritual movement created by our Lord. He came to our Lord with the words " Good Master," recognising that He was in a different category from the scribes. Our Lord referred him to the fundamental commandments. The young man replied that he had striven to keep these but still lacked the assurance of salvation in the kingdom of God. " Jesus, looking on him, loved him." He recognised his sincerity, and told him that to gain the kingdom he must sacrifice all his possessions. The youth could not stand the test. He went away sorrowful because he had great possessions. Our Lord set him midway between the man he was and the man he might become, but he made the great refusal. According to tradition his old contentment perished for ever. He could not forget Christ's appeal, and the memory of His face was a torment and a curse.

As our Lord saw this disciple whom He had hoped to secure take his departure, He sorrowfully told His disciples of the difficulty the rich had in entering the kingdom. It was as absurd, He said, to expect that earthly possessions could unlock the door of the kingdom, as it was to expect that the largest beast of burden could enter a small hole. Humanly speaking, He said, it was impossible for a rich man to enter the kingdom, but God could rescue the human heart from the bondage of riches.

Our Lord did not despise the wealthy. He dined with them on invitation. He received Nicodemus. He restored the daughter of Jairus, the ruler of the synagogue. He had a meal with the wealthy publican, Zacchaeus. But it is noteworthy that the names of all the rich with whom He came in contact are given, " and that shows us where the canker at the root is to be found. Names are only given when there are few to give. Jesus found the rich hard soil, in fact generally a soil that yielded nothing, and He only won individual rich people to Himself. There is a curse attendant on wealth, honour, high reputation, everything that brings celebrity in its train, even wisdom and learning. For such things make men satisfied, and they desire nothing more. It leads them to believe that they are well-pleasing to God and man, and thus bars the way to a change of heart. . . . Wealth, too, has this peculiarity, that it occupies a man's mind; and, at least when it becomes the master, it makes any division of service impossible. . . . The rich man is always afraid that people have designs on his pocket. He is afraid, too, of his own heart, in case it should carry him away, and so he allows it no freedom. Truly the barriers such a man erects against God are terribly strong."

At Jerusalem.

The Vineyard of The Lord—*Mark* xii. 1-12.

Our Lord made a first beginning of teaching by parables during His ministry in Galilee. A second beginning He appears to have made during His ministry in and around Jerusalem immediately prior to His crucifixion. The present parable belongs to the latter period. Spoken as it was on a day in Passion-week it must have been one of the very last of all His parables. While most of His parables were addressed to the disciples and to the people generally, this one was spoken in the first instance and especially to those in authority in the capital.

Its story is not, as some have supposed, an impossible one. In Palestine absentee landowners let their land to husbandmen, i.e., local cultivators not always upon the condition of their paying them a money rent but frequently on their agreeing to give them a definite portion of the produce. Such leases were sometimes by the year, sometimes for life, and sometimes even passed down from father to son. That the husbandmen should have treated the servants of the landowner so contumeliously as is related consists with what is known as to the difficulties experienced in the collecting of rents. In murdering the heir these husbandmen, if they did not suppose that the landowner was now dead, must have proceeded on the assumption that, being in a distant land, he would not return for a considerable time and in that assumption they may well have been confirmed by the fact that he had not come in person to avenge their ill-usage of his servants.

The present parable is an allegory rather than a parable. It is a presentation in a picture of Israel's history past, present, and future—on the one hand of God's infinite patience towards His people, on the other hand of their long continued rejection of Him and of the catastrophe in which it is to issue. This parable needed no interpretation. The meaning of it must have been at once apparent. In speaking of Israel as God's vineyard our Lord made a comparison which, occurring in the prophets and in the psalms, was well known to those whom He addressed. The details show that our Lord had principally in view the passage Isaiah v. 1-7. The hedge about a vineyard might be of thorns; frequently it was a wall of unmortared stones. The winepress consisted of two parts— the press which was a trough hewn in the rock in which the grapes were trodden by the feet, and the pit, a similar but smaller cavity lower down into which the juice was allowed to run. A vineyard had among its enemies jackals, foxes, and bears, thieves also and robbers. A watchman had to be continuously on duty. By night he moved about on foot. By day he sat in a watchtower. This might be but a booth hoisted in the air upon four long poles. Sometimes it was a more permanent structure of unmortared stones which served not only as a watchtower but also as a place of storage and as a shelter for the workmen. These details are interesting in themselves. They should not, however, be regarded as having each a special significance. Together they express God's great care for His chosen people and that is the one matter which, in speaking of them, one ought to stress.

In this parable severity and sorrow are intermingled. There is indignation in our Lord's setting of the attitude of the authorities towards Himself in line with Israel's cruel treatment of God's prophets through all her past. Yet He is also sad not in the contemplation of the death to which these same authorities are to put Him but in view of the doom about to come upon those who have despised a precious privilege and misused a great trust.

This parable shows that our Lord regarded Himself as occupying in relation to God a place higher than that of the Old Testament prophets; He claimed to be not God's servant but His beloved son. It shows further how large a place at this time the thought of His approaching death had in His mind and what far-reaching consequences He realised it would have. For those reasons this parable is one of importance.

Concluding it our Lord made a quotation from Psalm cxviii. In their original setting the words quoted refer to Israel despised by the world-powers yet destined in the purpose of God to occupy a place of pre-eminence amongst them. As used on the present occasion by our Lord they have been interpreted in two ways. By some they have been taken as referring to the true Israelites. Soon to be delivered from their unfaithful leaders they will be given others under whose guidance they will attain to great honour. By others they have been taken to refer to our Lord Himself. He was the stone which the builders rejected, which afterwards would be made the head of the corner. So understood the words supply a thought that could not be expressed in the parable proper, that namely of the Resurrection.

THE ANOINTING AND BETRAYAL—*Mark* xiv. 1-11.

(*a*) Verses 1 and 2.

The Jewish authorities in Jerusalem came to a momentous decision. They resolved to arrest our Lord. From verse 2 it is clear that they recognised that their doing so might result in an outbreak of disorder among the people. It is clear also that in their fear of that they recognised the need of acting with subtilty. It cannot, however, be made out with certainty whether they resolved to avoid arresting our Lord during the days of the approaching Passover feast and so were prepared to arrest Him before or after it as opportunity presented itself or resolved to postpone His arrest until the feast was over and the majority of His Galilean followers had departed to their homes. If they decided upon postponement it is conceivable that the unexpected offer of help made them by Judas led them to change their minds and act at once.

Verse 1 contains a time indication of considerable difficulty. This is seen on reckoning first backwards and then

forwards. According to all four Gospels the Crucifixion
took place on a Friday. The Lord's Supper was instituted
on the preceding evening, i.e., on Thursday. It would
appear, therefore, that the decision to arrest our Lord was
made on Wednesday, the anointing at Bethany as recorded
by Mark taking place on the evening of the same day. If
now the Passover took place two days after that decision
was reached then it took place on Friday. That means
that the Crucifixion took place as the Fourth Gospel indicates on the day in the evening of which the Passover was
eaten, that therefore the Last Supper was not, as the
Synoptic Gospels indicate, a Passover meal. A way out of
the difficulty is sought through the assumption that Mark
reckoned in the Jewish fashion, that consequently by
" after two days " he meant " on the evening of the next
day." The same verse distinguishes between the feast of
the passover and the feast of unleavened bread. The
former in the narrow sense denoted the feast observed on
the evening of the 14th Nisan, i.e. (since the Jewish day
began at 6 p.m.) immediately after the 15th day of that
month began. The latter denoted the feast observed during
the seven days following and throughout which in com-
memoration of their departure from Egypt the Jews ate
unleavened bread. Not infrequently the former name was
applied to the whole eight days' feast. The use here of
both names is remarkable. (See, however, 2 Chronicles
xxxv. 17).

(*b*) Verses 3-9.

See Senior (2nd Year): Jesus the Friend, Friends of
Jesus.

(*c*) Verses 10 and 11.

The Jewish authorities who had resovled to arrest Jesus
fully realised how necessary it was to do so secretly. Contrary no doubt to all their expectation but assuredly to
their great joy Judas Iscariot, here called " the one of the
twelve " possibly to distinguish him from some other Judas
and at the same time to emphasise the enormity of his
crime, came forward offering them the help that would
enable them to effect such an arrest.

About Judas Iscariot—the man from Kerioth—it is impossible to think without a feeling that we are in the
presence of what is strangely dark and mysterious and un-
fathomable. (The teacher might refer to Hazlitt, Ayrton,

Hunt, Matthew Arnold's "Saint Brandon," Robert Buchanan's "Ballad of Judas Iscariot." Lamb is quoted by Hazlitt as saying : " I would fain see the face of him who having dipped his hand in the same dish with the Son of Man, could after-- wards betray Him. I have no conception of such a thing; nor have I ever seen any picture (not even Leonardo's very fine one) that gave me the least idea of it.") There is the mystery that surrounds our Lord's choice of him to be one of His disciples. There is the mysterious fact that though he companied with our Lord and the other disciples, yet, in spite of all the gracious influences that must on that account have been about him and upon him, he became not a better but a worse man. Yet again there is the mystery that surrounds his deed of treachery. How is it to be explained ? There are several theories. There is the theory that Judas was an incarnation of the devil. There is a series of theories which agree in this, that they seek to make out that Judas was not so great a sinner as ordinarily he is supposed to have been. According to one of these, expounded in peculiarly attractive terms by Thomas de Quincey, Judas was convinced that Jesus was the Messiah but he grew weary of His long delay in mani- festing Himself as such. He resolved accordingly to place Him in the grip of the law that so He might be forced to manifest His Messiahship. But while it may well be that the motives of Judas were mixed there is reason to be- lieve that what principally prompted him to his great crime was greed. For money men will desecrate what God has sanctified : for money men will forsake religion : for money Judas undertook to deliver his Master into the hands of His enemies.

THE LAST SUPPER—*Mark* xiv. 12-26.

(*a*) Verses 12-16.

See Senior (2nd Year) : Jesus the Friend—*Luke* xxii. 7-13.

(*b*) Verses 17-26.

Our Lord and His disciples had assembled themselves in a large upper room in Jerusalem (verse 15). The tradi- tional site of this room is within a building known as the Cenaculum outwith the present south wall of the city and near the Zion Gate. Sanday believes " that of all the most sacred sites (in Jerusalem ?) it is the one that has the strongest evidence in its favour."

Mark records in the first place that, whilst the meal was in progress, our Lord startled His disciples with the intimation that one of them was to betray Him. When one by one they inquired of Him, " Is it I ? " he replied, " It is one of the twelve, he that dippeth with Me in the dish." Proceeding further and emphasising the divine necessity of His death He pointed out how dreadful none-theless would be the doom of the man through whom He would be betrayed.

Mark does not say explicitly that on this occasion Judas was of the Lord's company. Nothing in verses 17-21 neces-sitates his presence. " The twelve " in verse 17 may be conventional and in any case may not include the two dis-ciples (verse 13) who had been sent on ahead to make arrangements, while the words " he that dippeth with Me in the dish " may not indicate some particular person but mean simply " one of my intimate friends." The other evangelists, however, regard Judas as present and Mark doubtless implies that. That our Lord, as Mark records, should have spoken of him in general terms without de-finitely indicating him is altogether in keeping with what we know of our Lord. Without addressing Judas in person He let him know that the deed of treachery he contem-plated was not hid from Him: in words that are an appeal of love He warned him of the consequence to himself if he proceeded to so great a crime. It is possible that our Lord, still hoping to win Judas from his evil design, stayed this intimation of his treachery until after the institution of the Supper. That is the place given it in Luke who at this point appears to have followed an independent source. Mark, it will be observed, gives no hint as to the hour of Judas leaving the company.

There follows Mark's account of the Last Supper, the most concise of all the New Testament accounts of it. According to Mark (verse 12) and the other Synoptists our Lord had come with His disciples to the Upper Room in Jerusalem that He might eat the Passover with them and it was at the time of this Pascal meal that He instituted His Supper. According to the Fourth Gospel, on the other hand, the Crucifixion took place on the day in the evening of which the Passover was eaten and the institution of the Supper, of which this Gospel contains no account, taking place on the preceding evening, cannot be assigned to the time of the Pascal meal. That the Synoptics and the Fourth Gospel are in conflict in reference to this matter is now generally recognised. Moreover while the Synoptic date of the Crucifixion has still able defenders the majority of scholars appear to prefer that given by the Fourth Evangelist. It is conceivable that the early Church soon began to think of the Lord's Supper as a Passover, and that that thought of it influenced Mark from whose Gospel it passed into those of Matthew and Luke.

The meal of which we read here may not have stood alone. It may be, as some have suggested, that throughout His ministry our Lord had from time to time had meals with His disciples at which, as head of the company, after offering a solemn thanksgiving over bread and wine and then breaking the bread He had handed it and the cup to them. Be that as it may, this meal was different inasmuch as on this occasion in distributing the bread our Lord said, " Take, eat : this is My Body," and in giving the cup, " This is My Blood of the Covenant " and then, hinting that this would be the last occasion on which He would drink wine with His disciples, spoke of a more blissful fellowship which He would yet have with them. As recorded in this Gospel the Lord's Supper is a symbolic foreshadowing of His death. Throughout it we see our Lord seeking by word and by act to prepare His followers for the death He is to die and seeking also to make known to them its significance. His death, He sought to teach them, would be sacrificial: through it a new covenant would be made between God and man. " In the thirty-first chapter of Jeremiah we have the sublime prophecy of a new covenant —a new covenant which is indeed but the efficacious renewal of the old, for there is but one God, and His grace is one—a new covenant, the condition and foundation of which is the forgiveness of sins. ' They shall all know Me from the least to the greatest, for I will forgive their iniquities, and I will remember their sins no more' (Jeremiah xxxi. 34). It is this that is present to the mind of our Lord as He says of the outpoured wine, ' This is My blood of the covenant.' He is establishing, at the cost of His life, the new covenant, the new religious relation between God and man, which has the forgiveness of sins as its fundamental blessing. He speaks as knowing that that blessing can only become ours through His death, and as the condition upon which it depends His death can be presented as a propitiatory sacrifice. It is as though He had pointed to the prophecy in Jeremiah, and said, This day is this Scripture fulfilled before your eyes."

Neither the account of the Last Supper given by Mark nor that given by Matthew contains the injunction, "Do this in remembrance of Me." While it occurs in the received text of Luke xxii. 19 it is regarded by many as an interpolation there. It is clear, however, that in St Paul's time it was believed that our Lord had given such an injunction. It is possible that, though Mark is silent in reference to it, our Lord commanded a perpetual observance of the Supper on the occasion of which we read here. It is also possible that He gave His disciples that commandment after His Resurrection and before His Ascension.

GETHSEMANE—Mark xiv. 32-52.

(*a*) Verses 32-42.

The Garden of Gethsemane will never be forgotten. To the end of time it will remain associated in men's minds with the most deeply moving conflict of soul of which we have record. The traditional site of it is most easily reached by a road which, passing through the St Stephen's Gate in the east wall of the Holy City, runs down thence to the Kidron bridge. The Garden, distant but a few paces beyond the bridge, is a square piece of ground now enclosed and having eight olive trees of a great age growing in it. The place of the Agony, if not within this Garden, cannot have been far from it.

It is not likely that our Lord accompanied by the Eleven came down to Gethsemane by the road just mentioned. Probably He approached it from the south-west. That matters little. What impresses us is the fact that at so late an hour—it must have been about midnight—He should have left the city, that at a time when Jerusalem was hushed in sleep He should have sought the deeper stillness that reigned down in the dark Kidron valley. Even more significant is His action on arriving. At the entrance to the Garden He left eight of His disciples. Taking the remaining three — Peter, James, and John— with Him to some point within, He bade them tarry there. He himself went on still further, then fell upon His face and prayed. All this isolating of Himself, first from the world generally, then from the body of His disciples, and then finally even from the chosen three indicates that on this night a great desire to be utterly alone possessed and moved our Lord. Along with this, however, there are other facts which cannot but be noted. Our Lord did not go down to Gethsemane unaccompanied. He took the Eleven with Him. When He retired within the Garden He did not leave them all by its entrance. He took three of them with Him. When He parted from them it was not His will that in spirit they should be separate from Him. His word to them on leaving was that they should watch with Him (verse 34). Even more significant, perhaps, is the fact that He came back seeking the fellowship of these three not once but a second and a third time. In all this there is ample evidence that on this night another desire of a contrary nature possessed and moved our Lord. Longing to be by Himself, He also longed to have the company of others. Seeking solitude He also sought sympathy.

Why on this night did our Lord seek thus diligently to be by Himself?

What He had to experience on this occasion no man could experience with Him. The burden that He had to take upon Himself was one which neither Jerusalemite nor disciple, even the most devoted, could share with Him. He had to tread the winepress alone. His desire for solitude relates itself to that necessity.

Why on this night did our Lord long for human fellowship?

It is not with man as it is with the beast of the field. The beast of the field receiving a mortal wound retires to its lair and dies alone; man in that last hour when he knows that all the help of man is vain yet yearns for some brother, some sister nigh at hand. In Gethsemane our Lord longed for the assurance that in His agony some human eye would be upon Him, that some of those who had learned to know and love Him would behold Him and feel for Him. In Gethsemane He who was made in the likeness of men yearned for human sympathy. But He found it not. In that hour when the Saviour of mankind agonised for all mankind, in that hour all mankind left Him alone. Surely it was the unkindest thing that ever could be. Yet so it was. Coming to His disciples He found them sleeping.

What was the nature of the agony that our Lord endured in Gethsemane? That is the most important question the verses before us present: it is a question also to which many answers have been given. It has been urged, for instance, that in the Garden our Lord fell into a retro-

K

spective mood. He began to look back over His brief ministry, to review and estimate it and it was then that suddenly the painful truth flashed upon Him that all the great expectations He had entertained were now beyond realisation. Disappointed and broken in spirit He cried, " My soul is exceeding sorrowful even unto death." Others associate our Lord's agony with fear of the terrible sufferings that He knew awaited Him in the immediate future. Having a presentiment of the several agonies that He would have to endure on the cross He shrank back in fear and trembling: henoe His prayer that the hour might pass away from Him and that the cup might be removed from Him.

To such theories there are at least two fundamental objections :—(a) We nowhere else read of our Lord flinching at the thought of death. He feared neither man nor wicked spirit. He knew that the former had power that went no further than killing the body. His counsel to His disciples was that they should not stand in fear of such. He returned to Judaea from Peraea despite the protest, " Master, the Jews of late sought to stone thee, and goest thou thither again ? " Of the prince of this world He said, " He cometh and hath nothing in Me." (b) Such theories, while they may satisfactorily account for a passing mood of sorrow or despair come far short of an adequate explanation of that agony which our Lord endured in the Garden of Gethsemane. It is no commonplace experience of which we read here. It is no ordinary sorrow. It is no agony with parallels. It is something altogether unprecedented, altogether unique. This truth is borne in upon us as we seek to enter into all that the Greek words and phrases used by Mark convey or rather seem to labour to convey: for in truth one gets the impression that here he is struggling to describe what he feels it is beyond his power adequately to describe. Our Lord was demented or beside Himself: He was on the brink of despair: He was not merely surrounded or compassed about by sorrows but reduced to that hapless condition wherein sorrow masters the whole consciousness: so full was His heart of sorrow, the least little more of it would have meant death. My soul, he said, is exceeding sorrowful even unto death. To this unprecedented character of His agony our Lord's longing for the fellowship of His disciples, spoken of above, bears further witness.

Our Lord prayed and said, " Abba, Father, all things

are possible unto Thee; take away this cup from Me: nevertheless not what I will, but what Thou wilt." If we could but understand what the cup of which He spoke stood for in His thought we would come near to an understanding of the nature of that agony which He endured in the stillness of the Garden retreat. It was not anything that could come from man though it might and indeed did come through man. That we have seen. It must then have been something in the will of the Father from which the will of our Lord shrank. Our Lord, it would seem, fell back for the moment not before the physical pain of the death He was to die but at the thought of all that that death was to involve as a sacrifice for the sin of the world, above all at the thought of the interruption it would involve in that sacred, loving communion He had always had with the Father. If that was the nature of His agony His prayer in Gethsemane and His cry from the Cross, " My God, my God, why hast Thou forsaken Me? " belong together. The one anticipates the dread experience to which the other bears witness.

In the Garden our Lord looked into the darkness and the blackness of death which is the wages of sin; and then He said, " Yea Father, even into this I shall go." So great His filial obedience. So great His love of man.

Teachers will find it profitable to ask their pupils to compare this scene with that of the Transfiguration, also to compare our Lord's words here with certain of those in the Lord's Prayer. With reference to the familiar words, " the spirit indeed is willing, but the flesh is weak " (verse 38) the question needs to be asked whether they are a doctrinal platitude or an excuse or a reason.

(*b*) Verses 43-50.

See Senior (1st Year) : Facing Death, The Arrest of Jesus.

(*c*) Verses 51 and 52.

Mark does not give the name of the youth who figures in the little incident he records in these two verses. A conjecture that has been widely received with favour is that he was none other than the Evangelist himself. At the time he was but a lad, the son of the owner of the house in which the Last Supper had been eaten. He was in bed when our Lord and His disciples left for the Garden of Gethsemane; but hearing them go he rose, hurriedly threw a wrap about him, and with a lad's curiosity followed them across the Kidron and into the Garden, overheard the words in which our Lord prayed there, was still near to Him when the multitude arrived to arrest Him, and fled only when they sought to lay hands upon himself.

This theory that the young man was Mark may explain how the incident has been recorded by Mark and by him alone. It also consists with the fact known from the Acts (xii. 12) that the house of Mary the mother of Mark was a place where Christians met in the early days of the Church.

THE DENIAL OF PETER—*Mark* xiv. 53-54, 66-72.

Each of the Evangelists tells of Peter's denials. The four accounts differ considerably in particulars but the main facts are clear.

According to Mark those who arrested our Lord led Him away to the high priest (verse 53). His residence, like most Oriental houses of any size, was built round and had its doors and windows looking out upon an interior rectangular court. A broad passage piercing the front part of the building led from the street into this courtyard and was closed at the end towards the street by a heavy folding gate having in it a smaller wicket by which individuals were let out and in. On one side of this passage and within the gate was a room for the porter or portress. On the arrival of the party that had arrested our Lord the portress (John xviii. 16) doubtless opened the big gate and then, when all were through, closed it again. Having handed over the prisoner to the high priest the members of the party, their work being now done, lit a fire and, clustering round it in the cold of the early morning, began to warm themselves.

At the time of the arrest of our Lord His disciples forsook Him and fled. Two of them, however, soon rallied somewhat from their panic. Of these the one was Peter, the other " another disciple " (John xviii. 15) who, if not John the son of Zebedee, may have been a resident in Jerusalem. These two followed the party that led our Lord away to the high priest. They kept, however, at a safe distance behind. Consequently by the time they arrived at the residence of the high priest the party had entered and the big gate was already shut. The " other disciple," however, was " known to the high priest " and not only did the portress at once admit him, she also at his request allowed Peter to follow.

Once inside Peter joined the men who were warming themselves round the fire in the courtyard. One of the maids of the high priest, in all likelihood the portress who had given him admittance, seeing him there in the light of the fire as she chanced to pass charged him with being with our Lord. Peter at once denied; in his embarrassment he declared that he did not even understand her meaning, "I neither know, nor understand: thou, what sayest thou?" In his uneasiness he withdrew from the brightness of the fire into the passage leading from the street. There, however, he was near to the portress' lodge. She, returning there, saw him again and called the attention of the bystanders to him. Again Peter denied. But his speech convicted him. The bystanders noted his broad northern accent and now they took up the charge saying to him, "Of a truth thou art one of them; for thou art a Galilean." A third time Peter denied his Lord, this time cursing and swearing as he did so. Immediately the cock crew, and Peter, recalling our Lord's warning that he would deny Him before cock-crow, "burst into tears."

In treating of Peter's denials care is needed that his conduct be not represented as worse than it actually was. At the time he was tired in body and perplexed in mind. It was desire to be near his Master that had brought him into the court of the high priest's house and, it may be, that it was in part at least to the end that he might not be excluded from the place where his Master was that he spoke as he did. That his love to his Lord had not failed is proved by the sincerity of his contrition.

On the other hand, care is needed lest we appear to defend his action. Peter had been warned: Peter had made a solemn promise (Mark xiv. 26-31). That warning he neglected: to that promise he proved unfaithful. To think of Peter at Caesarea Philippi and then here in the courtyard of the high priest's residence is to realise how a man may confess Christ in the company of His disciples and then deny Him among strangers. To think of Peter in Gethsemane and then here is to realise how soon courage may give place to cowardice. Yet again, to think of Peter ready to draw his sword in the presence of the whole company that has come to arrest his Master and then here incapable of giving a straight answer to a maidservant's taunt is to realise how a man may rise to the necessities of a great occasion and yet go down before a lesser test.

THE TRIAL—(a) *Mark* xiv. 55-65; (b) *Mark* xv. 1-20.

It was not the policy of Rome to deprive the countries of which she became mistress of all their former powers. Judaea, associated since the removal of Archelaus by Augustus in A.D. 6 with the province of Syria, was administered by a resident governor (procurator): but the ancient Jewish ecclesiastical court, the Sanhedrin, still exercised certain functions.

In recent times there has been considerable discussion as to the extent of the powers retained by the Sanhedrin. Mainly on the basis of a passage in the Palestinian Talmud some have argued that from the time when Judaea passed more directly under Roman administration the Sanhedrin lost its right of trying capital cases, that consequently in the case of our Lord there can have been no ecclesiastical trial in the strict sense nor any actual condemnation of Him by the Jewish authorities. They had power only to take the initial steps. Having arrested our Lord they could examine Him and make investigations regarding Him but only with a view to the presentation of a case against Him in a Roman court. In point of fact the Fourth Gospel contains no record of an actual trial of Jesus by the Sanhedrin. According to it He was first examined before Annas a former high priest and still the *de facto* leader of the Sanhedrin, then further examined before Caiaphas the high priest *de jure,* then finally was taken from the house of Caiaphas to the praetorium, the residence in Jerusalem of the Roman governor, and tried before him. The Third Gospel also, while it reports proceedings at a hastily convened meeting of the Sanhedrin, does not record a formal verdict of that court. There are many, however, who are not satisfied that the Sanhedrin had no power to condemn. That it had such power is certainly assumed in Mark's account of the trial of our Lord (cf. that of Matthew). As for the passage in the Talmud alluded to above its tradition, being of uncertain origin, is of doubtful value as evidence. One thing, however, is certain—whether or not the Sanhedrin had power to pronounce a capital sentence, it had no power to execute it. Such a case had to be carried before the Roman governor for re-trial. The *jus gladii* or power of life and death was vested in him and in him alone and only if he confirmed it could a death sentence be carried out. For these reasons the trial of our Lord proceeded in two stages. There was first the ecclesiastical or Jewish trial. Upon that there followed the civil trial or the trial before Pilate the Roman governor.

Mark's account of the first stage of the trial is contained in xiv. 55-65 and xv. 1. The passage xiv. 55-65 contains a report of proceedings at a meeting of the Sanhedrin held in the early hours of the morning. The meeting of that court mentioned in xv. 1 was a formal one held in the daylight merely, as it would appear, to confirm and regularise the findings already reached. That there were informal investigations from the time of the arrest on through the early hours of the morning till daybreak seems quite certain: but that within that time there was any full meeting of the Sanhedrin such as Mark reports at which our Lord was tried and condemned has seemed to many unlikely. The difficulties of convening the members of that court so early are obvious. There is, moreover, no report of a trial by night in the Lucan narrative. It is possible, therefore, that much that Mark reports in xiv. 55-65 belongs properly to the meeting of the Sanhedrin mentioned in xv. 1.

The informal investigations of the early morning were conducted partly in the house of Annas, and partly in that of Caiaphas and it was in the latter place, as it would seem, that the subsequent regular meeting of the Sanhedrin took place. It is supposed by not a few that Annas lived at the Tabernae or Booths on the Mount of Olives and not far from Gethsemane. Mark makes no reference to any examination of our Lord before him. The view that Annas and Caiaphas his son-in-law had a common residence seems unlikely. Some think that, since Caiaphas was high priest, his house was an official residence within the Temple area and included the hall where the Sanhedrin had its sessions. Others deny this and seek the house of Caiaphas elsewhere. To-day a claim is made for a site outside the south wall of the city where stood a church of St Peter called *in gallicantu* and where is to be seen a stoneway cut in the living rock, the very road, it may be, over which our Lord was led to be tried by the Jewish authorities.

Mark reports that the chief priests and the whole council sought evidence against our Lord. Witnesses were got together but many of them were false and there was conflict of evidence. At last there stood up certain who gave a garbled version of a saying of our Lord (cf. John ii. 19). In some respect, however, which the Evangelist leaves unmentioned their testimonies also were found wanting in consistency. Meanwhile our Lord held His peace and answered nothing. The high priest, confronted with the possibility of the case breaking down and chagrined at the silence of our Lord, took an extraordinary step. He himself put to our Lord the question, " Art thou the Christ, the Son of the Blessed? " Challenged thus in the supreme ecclesiastical court of His nation to say whether or not He claimed to be the Messiah our Lord at once admitted the claim and then, in words which seem to be expressive of His assurance that some day His claim would be gloriously vindicated, added the triumphant prophecy, " Ye shall see the Son of man sitting at the right hand of power, and coming with the clouds of heaven." This claim was forthwith interpreted as blasphemy. All had heard it made. There was no further need of witnesses. All condemned Him to be worthy of death.

The mocking and ill-treatment of our Lord which Mark reports to have followed this condemnation is put before the trial in Luke's narrative. Those who indulged in these indignities were not members of the Sanhedrin but certain of the party that had arrested our Lord and were still in charge of Him. No doubt they were emboldened by the conduct of their superiors.

The question of the extent to which the Jewish authorities acted legally in their conduct of the trial of our Lord is a difficult one. Usually it has been assumed that the laws governing the procedure of the Sanhedrin as contained in the Mishnah, obtained in the time of our Lord, and judged in the light of them His trial by that court has been pronounced grossly unfair. Now, however, it is held by some that these laws of the Mishnah represent a later phase of Jewish jurisprudence and that while the Sanhedrin was far from faultless in its action, it cannot be made out with the old-time certainty that it did not observe the usual forms of legality.

Pontius Pilate before whom our Lord was now taken for trial was the fifth in succession of the Roman governors of Judaea. The office, to which he was appointed in A.D. 26, was one of considerable difficulty. That Pilate did not possess all the gifts of statesmanship it needed is clear. There were weak points in his character: on occasion he proved obdurate: sometimes he displayed hot temper and acted with cruelty. The fact, however, that he was allowed to retain the office for 10 years is a proof that his administration was not so unsatisfactory as it has been represented. In Palestine Pilate resided normally at Caesarea: but he came up to Jerusalem at the time of Passover to maintain order there. Where he stayed in the Holy City and where therefore the Roman trial of our Lord took place cannot be made out with certainty. It may have been in the Tower of Antonia which overhung the Temple area or in the Palace of Herod near the Jaffa Gate.

From the narrative of Mark it appears that, when the Jewish authorities brought our Lord before Pilate, they began by alleging that He claimed to be Messiah in a political sense. This explains the question that the governor put to our Lord, "Art thou the king of the Jews?" He in reply neither admitted nor denied the charge. At this point there is a certain vagueness in Mark's account of the proceedings. It is clear, however, that Pilate grew in the conviction that the prisoner was guiltless and sought to escape the odious necessity of condemning Him. An opportunity of doing so seemed to present itself when during a pause in the trial a crowd of people came streaming in before his judgment seat. They came not necessarily interested in the trial then in progress but reminding Pilate of a custom that prevailed at the Passover season and loudly demanding the release of a prisoner. Of this custom—that of setting some one prisoner at liberty as often as the season of Passover came round—singularly little is known, the only evidence of it being that afforded by the Gospels. Pilate seized the opportunity. Before the multitude had time to name the prisoner whom they wished he suggested our Lord. "Will ye," he at once inquired, "that I release unto you the King of the Jews?" He perceived that if only the people agreed all would be well. But they, instigated by the chief priests, called for the release of Barabbas, a notorious robber and murderer who had been arrested and cast into prison. When Pilate again asked, "What then shall I do unto him whom ye call the King of the Jews?" they replied, "Crucify Him." To Pilate's further question, "Why, what evil hath He done?" their only reply was a more clamorous repetition of their cry, "Crucify Him." Mark who makes no mention of a threat being held over Pilate's head to report his conduct to the Emperor represents him simply as having given way before the persistent, frantic demand of the people. Releasing Barabbas and delivering our Lord to be crucified Pilate gratified both their requests.

The scourging mentioned in verse 15 was a regular part of the sentence of crucifixion. The mocking, of which details are given in verses 16-20, took place after our Lord had been taken into the courtyard of the praetorium.

With regard to the action of Pilate the following is quoted from Taylor Innes, " He (Pilate) believed Jesus to be both just and harmless; and, so believing, he sinned in corruptly swaying from his first judgment, and betrayed the innocent blood. Yet had he adverted to the claim of his City to regulate religious opinion and conscience, and compared it deliberately with the counter claims of the prophet before him, or had he sent on his prisoner to answer for Himself at the imperial tribunal, it seems certain that in either case the trial would still have been followed by the tragedy which the world knows so well. . . . For in point of fact, when Pilate ultimately sent Jesus to the cross, it was as claiming to be a King, and on the original charge of acting *adversus majestatem populi Romani.* The judgment was legal, though the unjust judge did not believe it. For whatever Caesar's deputy may have thought, the claim of Jesus was truly inconsistent with the claim of the State which Caesar represented; and the world must judge between the two."

The Crucifixion. See Senior (1st Year), Facing Death.

The Resurrection—*Mark* xvi.

(*a*) Verses 1-8. See Junior (2nd Year), Stories of Jesus.

(*b*) Verses 9-20.

It is now widely recognised that these last twelve verses are not by Mark. Either he was unable to complete his work or its original ending has been lost.

The passage before us is assigned in an Armenian MS. discovered in 1891 to Ariston who may be the Ariston described as " a disciple of the Lord " by Papias *c.* A.D. 130. Whether or not it was actually written by him, its composition must be put towards the end of the first or early in the second century. It is a summary based upon the Gospels and the Acts:—

Verses 9-11, cf. John xx. 11-18, and see Junior (2nd Year), Stories of Jesus.

Verses 12, 13, cf. Luke xxiv. 13-35, and see Senior (2nd Year), Friends of Jesus.

Verses 14-18, cf. John xx. 19-23, and see Senior (1st Year), Facing Death.

Verses 19, 20, cf. Luke xxiv. 53 and Acts i. 3,12, and see Junior (2nd Year), Stories of Jesus.

A shorter ending found in four uncial MSS. runs as follows:—" But they gave Peter and his companions a brief account of all that had been enjoined. And after that, Jesus himself sent out by means of them from east to west the sacred and imperishable message of eternal salvation." (Moffatt's Translation.)

SENIOR (Third Year).

B.—THE EARLY CHURCH.

THE BOLDNESS OF PETER—*Acts* iv. 1-22.

The healing of the lame man at the Gate Beautiful marked the first open breach between Judaism and the Christian Church. The Jewish religious authorities became alarmed at the success of the new movement and action was taken by the Sadducees. Peter and John were arrested but as they had committed no crime they could not be kept in prison. The purpose of the Sadducees was to prevent the spread of the preaching of the Gospel by silencing the leaders.

After a night in prison, the two apostles were brought before the Sanhedrin, composed of Sadducees and Pharisees. Caiaphas, son-in-law of Annas, was the official high-priest, but Annas, though deposed in 14 A.D., still retained the title. Of John and Alexander nothing is known. The indictment against the apostles was that they were stirring up Messianic enthusiasm that might lead to trouble with Rome, that they were unlearned and ignorant, *i.e.*, unprofessional teachers, and that in the Temple they not only proclaimed the doctrine of Resurrection (which the Sadducees refused to accept), but the Resurrection of Jesus who, by the intervention of the Sanhedrin, had been put to death.

Peter boldly proclaimed that the cure of the lame man had been effected " by the name of Jesus of Nazareth." The invalid was there, healed, and Peter's claim could not be denied. The Sanhedrin was impotent. Pilate would not take action against the members of the new sect on religious grounds, and as among "the brethren" there were several Pharisees, the Pharisaic section of the Sanhedrin would not permit of any persecution of a sect that included some of their own number. To the Pharisees the identification of the crucified Jesus of Nazareth with the Messiah might appear ridiculous but there was no valid ground on which they could proceed to persecution. Therefore Peter, although he flung defiance in the face of the High Court, was, with John, dismissed with a caution.

STEPHEN—*Acts* vi., vii. 51-60.

The Church, to begin with, was confined to Jerusalem, its members being Jews and Jewish proselytes, chiefly "Hebrews," *i.e.,* Aramaic-speaking Jews, and "Hellenists," *i.c.,* Jews by birth but Greek in speech. But within the new movement there were differing elements. In the first place there were Pharisees, zealous for the Law, the divinely-appointed means by which God would give them the victory over their oppressors. Through the keeping of the Law, they believed the time of God's vengeance would be fulfilled. To the Hellenists who had come from distant lands to reside in Jerusalem, the Law was the means whereby they were kept on a higher ethical level than the Gentile world, and they valued the Law not for its ritual but for its spiritual and ethical teaching. They were zealous for the Law as the means of converting the Gentiles.

At first the members of the new sect had all things common. But with increase in numbers dissentions arose, and the attempt to preserve equality in possessions led to grievances. Complaints were made that in the daily administration of the bounty, the widows of the Hellenists were overlooked. Therefore seven administrators were appointed from the Hellenistic section to look after the needs of their own members. But the gifts of the seven made them effective missionaries of the Gospel, a Gospel of which they took a much wider view than did the "Hebrews." The lead was taken by Stephen who recognised the true inwardness of the new religion as implying the passing away of Judaism. To Stephen the Christian system was not the completion of the old system, but meant its abolition. In the Hellenistic synagogues he proclaimed that belief in the Resurrection of Jesus and in His imminent second-coming, together with the gifts of the Spirit, imparted a greater power than the Law could supply, delivering the believer from bondage to the letter of the Law. There was, he argued, no further need for Law or Temple. His teaching aroused the fury of all sections of the Jewish community. The Sadducees could not tolerate the doctrine that the Temple system on which their prestige and power and wealth depended was doomed to go, nor could the Pharisees accept the teaching that the Law was temporary. The Sanhedrin, therefore, felt bound to suppress the new teaching, and Stephen was tried on a charge of blasphemy.

Stephen, in his defence, argued that the devotion of the Jews to Palestine, the Law and the Temple, had from the first been a mistake. He reminded them that Joseph had attained to power in a foreign land, that Jacob had died in Egypt and was buried in the country of the hated Samaritans, that God had revealed Himself to Moses in Midian and again in Sinai, that the degenerate Solomon had built the Temple and committed them to the belief that God dwelt in a house made with hands. He then condemned them because they had murdered God's last and greatest Witness. They and their fathers had all alike resisted the Spirit of God and the crucifixion of our Lord was the natural act of the children of those who had murdered the prophets. The Sanhedrin, gnashing their teeth with rage, refused to hear him further. Amid the uproar, Stephen, raising his eyes to heaven, declared that he saw the Son of Man standing on the right hand of God. This statement proved too much for the Sanhedrin. Stephen was dragged outside the city and stoned to death. According to the Law, death had to be inflicted outside the gates, the witnesses placing their hands on the head of the condemned as evidence of his guilt. A leading part in the proceedings was taken by a young man, named Saul, who held the outer garments of those who cast the stones. The murder of Stephen was possibly illegal. It shows the extent to which Pilate had lost control of the situation in Judaea.

STORIES OF PAUL.

(a) THE SCOURGE OF THE CHURCH—

Acts viii. 1-4; ix. 1-9, 10-22, 22-30.

The death of Stephen marked the beginning of a policy of persecution, and the exponents of the new teaching fled the city. At Caesarea with its Roman garrison and Gentile population, in Galilee, the territory of Herod Antipas, and in Samaria, the brethren were beyond the reach of the Sanhedrin's arm. But in Damascus the situation was different. Damascus was in the hands of Aretas, who was at war with Herod Antipas. Aretas, anxious to secure the support of Judaea, consented to the arrest of the Christian refugees in his territory. Saul, armed with letters to the synagogues, set out for Damascus, to call for the surrender of the brethren whom he intended to bring back to Jerusalem to meet the fate of Stephen.

His plans had a dramatic ending. On the way he became converted to the new faith. His conversion was not so sudden as would appear. Saul had been powerfully influenced by Stephen's demeanour and arguments, and the martyr's faith and fortitude in the presence of death gave rise to doubts in his mind. He tried to stifle these doubts by behaving like a madman, by endeavouring to uproot the new religion. On the way to Damascus the battle was raging in Saul's breast, and in a moment the truth burst on him like a flash of light that the dead Stephen was right. Saul consciously accepted Christ in that hour as his Lord and Master. Although psychologically the vision was the solution of a doubt already present in the unconscious mind, its genuineness as a manifestation of the Risen Lord is in no way affected. The hand of God was in it in an extraordinary way. The wonder of it, not its naturalness, will appeal to the child.

Commanded to complete his journey and to await further orders, Saul was visited at Damascus by a pious Jew, named Ananias, was baptized by him, and had his sight restored. At Damascus he preached the Gospel he had come to destroy. But the atmosphere was not favourable. Judaism was making many proselytes amongst the Gentiles there, and could not tolerate the preaching of the abolition of the Law, and Aretas, the king, was pro-Jewish in sympathies. A plot to kill Saul was hatched, but, being forewarned, he made good his escape, being lowered over the wall in a basket.

Saul made for Jerusalem, but naturally the Church there regarded him with suspicion. Barnabas, however, accepted him on trust, with the result that he was given a leading place in the Christian community. Hoping that the Gospel would be carried by the " Grecians," i.e., the Hellenists, to the Jewish communities throughout the Roman Empire, and through these communities to the Gentile World, Saul took up the work of the martyred Stephen. But because his teaching involved the abandonment of the Jewish claim to exclusiveness, he aroused amongst the Hellenists as bitter feeling as had Stephen. So, with the approval of the Church, he gave up his ministry in Jerusalem and set out for Tarsus. Tarsus was an intellectual centre with a large Jewish population. It was the city of his birth and there he would be free from persecution and his doctrines would have a chance of reaching the Gentile world through the synagogues.

(b) HAILED AS A GOD, AND LATER, STONED—*Acts* xiv. 1-22.

At Antioch in Syria there was a considerable colony of Jews living on friendly terms with their Gentile neighbours, and amongst these the refugees from Jerusalem after the first persecution found a fruitful field. There sprang up in the city a branch of the Christian Church composed of Jews and Gentiles, not marked off by any schism from the rest of the Jewish population. Barnabas was sent from the Jerusalem Church to supervise this new body, but finding the work of supervision greater than he could accomplish single-handed, he sent to Tarsus for Saul as colleague. Their joint ministry in Antioch was attended with such success that they decided to go further afield, and to appeal to a wider Gentile circle. After visiting Cyprus they left for Pisidian Antioch where there was a large Jewish colony on friendly terms with the Gentiles. They preached the Gospel with such marked success in the synagogues that the Jews adopted a policy of opposition. It became apparent to Paul that the majority of the Jews would not accept his views and he decided that, as by their opposition they had forfeited their right to hear the Gospel first, he would in future appeal to the Gentile world directly without the intervention of the synagogue. At Pisidian Antioch he succeeded in founding an enthusiastic branch of the Church apart from the synagogue, but Jewish hostility led to his expulsion.

Paul and Barnabas then set out for Iconium, an important city on the border of Galatia. There they conducted a lengthy mission, converting both Jews and Gentiles. Owing to the opposition of the orthodox Jewish party the magistrates feared a disturbance, and, although refusing to take direct action, arranged to refrain from interfering with a mob attack on the two apostles. The plot was made known to Paul and his companion who made a hurried departure for Lystra and Derbe, two small Lycaonian towns off the beaten track, where the old Greek gods were still worshipped.

At Lystra Paul's cure of a cripple led the community to believe that he and Barnabas were the Greek gods Mercury and Jupiter, and preparations were made by the priesthood to

offer them sacrifices. Emissaries from Iconium put an end
to the activities of the Apostles. They stirred up the people
with the result that Paul was dragged outside the city, stoned,
and left for dead. Paul, however, recovered, made his way
back to the city, departed for Derbe and founded a Christian
community.

(c) In Prison at Philippi—*Acts* xvi. 12-40.

From Derbe Paul and Barnabas returned to Syrian Antioch
and to Jerusalem where they reported on their work. Thereafter they decided on a second missionary journey to con-
solidate their gains. As Mark had been a deserter Paul
refused to have him as a companion on the journey, contrary
to the wishes of Barnabas, and Paul and Barnabas agreed to
part. Barnabas with Mark sailed for Cyprus, and Paul with
Silas, a Jerusalem Christian and a Roman citizen, set out
for Galatia.

At Lystra Paul and Silas were joined by Timothy. They
proceeded to Troas where they were joined by a Christian
convert, believed to be St Luke. While waiting for a ship
Paul had a vision of a Macedonian pleading with him to
come to Europe. He decided to respond to the call and
landed at Neapolis, the port of Philippi. Philippi was an
important commercial centre and as the locale of the defeat
of Brutus and Cassius by Anthony and Octavian had been
made a Roman colony. The Jewish population, however,
was small, so small that there was no synagogue. The Jews,
therefore, met on the Sabbath day in an open space by the
river-bank—running water being necessary for their rites of
purification—and there Paul expounded his teaching to the
women. His first convert in Europe was a proselyte of
Thyatira, named Lydia, a woman of substance. Lydia's
house became a Church and many of the local Jews were converted to the new doctrine.

The Mission, which continued peacefully for some time,
came to a sudden end. A lunatic slave-girl, credited with
powers of divination, was cured by Paul in the name of
Christ. Her owners were incensed at the loss of one who
had been to them a source of much gain and stirred up a riot.
Paul and Silas were arrested and brought before the magistrates. They were charged with carrying on propaganda
for the purpose of converting Roman citizens to a foreign
superstition, were scourged without a trial, and cast into a
dungeon.

During the night there took place an earthquake that shook

the prison to its foundations. The gaoler, fearing that his prisoners had escaped, and unprepared to face the magistrates in the morning for neglect of duty, was about to commit suicide but was stopped by Paul. In the morning the magistrates had reason to regret their hasty action. It became known that Paul and Silas were Roman citizens, and a Roman citizen might not be scourged. Had the Apostles reported the matter to the higher authorities the magistrates would have been deposed, and perhaps punished. An apology was tendered and accepted, and Paul and Silas left the city, leaving behind them the first Christian Church in Europe.

(d) SHIPWRECKED ON THE WAY TO ROME—*Acts* xxvii.

On his return to Jerusalem Paul was saved from death at the hands of a Jewish mob by the intervention of the Roman guard and was lodged in prison in Caesarea for safety. In Caesarea he spent two years. He was tried by Felix and should have secured an acquittal, but Felix detained him in the hope that his friends would pay a big ransom for his release. Felix was replaced by Festus who instituted a fresh trial. Festus was inclined to send the prisoner back to Jerusalem but Paul decided to exercise his privilege of Roman citizenship and appealed for a trial before Caesar at Rome.

Under the charge of Julius, a centurion, he set sail from Caesarea, and at Myra transhipped to an Egyptian grain vessel bound for Rome. The winter season was at hand and the ship encountered bad weather. At Fair Havens Paul warned the captain to lie up until the spring but the captain decided to make for Phoenix and winter there. Off the coast of Melita (Malta) the ship was wrecked. " Ships were rude in design, and built the same fore and aft; one large mainsail, with an enormous yard, was carried on a single mast; was steered by two large paddle-rudders. The concentrated strain of the single mast frequently caused ship's timbers to open, so that more ships were lost through foundering than any other cause; to reduce this danger ships were frapped or undergirded (verse 17), *i.e.,* bound round the middle with strong ropes to prevent planks from starting." Throughout the thrilling story the teacher will emphasise Paul's courage and faith in God.

L

JUNIOR (First Year) — OLD TESTAMENT.

C. STORIES JESUS HEARD.

How the World was Made—*Genesis* i.-ii. 3.

It is generally admitted that the Book of Genesis is of composite structure, compiled from different sources and materials of different age. The aim of the men who compiled an account, from these sources, of the origins of their race, was to teach religious history, to show the hand of God in the nation's life and in the life of mankind as a whole. The early narratives in Genesis, based upon folk-lore, are used not so much to give history as to teach divine truth.

There are two accounts of Creation in the first two chapters of Genesis, and there is general agreement among scholars that the first account is the later of the two. Because of certain resemblances between this magnificent hymn of Creation and the Babylonian account of the beginning of the world it would appear as if the poem in the first chapter of Genesis were written during or shortly after the Babylonian Exile. During the Exile the Jews would become familiar with Babylonian ideas. They would hear of Marduk, the god of light, fighting with the gods of the abyss, slaying the dragon Ti'amat and using part of her body to make the earth and part of her skin to make the firmament. They knew this conception of creation to be false. In the beginning, they maintained, was God, and the heavens and the earth were the work of His hands; and one of their number wrote for mankind this inspired account of creation.

The story is not a scientific but a religious story. Its purpose is to show that there is but one spiritual God, that all that He does is very good, that He brought order out of chaos, and that man is the highest of all created things in this world. Although the writer thought of the earth as flat with Sheol in its centre, and resting upon the great deep, there is no contradiction between his account and our scientific hypothesis to-day. To begin with there was darkness and God said "Let there be light." Is not that what the astronomer tells us to-day when he says that there was a fiery mist, part of which cooled and hardened, and that the rays of the sun dispelled the vapour from the earth? On the

second day God made the firmament, a solid arch supporting
the waters above the earth. The scientists says that after the
vapour was dispelled by the rays of the sun the winds collected the clouds above the earth. On the third day God
made the dry land and vegetation. The scientist traces for
us the evolution of plant life from the sea through the various
stages of mosses and ferns and trees, all marvellously adapted
to their environment. "And God saw that it was good." On
the fourth day God made luminaries or lights, and on the
fifth day birds in the firmament and fishes in the waters.
According to the scientific hypothesis animal life began in
the sea, fish being the oldest of the larger forms. Then there
came frogs, crocodiles, etc., which live in water and on land,
then flying reptiles, and then the birds. "And God blessed
them, saying, Be fruitful and multiply, and fill the waters in
the seas, and let fowl multiply in the earth."

On the sixth day God made animals and man. And He
made man in His own image to have dominion over His
creatures. Man, made in the image of God, must therefore
be Godlike. He must bring order out of chaos, beauty out
of ugliness, and use his power to preserve the creatures of
God's handiwork. Like Francis of Assisi he must regard
the birds and the animals as his brothers and sisters. The
teacher should not lose the opportunity of impressing the
need for kindness to animals and should form a "Kindness
to animals" Club among the children.

On the seventh day God abstained from work. "He made
the world complete by introducing rest," and for man the
seventh day is to be a day of refreshment for body, mind and
spirit. The Sabbath was a long-standing institution in Israel,
its purpose being humanitarian, the securing of a complete
break for every member of the community once in seven
days. The writer of the Creation Hymn, alive to the value
of the day of rest for man, traced its origin back to the beginning of things and insisted that even God desisted from
labour. Much of the neuroticism of our age is the result of
restlessness and one of our direst needs is the need for a
day free from noise and bustle, a day in which we can be
still and hear the Voice of God in the silence.

The Creation Hymn is a masterpiece. M'Fadyen says:
" There is much artistic skill as well as religious insight and
power in the construction of the story, which reflects the
comeliness and order visible everywhere throughout the
universe. . . . Those who described the creation of the world
in this way must have been deeply impressed with the sym-
metry and order of the universe, with the wonderful adapta-

tion of life to environment, and with the traces of development, progress and purpose running through phenomena, which we are now only beginning at all adequately to appreciate."

The teacher should first read the story to the class and tell it as given. He will note that God *divided* the light from the darkness; that He *divided* the earth from the heavens; that He *divided* the waters from the earth. On the fourth day, corresponding to the light of the first day, God commanded the sun, the moon and the stars to appear. On the fifth day, corresponding to the firmament and the waters of the second day, God created the fish of the sea and the fowl of the air. On the sixth day, corresponding to the earth with its herbage, God created animals and man. Each day there is repeated the phrase : "and God saw that it was good." With regard to the rest of His creation we are told that God spoke, but in the case of man there was no speech. God made man in His own image, placing him on a higher plane than the animal kingdom. On the seventh day there is the grand climax—God resting not in inactivity, but in the maintenance and restoration of His creation.

ADAM AND EVE—Genesis ii. 4-24.

The interest of the writer of this early account of Creation is in man and man's responsibilities. The writer places the first scene of the drama of human life in a garden. God provides the garden with water and with trees to furnish man with food. He takes a piece of clay, kneads it into the form of a man and breathes into it the breath of life. The writer emphasises that man is dust of the ground but spirit of God, a divine being with animal instincts. God brings the animals to Adam and Adam gives them names. Who that has studied a child does not recognise something with which he is familiar? But man is higher than the animal kingdom. He can have fellowship only with his own kind and with God. And so God provided him with a wife. The writer, to emphasise the relationship which should exist between husband and wife, represents God as making the woman from one of Adam's ribs. In order that perfect communion between Him and His creature might remain unbroken God demanded of Adam implicit obedience. Of the tree of the knowledge of good and evil he might not eat.

NOAH AND THE FLOOD—*Genesis* vii., viii., ix. 1-17.

To the ancients only a small part of the world was known, each race being more or less cut off from the others. In the

legends of most races there is a story of a flood that affected
only the part of the world known to them.   In 1864 a cyclone
in India caused the loss of 60,000 lives, and it is not surprising that in the ancient world a local flood should seem a
universal deluge.

That the flood story in Genesis is not pure legend is confirmed by recent archaeological discoveries that have proved
that a large part of Babylonia lay under water for a long
period.   Dr Woolley, writing of his excavations at Ur, says :
"The shafts went deeper and suddenly the character of the
soil changed.   Instead of the stratified pottery and rubbish
we were in perfectly clean clay, uniform throughout, the
texture of which showed that it had been laid there by water.
The workmen declared we had come to the bottom of everything, to the river silt. . . . I sent the men back to deepen
the hole.   The clean clay continued without change until it
had attained a thickness of a little over 8 feet.   Then, as
suddenly as it had begun, it stopped, and we were once more
in layers of rubbish full of stone implements and pottery. . . .
The great bed of clay marked, if it did not cause a break in,
the continuity of history ; above it we had the pure Sumerian
civilisation slowly developing on its own lines ; below it there
was a mixed culture . . . no ordinary rising of the rivers would
leave behind it anything approaching the bulk of this clay
bank ; 8 feet of sediment imply a very great depth of water,
and the flood which deposited it must have been of a magni-
tude unparalleled in local history.   That it was so is further
proved by the fact that the clay bank marks a definite break
in the continuity of the local culture ; a whole civilisation which
existed before it, is lacking above it and seems to have been
submerged by the waters . . . there could be no doubt that the
flood was the Flood of Sumerian history and legend, the
flood on which is based the story of Noah."   Apart from
the alluvial deposits there is ample confirmation of the fact
of the Flood in the numerous cuneiform tablets discovered
and found to be dated so many " years after the Flood."

In the biblical story two narratives of the Flood have
been dovetailed together.   For example, there are two
accounts of the number of animals and two accounts of
entering   into   the   ark.   The   central   thought   in   the
story is that God rewards the righteous and punishes the
wicked.   A great deal of nonsense is talked about the difficulty of this story for the teacher and the child.   Punishment
is not inconsistent with love.   It is still true that national
iniquity leads to national disaster and that the righteous reap

a spiritual if not a material reward. Although the writer of
the Flood story depicts Noah's reward as an earthly one, it
does not follow that he had no idea of a reward in a life
to come. Dr Langdon says : " The theological view running
through Babylonia before 2000 B.C. was of a heaven for the
righteous, whom the gods might choose to receive into Paradise where is the Bread and Water of Eternal Life." The
teaching of the Scriptures is that those who serve God will
receive a reward here and hereafter.

The teacher will show that the God who brought order
out of chaos and made man in His own image, hated iniquity
as unworthy of His creation. Because of the wickedness of
men God decided to send a flood but resolved that the
righteous would be spared. If there had been ten righteous
men in Sodom God would have spared that city and if there
had been a few righteous in the land He would have stayed
the flood. Noah, a righteous man, tried to move the people
to repentance. He told of judgment to come, only to be met
with scoffing. During the period taken to build the ark and
to gather the animals together, not one sinner turned from his
evil ways. For Noah's sake God had to send the flood, as
he and his family might have been corrupted by the evil
community. To children the punishment is just. The child
recognises that the evil doers were not destroyed without
warning and that if they had repented, they would have been
saved. The ending to the story about God setting the rain-
bow in the sky as a promise makes a tremendous appeal to
the child as it does to primitive peoples. There is a glimmer
of our Lord's conception of God as Love inasmuch as God
gave the promise that He would send no more floods on a
similar scale.

The Tower of Babel—*Genesis* xi. 1-9.

As Greek fable told of the giants who strove to scale
Olympus, so Semitic legend told of the impious act by which
the sons of men sought to erect an enduring emblem of human
achievement and human unity. It contains the answer given
by Hebrew folk-lore to the question suggested by differences
in nationality and language. The writer of the Genesis story
assumed that there was one original language but that God
confounded men's speech lest they should attribute their
achievements to themselves and forget Him, and he represents
Babel, a form of Babylon, as a contraction of the word
" Balbel," meaning " confusion."

In Babylonia there were no stones. Bricks were made from mud poured into moulds, dried in the sun and then baked in a mud-built oven. For mortar bitumen was used. The bricks measured some 20 by 12 by 4 inches and were frequently stamped with the name of the reigning king. They were used not only for house-building but for the building of the temple-towers or ziggurats to be found in every important city. The ziggurat was made in 7 stages and was used both as an observatory for the study of the heavenly bodies and for religious purposes. It may also have served as a place of refuge in time of flood. The writer of the Genesis narrative, seeing such ziggurats in Babylon at the height of her power, and knowing that she would fall as she was not founded upon divine principles, was inspired to write this story. His aim in telling it was to convey certain spiritual truths—that God is Sovereign, that He checks self-exaltation, and that, for the development and progress of the race, He destroys the work of man's hands.

ABRAHAM, THE SHEPHERD—*Genesis* xiii.

In Genesis xi. we are informed that Terah with his family migrated from Ur of the Chaldees to Haran, his objective being Canaan. The archaeologist has revealed that at Ur, one of the chief cities of Sumer, there was a rich civilisation as far back as 3500 B.C. The citizens of Ur lived in houses two storeys high with some dozen rooms round the courtyard. There was a kitchen, a reception-room and a family chapel. The citizens could read and write and extract cube roots! The Haran to which Terah migrated may have been in the North-West of Mesopotamia and in that case there is a probability that he was a moon-worshipper as *that* Haran was devoted to the cult of the moon-goddess. But as Terah's goal was Canaan it seems more likely that Haran lay near Damascus.

Abraham, son of Terah, at the call of God, broke away from his people and made his way to Egypt via Canaan. From 2371 B.C. to 1583 B.C. Egypt was ruled by the Hyksos or Shepherd-Kings, who owed their supremacy to the use of horses and chariots and iron weapons. These Hyksos came from the north and from about 2800 B.C. had established their supremacy in Babylonia and the surrounding districts. In consequence, in Canaan and Egypt, Abraham was in territories ruled by those of his own race. In Genesis xiv. we read of a battle between 4 Mesopotamian kings with 5 kings whose cities were in the neighbourhood of the Dead Sea. Lot, Abraham's nephew, was taken captive, but Abraham, with 318 " retainers "—a word used for the followers of Palestine chieftains about 2000 B.C.—gave chase and recovered Lot with the stolen plunder. Amraphel of Shinar is generally identified with Hammurabi of Babylon whose date is 2100 B.C.

In Genesis xiii. we read of the return of Abraham and Lot with their servants and herds from Egypt to Canaan, which was inhabited by a large number of tribes, some wandering, some living in walled cities and ruled by their city-kings. The deadly enemy of the nomad is drought and there were frequent quarrels between the shepherds of Abraham and those of Lot about access to the wells. A way out of the impasse had to be found and Abraham magnanimously gave Lot the first choice of unoccupied land. Although as the older man and the one to whom Lot owed his all, he had the right to make the first claim he felt that the way of self-surrender was the way of God. That night he received the divine blessing and the renewal of the divine promise that the land would be his.

Isaac—*Genesis* xxvi. 12-33.

Gerar was a large grain-growing centre, controlled by the Philistines, who exported grain to their relatives in Crete. It is not surprising that Isaac made his way thither during a shortage of food. Sir Flinders Petrie discovered at Gerar grain-stores and flint sickles belonging to the Hyksos period. Isaac traversed his father's routes and settled down to an agricultural life in the neighbourhood of Gerar. So successful was he as a farmer that the Philistines, envious and alarmed, stopped up his wells and ordered him to move on. Isaac was a man of peace. He felt that those who served God should settle their differences without fighting. Accordingly he removed his camp and digged well after well, only to have these claimed by his Philistine neighbours. Ultimately he ordered the camp to move south to Beersheba where already there were 7 wells and where they could live undisturbed. To Isaac there was vouchsafed a clearer vision of God than was given to those of his age and God gave his approval of his way of living at peace with all men. " Fear not," He said, " for I am with thee, and will bless thee." " The life of Isaac," says Matheson, " is from beginning to end a suffering in private. His was that form of sacrifice which does not show, which wins no reputation for heroism. But just on that account it had a value all its own. . . . The sacrifices of Isaac came from the unaided heart. . . . They were the revealing of private sentiments, of strength exhibited in seclusion. He is like an artist painting in a desert—painting in the firm belief that none will ever see his work. . . . He has submitted to self-effacement for the sake of his family. . . . He is the forerunner of all domestic drudges, of all who lose promotion through the impediments of home."

JACOB AND ESAU—*Genesis* xxvii.

The interest of this story lies in the contrast between the two brothers, each with his good qualities and his glaring faults. Esau was impulsive, impetuous, sensuous, fond of out-door life. Jacob was cautious, cunning, envious, a stay-at-home. The name Jacob means the supplanter, the cheat, the deceiver. But Jacob was the bigger man of the two. He was far-seeing and ambitious. He appreciated the value of the blessing, highly valued in the East as the means of bestowing good-fortune, and of the birthright which gave to its possessor the right to inherit the father's position with a double portion of his property. Esau was a materialist without spiritual apprehension. To the Hebrew writer Esau was the more culpable of the two. While Jacob's conduct cannot be condoned it must not be forgotten that his mother, the instigator of his crimes, was the real sinner.

As the result of his trickery Jacob, the stay-at-home, had to flee like a vagabond and his mother was destined never to see her favourite son again. " The lesson is plain, that deception is heavily punished. . . . Deceit may be clever, but in the long run it is costly. It brought to Jacob separation from those whom he loved, exile in a foreign land, and many a trial and sorrow there. The days are linked each to each, and the falsehood which we sow to-day we shall reap in sorrow and disaster to-morrow, or if not to-morrow, after many days."

JACOB AT BETHEL—*Genesis* xxviii. 10-22.

The home-sick boy—he may have been just a lad of some 15 years—as he trudged the dreary miles in constant fear of attack from wild-beasts or robbers had time and opportunity to reflect on his trickery. Away from his mother's evil influence he saw his sin in its true light. Penitent and praying to God for forgiveness he lay down on a piece of rocky ground with a stone for pillow and cried himself to sleep. He dreamed that he saw a ladder connecting earth and heaven with the angels of God ascending and descending. The dream may have been suggested by the terraced hillside or Jacob may have heard from his father of the Babylonian ziggurats seen by his father, Abraham, with the priests ascending and descending the Hill of Heaven. Jacob experienced an awakening to and an awareness of other things in life than the merely material. He felt that he had had a revelation from God and an assurance of the divine forgiveness and the divine presence with him in days to come. Reverentially he removed his sandals, poured oil upon the stone associated in his mind with this transforming experience, and, still the bargaining Jew, vowed that if God would help him in his new way of life he would endeavour to serve Him with faithfulness. In God he had found a friend and his response was the emotion of gratitude and the resolve to live a Godlike life.

JOSEPH AND HIS BROTHERS—*Genesis* xxxvii.

For Jacob the question of the selection of his successor as head of the clan was a matter of grave importance, and subsequent events proved his choice of Joseph a wise one. By his favouritism, however, in giving the elder son of his favourite wife a robe with long sleeves that absolved Joseph from manual labour, he aroused the envy of the rest of the family and was not free from responsibility for his own later sufferings when his sons wrung his heart with their lying story. Joseph intensified the spirit of hate by the stories of his wonderful dreams. Dreams, it was recognised, had a meaning. The modern psychologist regards certain dreams as foreshadowings of the future—the life-force pushing itself out in new directions first finding expression through the symbolism of the dream.

Joseph was his father's confidant. If his brothers wrongly reported losses of sheep that they had sold he had the courage to prove loyal to Jacob. In obedience to his father he was persistent in his search for the brothers. For his loyalty he was hated and when the opportunity presented itself his brothers took their revenge. They placed him in one of the underground reservoirs at Dothan—abandoned cisterns were not always filled in—and then sold him to Ishmaelites for 20 pieces of silver. The lesson might be taught as an illustration of the terrible results of envy-suffering for Joseph, for the brothers and for the father of both.

Joseph in Prison—*Genesis* xl.

Joseph was bought by Potiphar, governor of the prison, when the slaves were up for auction. Instead of brooding over his loss of liberty he resolved as a servant of God to serve his master to the best of his ability and for his trustworthiness was promoted chief servant. As the result of a lying story by a woman he was disgraced and thrown into prison, a fortified palace where State officers were interned on parole. On Egyptian wall-sculptures figures of the butler and the baker with his basket may be seen to-day. In prison Joseph's power to read and interpret the symbols of the unconscious mind again came into prominence. His interpretation reflected the thoughts of the two men about the poison-plot against the king, and he had hopes of release through the instrumentality of the butler. But his hopes were doomed to disappointment. "Yet did not the chief butler remember Joseph, but forgat him," as is the way of the world.

Joseph Interpreting King's Dreams—*Genesis* xli. 1-43.

At last promotion came to Joseph through the butler. The magicians failed to interpret the Pharaoh's dreams and Joseph was called for. The gift which aroused the ire of his brothers and led to his exile saved not only Egypt but his own family. His sudden elevation to the premiership was quite in keeping with Egyptian custom as it was not unusual for Semitic slaves to attain to high position. The ruling Pharaoh was probably one of his own people, a Hyksos king, for we read that he made Joseph ride in the second chariot; and we know that horses and chariots were introduced into Egypt by the Hyksos. Joseph probably originated the policy of grain-storing which became the usual practice. He suggested the appointment of officials to take up the fifth part during the years of plenty. In Palestine at a later time the Pharaohs appointed a head official to whom the sub-officials brought their revenue in the form of corn, wine and oil. Joseph was given a new name, " Zaph-nath-paaneah," meaning " the ruler of the realm of life." During the years of plenty his policy must have been unpopular in the extreme, demanding of him great faith and strength of character. Joseph had been loyal to his father as a boy, he had been loyal to God as a man, and God rewarded his loyalty.

JOSEPH RECEIVING HIS BROTHERS—*Genesis* xlii.-xlv.

There were years of drought in Egypt and years of drought in Canaan, and Joseph's brethren who had heard of corn in Egypt came down for supplies. An inscription of Merneptah, Pharaoh in Egypt in the 13th century B.C., tells of Bedouin tribes who came from Edom to obtain food for themselves and their cattle in the field of the Pharaoh. So the action of the brethren was in keeping with the custom of the times. Joseph's brethren failed to recognise him. He was clean-shaven, following the fashion of Egypt, and they believed him dead. How would he use his power? Would he do unto them as they had done unto him? Not a trace of vindictiveness appears in his nature. But he had his doubts about his brothers and may have suspected them of cruelty to Benjamin. The plan which he devised revealed in them a complete change of heart as they all stood by Benjamin to save him for their father's sake. At Judah's offer to become a slave in order that Benjamin might go free Joseph broke down and revealed himself and dispelled their uneasiness by saying that God had turned their evil to good. He gave further evidence of his greatness in making public acknowledgment of his relationship with this nomad clan whose calling rendered them unclean in the eyes of Egypt. All through life Joseph remained true to himself and true to God and in his spirit of forgiveness and in his provision for the needs of others he typifies our Lord.

MOSES, THE SLAVE'S SON—*Exodus* i. 7-iii. 18.

It seems certain that the Pharaoh of the oppression was Thotmes I. (1539-1514 B.C.) and that it was his daughter, Hatshephut, who played a leading part in the government of Egypt during the two succeeding reigns, that found Moses in the ark of bulrushes. The name Moses is Egyptian and the massacre of unwanted children was common in the ancient world. During the reign of her half-brother, Thotmes II. (1514-1501 B.C.) Hatshephut was the real ruler of Egypt, and to retain her control she married her nephew, Thotmes III. (1501-1447). She died about 1482 and Moses, as her favourite had to flee to Midian as Thotmes III. so thoroughly detested her that he defaced her monuments.

The biblical narrative informs us that Moses, Egyptian by name and education, remained a Hebrew at heart. In a moment of anger he smote an Egyptian and had to flee like a vagabond for his life. By his rash act he proved himself lacking in control, unable to effect the deliverance of his people. He who cannot control himself cannot control others. The 40 years that he spent in Midian as shepherd are memorable years. In the desert Moses learned the secret of success and the cause of failure. He acquired self-control, for merely to exist in the desert he had to keep a constant rein on his inclinations. He never ceased to think of his enslaved people, and hearing of the death of Thotmes III., he wondered if he ought to return and lead them from the land of bondage. In the desert of Horeb where he had gone with his flocks he saw a bush in flame, yet unconsumed, possibly one of those desert shrubs that emit combustible gases. He was struck by the wonder of the divine Presence and heard the Voice of God calling upon him to deliver his people. But remembering his hasty blow he asked if he, the rash avenger, was fitted to be God's instrument. He received the assurance of God's help and presence. The God of the past will be the God of the future. He is the same yesterday, to-day and for ever.

The Pharaoh whom Moses interviewed was Amenhetep II. (1447-1423). Moses asked that the Hebrews be allowed to go 3 days' journey into the desert to sacrifice. We learn from Exodus viii. 25-27 that the Hebrews could not sacrifice in Egypt the " abomination of the Egyptians "—the sheep?— and hence Moses' request. Sir Flinders Petrie thinks that " the three days' journey " was the phrase used in Egypt for going down to Sinai. In Sinai he has excavated on one of the hills the Temple of Serabit in which burnt sacrifices— foreign to Egypt—were offered. The Temple lies near the Egyptian turquoise mines and there is a possibility that these mines were worked by Semitic slaves and that the Temple had been built by Hatshephut to enable them to worship their God according to their own ritual.

Pharaoh refused to grant the request and on the ground that Moses was encouraging the Israelites to neglect their work he gave orders that they were to find their own straw for brick-making, and when the tale of bricks was not made up they were beaten. The Israelites were unable to find sufficient chopped straw—the chief item of fodder for animals in Egypt—without impoverishing their beasts of burden, and had to collect grass, with the result that their bricks were not up to the standard requirements. " Their hardships assumed gigantic proportions in their eyes . . . and the decision to escape from their serfdom was made even though it meant exchanging the more or less fruitful land of Goschen for the wilderness of Sinai."

THE DELIVERANCE—*Exodus* xiii. 17-22.

What route did they take? The popular view is that they crossed the Sea of Reeds—wrongly translated the Red Sea— at the northern part of the Red Sea and made their way south. But an attractive theory has lately been worked out by Major Jarvis, Governor of Sinai. Although the Israelites lived for a time on manna and quails they could have subsisted in Sinai for 40 years, only through the cultivation of the soil and the grazing of sheep and goats. Now Southern Sinai, "a tumbled mass of pure granite," could not have produced the food necessary for the flocks. In Northern Sinai, on the other hand, first-class crops can be produced. Manna is seldom to be found in the South whereas it is plentiful in the North. In the South quails are conspicuous by their absence while in the North during the migration season they are to be found in large numbers. In the South the turquoise mines would be under a strong guard of Egyptian troops and Moses would be likely to avoid that area. In the North there is a mountain called the Mount of the Law and a number of place names bearing a close resemblance to places mentioned in Exodus. In the Red Sea there are no reeds but in Lake Sirbonis on the Mediterranean coast there are big areas of rushes. On these grounds, Major Jarvis argues that the Israelites made for Lake Sirbonis, a clay pan about 6 to 10 feet below the level of the Mediterranean, and separated from the sea by a strip of sand from 100-300 yards wide. On this strip of sand, states Jarvis, one has the illusion of walking between two walls of water. Moses took the route along the sea-shore, the Egyptians tried to cut across the clay-pan to head him off, a gale arose and the Mediterranean broke through at certain points, flooding the Lake—as happened during the 1914-18 war—and the Egyptians were trapped. (The teacher might refer to Milton's lines—" That Sirbonian bog . . . where armies whole have sunk.") " This is a catastrophe that could happen to-day if an army were foolish enough to try to cross the clay pan with bad weather in the offing."

With regard to the pillar of cloud by day and of fire by night, Major Jarvis states that when heavy weather is impending " there is a most remarkable cloud formation— namely, a huge column of cumulus, black in the centre with hard white edges. This column which begins at the sky-line and is most impressive, extends to the zenith, constantly emitting lightning, and at night is an intermittent blaze of fire. This cloud was coming in from the eastward as it has done since I have been in Sinai." To Moses it was a sign that God would be their leader and grant them deliverance.

CARE IN THE WILDERNESS—MANNA, QUAILS AND WATER— Exodus xvi., xvii. 1-6; Numbers xi. 31, 32.

As soon as the Israelite hosts were embarked on their perilous journey they were faced with the problem of supplies, and murmured against Moses and against God for bringing them out to the wilderness to die of starvation. Moses, with unquenchable optimism, turned to God and received the assurance that He would make provision for their needs. In the morning when the dew had gone up large quantities of grains of manna, the size of coriander seeds, lay upon the ground. Manna is the deposit left by a small insect that feeds upon the tamarisk tree, and on the Mediterranean coast " it is obvious, from the stumps of semi-fossilised trees, that there was a veritable belt of tamarisk which would have supplied sufficient manna for the Israelites." The fact that the manna is capable of a natural explanation makes it none the less miraculous. The bread that is delivered regularly by the baker's boy is no less a miraculous gift of God than the manna to the Israelites. " For our daily bread we are ultimately dependent upon God, who for our sakes works His perpetual miracle."

One of our needs is for variety in food. The Israelites, tired of manna, longed for flesh. And God sent them quails in abundance. In September and October clouds of quails come in from the Mediterranean "so completely exhausted that they pitch on the sea-shore and stagger into the nearest scrub for cover." They are netted to-day by the Egyptian Arabs in large numbers. The exhausted quails take refuge in small bushes to the south of which the Arabs place small hand-nets in which the birds become entangled. Large trammel-nets are also erected in the open desert and as the birds arrive at dawn, they fail to see the nets in the uncertain light. Large numbers are dispatched annually to London and other centres.

In the wilderness the most dreaded enemy of man and beast is drought. During a water famine the Israelites again murmured against Moses and against God for bringing them into the desert to die of thirst. Moses appealed to God, in whom he had implicit faith, and was commanded to strike a rock. He did so and there came forth a stream of water. Major Jarvis records a similar occurrence. " Some of the Sinai

Camel Corps had halted in a wadi and were digging in the loose gravel accumulated at one of the rocky sides to obtain water that was slowly trickling through the limestone rock. The men were working slowly, and the Bash Shawish, the Colour-Sergeant, said, " Give it to me," and seizing a shovel from one of the men he began to dig with great vigour. One of his lusty blows hit the rock, when the polished hard face that forms on weathered limestone cracked and fell away, exposing the soft porous rock beneath, and out of the porous rock came a great gush of clear water."

A NEW LEADER—Numbers xiii. 8; xiv. 6-9, 14, 30; xxvii. 18-23; *Joshua* i. 1-11.

The original inhabitants of Palestine were cave-dwellers, but by 2000 B.C. their civilisation had almost disappeared, being merged in that of their conquerors who dwelt in houses and within walled cities. About 3800 B.C. Palestine was known as the land of the Amorite, and Amorites and Hittites were the predominant peoples, the other Canaanite tribes being branches of these two. It is probable that these Canaanites were the Hyksos, descendants of Eber, ancestor of Abraham, who on their march south to Egypt inter-married with the cave-dwellers and imposed upon them their arts and civilisation, which can be traced to Babylonia. From about 1600-1400 B.C. Egypt was dominant in Palestine and had governors in all the important towns. In 1580 the Hyksos were expelled by Aohmes I. and Egypt became a military state. The quiver had been introduced from Asia and there were thousands of horses and chariots. As Egypt aspired to control of the Euphrates she had to keep Palestine in subjection in order to safeguard her line of communications. The Canaanites were organised into numerous city-kingdoms, each under the rule of a local king with an advanced civilisation. They were inveterate traders and through contact with other races they had learned to cast hollow bronzes and to make glass vessels. Amenhetep I. (1560-1539) penetrated as far as the Euphrates, and Thotmes I. (1539-1514) boasted that he made the boundary of Egypt as far as the circuit of the sun and every land her serfs. Under Hatshephut, who married Thotmes III. (1501-1447), the Syrian dynasts revolted against Egypt but Thotmes took the field and inflicted defeat upon the Asiatic allies at Megiddo. The catalogue of his spoils from Megiddo is a surprising revelation of the wealth of the country. It included 924 chariots, 2238 horses,

200 suits of armour, the gorgeous tent of the king of Kadesh, together with his household furniture and royal sceptre. Thotmes supplanted the city-kings with those who would be loyal to Egypt and carried off their eldest sons to the " Castle of Thebes," where they were given the best of educations and made friendly. When a city-king died Thotmes " caused his son to stand in his place." He stationed Egyptian garrisons throughout Syria and campaigned year after year, exacting heavy tribute. Amenhetep II. (1447-1423) and Thotmes IV. (1423-1413) maintained the Egyptian Empire in Asia and the time was not propitious for the Hebrew invasion of Palestine. When news of the death of Thotmes III. came the city-kings were prepared to revolt and it was at that time that the spies were sent out by Moses to survey the land. Under Amenhetep III. (1413-1377) Egyptian power in Syria was on the wane, and under Akhenaten (1377-1361), an idealist whose sole interest was in religion, there was chaos. Egypt's power was undermined and city after city was lost. The Hebrews were not slow to take advantage of the laziness of Amenhetep III. Under Joshua they succeeded in establishing a footing in the Promised Land, and taking advantage of the anarchical state of the country later succeeded in establishing themselves as the dominant people on the Highlands where they settled down to an agricultural and pastoral life.

The Hebrew conquest was rendered easy by the policy of the Pharaohs. In Exodus we read : " I will send the hornet before thee which shall drive out the Hivite, the Canaanite and the Hittite from before thee," and in Joshua : " I sent the hornet before you which drove them out from before you." The hornet was the badge of Thotmes and his successors. Thotmes' spoils at Megiddo, in addition to those already mentioned, included 2000 sheep, 20,500 goats, and 208,200 fourfold measures of grain. Other places were visited year after year and the country drained of its resources. " If the spoliation was in fact anything like that depicted in the records, the triumphs of Egypt meant in effect the ruin of the country and account in large measure for the decay of the old Canaanite power and civilisation." When the Egyptian garrisons were withdrawn the Canaanites were at the mercy of any foe. " The reaction to the Pharaoh's continuous apathy was profound, and coupled with the menace of the Hittites from the north it rapidly proved fatal to Egyptian prestige and authority. Unrest led to disorder. The resident Governor, the inspectors, and loyal chieftains, were

M

alike powerless without troops to stem the growing revolution, much less protect the frontiers of Canaan. It was at the opening of this period, according to Biblical chronology about 1406 B.C. and therefore in the earlier years of Amenhetep's reign, that Joshua and the Israelites appeared from the east before the walls of Jericho."

The name Joshua means " God is Salvation," and appears ultimately in Greek as " Jesus." Of the tribe of Ephraim, Joshua came into prominence as a military leader under Moses with whom he shared in the revelation at Sinai. He was one of the two spies who brought back to Moses a favourable report. Canaan had been weakened by the campaigns of Thotmes III. and immediately after the Exodus Joshua and Caleb recognised that an opportunity of entering the Land of Promise had presented itself. Through neglect of that opportunity the Israelites were doomed to wander for years in the Wilderness. Joshua had always shown himself to be a man of great courage and of loyalty to Moses and to God and was recognised by the Israelite warriors as the only worthy successor to their great leader.

The discipline of 40 years of desert life had converted the turbulent, undisciplined horde of slaves into a strong and conquering host. God deals with us not only according to our abilities but according to our disabilities. Moses, the law-giver, was God's instrument for welding the tribes into a nation, then for him " Nebo's lonely mountain." Joshua, the military leader, was best fitted for the fighting that must follow the crossing of the Jordan and for the settlement of the tribes in the Promised Land.

JUNIOR (Second Year) — OLD TESTAMENT.

C.—STORIES JESUS HEARD.

THE SPIES—*Numbers* xiii.

CANAAN had been weakened by the campaigns of Thotmes III., and immediately after the Exodus the opportunity was given to Moses of leading his people into the Land of Promise. Moses sent out 12 spies to make a survey and to report. The spies, doubtless in twos and threes to avoid arousing suspicion, traversed the whole land and brought back samples of its produce and reports concerning the various tribes inhabiting it. But, with the exception of Joshua and Caleb, the former of whom here first comes into prominence, they considered the time inopportune for attack. In particular were they terrified of the " sons of Anak." Evidences of the existence of the " sons of Anak " appear in a series of remarkable underground dwellings in the territories between Hebron and Ashdod. It is possible that the Israelites subsequently occupied some of their homes. The spies reported that the land starved its inhabitants to death (verse 32).

Apparently there are two accounts of this mission of the spies dovetailed together. According to the earlier account (17b-20, 22-24, 26b-31, 32b-33) the spies explored only Hebron and neighbourhood and reported the land as unproductive; according to the later account (1-17a, 21, 25-26a, 32a), they traversed the whole land, which they reported as barren and unfruitful. But even the earlier report was discouraging. " We came unto the land whither thou sentest us; and surely it floweth with milk and honey; . . . howbeit the people that dwell in the land are strong and the cities are fortified and very great." Through neglect of opportunity and cowardice the Israelites were doomed to wander for years in the wilderness.

CROSSING THE JORDAN—*Joshua* iii. and iv.

As we have seen, conditions were favourable for the invasion of Canaan. The date is reckoned to be about 1400 B.C. Joshua had always shown himself as a man of courage and of loyalty to Moses and to God. Now 80 years of age and tested as a leader, he felt that the time had come to lead the Israelites into their inheritance. A new king, Amenhetep III., reigned in Egypt. The hold of that land upon Palestine being relaxed, Joshua knew that its people would be unable to offer a stubborn resistance to men of faith and courage.

The Israelites were encamped at Shittim, and to reach the Jordan they had to cross a sandy plain about 8 miles wide. In moving camp the flocks came first, followed in order by the herds, the fighting men, the women and families with the baggage, the elders and the chief. At the fords of Jordan Joshua found the river running high and realised that only by the intervention of God could a crossing be effected. Within the Tent of Meeting he had, with Moses, gone into the presence of God at every crisis and sought divine help and guidance. At the Jordan he knew that God would not fail him. "Sanctify yourselves; for to-morrow the Lord will do wonders among you," he said; " behold the ark of the covenant of the Lord of all the earth passeth over before you into Jordan. . . . And it shall come to pass that the waters of Jordan shall be cut off, even the waters that come down from above." His expectations were not disappointed. " The waters which came down from above stood, and rose up in one heap, at Adam, the city that is beside Zarethan; and those that went down toward the sea of the Arabah, even the salt sea, were wholly cut off; and the people passed over right against Jericho." It may be that high up the course of the river a landslide dammed the waters. Similar occurrences took place in 1267 A.D., 1906 and 1927. " On this last occasion," writes Garstang, " the high west bank immediately below the ford collapsed, carrying with it the roadway . . . and just below, a section of the cliff, which here rises to a height of 150 feet, fell bodily across the river and completely dammed it, so that no water flowed down the river bed for 21½ hours. Meanwhile the waters gradually filled up the plain around Tell el Damieh, and found their way eventually back to the river bed when the temporary barrage was in turn destroyed, and normal conditions were gradually resumed.

" During this time, it is asserted by several living witnesses that they crossed and recrossed the bed of the river freely on foot."

THE FALL OF JERICHO—*Joshua* vi.

Jericho stood isolated upon a mound at the foot of the hills barring the route to the western plateau, the objective of Israel. It was built in the early Bronze Age (2500-2000 B.C.), rebuilt in the middle Bronze Age (2000-1600 B.C.), but again destroyed. It was rebuilt in the late Bronze Age (1600-1200 B.C.), and Professor Garstang has given much reason to believe that it was destroyed by the Israelites about 1406 B.C. The walls of the city attacked by the Israelites ran parallel, the outer wall 6 feet thick, the inner wall 12 feet thick, and both walls were 30 feet in height, with a space of 15 feet between them. But the bricks were sun-dried with no binding straw, and as they were of different lengths the spaces between them were filled with mortar. The foundations were faulty, the inner wall overhanging an earlier wall, and the outer wall being built of debris at the edge of the mound. The walls in places were linked together by houses built across them, and when, as Professor Garstang has shown, the outer wall collapsed as the result of an earthquake, it involved the inner wall in its downfall. " The ceremonial specially instituted for this occasion, the daily carrying of the Ark in solemn procession around the walls, followed by the massed host of the Israelites in solemn silence, must have presented indeed a grim and terrifying spectacle to the besieged inhabitants, to whom it foreshadowed their impending doom. History hardly bears witness to a design so frightful, accomplished with such deliberation."

As the first-born of Israel and the firstlings of the flock were dedicated to God, so was Jericho " devoted " as the first fruits of the Land of Promise. There were neither spoils nor captives. Only a woman, Rahab, who had given assistance to the spies, was suffered, together with her household, to escape.

The God of Israel was " the Lord of Hosts," a God of battles, and to Him, as the Giver of victory, Jericho was put under the ban, " devoted " to destruction. While we may find it difficult, if not impossible, to believe that God approved of such " devotion," we must bear in mind that the people of Jericho were a debased type, given to the worship of Astarte, the goddess of love. If certain earnest Christians to-day believe in the sterilisation of the unfit, we can hardly cavil at Joshua for thinking that it was the will of God that degenerates should be exterminated. The lesson of the story is that the secret of victory lies in faith in God and in the righteousness of one's cause.

The Taking of Ai—*Joshua* vii., viii. 1-28.

The capture of Jericho put Joshua in control of a strategic centre whence he could set out on any one of three possible routes. Of these the easiest was the route *via* Ai, a city larger than Jericho, with some 2000 inhabitants and with formidable defences. The spies sent to reconnoitre the city underestimated its strength. The Israelites made attack from the wrong side as they had to cross exposed and difficult ground, and suffered defeat. Dreading the consequences of this blow to their prestige, Joshua and the elders gave way to despair. " O Lord, what shall I say after that Israel hath turned their backs before their enemies! For the Canaanites and all the inhabitants of the land shall hear of it, and shall compass us round, and cut off our name from the earth." The reverse was attributed to the sin of Achan who, at the sack of Jericho, had, in his greed, taken of the spoil that was devoted to God. Achan's sin was the sin of disobedience to what was regarded as the divine will, and Achan and his family were taken to the valley of Achor and put to death by stoning and burning. While it is true that the family often suffers for the sins of an individual member, it is no less true that the individual is largely the product of the environmental conditions of the home, and in holding the family responsible for the sin of the individual, the Hebrews called attention to this great truth. Almost without exception, the problem-child is the product of the problem-home, and many of the criminals and social misfits have to pay a heavy price for parental indifference and neglect. In O'Henry's story of the girl arraigned before the Heavenly Court, the Judge informed her accusers that they had brought the wrong person for trial and must make search for her father.

With the expiation of Achan's crime Joshua took fresh courage and decided to seize Ai by stratagem, and to strike terror in the hearts of the peoples of the land by a terrible deed. Bethel, though but a mile away, was invisible from Ai, and Joshua, under cover of darkness, sent a detachment of troops to take up position to the west of the doomed city while he himself with the main body made for the north side of Ai, " there to take up such a position that the first light of morning would disclose the hosts of Israel to the inhabitants." The manœuvre was a success. The men of Ai, with the first streaks of dawn, made for the Israelite hosts, who fled to the north and the east, thus gaining the advantage of the higher ground for their subsequent counter-attack. The storm-troops fired the city, " and when Joshua and all Israel saw that the ambush had taken the city, and that the smoke of the city ascended, then they turned again, and slew the men of Ai. And the other came forth out of

the city against them; so they were in the midst of Israel,
some on this side, and some on that side; and they smote
them so that they let none of them escape." A large number
of men and women were massacred, and Joshua burnt Ai
and made it an heap for ever. Professor Garstang has shown
that Ai was destroyed by fire about 1400 B.C., and it has
remained a desolation to this day, its site never having been
reoccupied.

THE GIBEONITES—*Joshua* ix.

The successor to Amenhetep III. in Egypt was Akhenaten
(1377-1361 B.C.), a thinker and a psalmist, a dreamer and an
idealist, who lost for Egypt her Syrian Empire. At Tel el
Amarna, the capital of Akhenaten, there were discovered, in
1887, 320 contemporary clay tablets, letters from the kings and
governors of Syria and Palestine to Amenhetep III. and Akhenaten. These letters tell of the revolt against Egypt and are
full of frantic appeals for help. In the north the Hittites and
the Amorites were in league against Egypt, and from the east
marauding bedouin were forcing an entry into the country.
Some of the tablets speak of the invasion from the east of
the Jordan by the Habiru. The Habiru are probably to be
identified with the Israelites.

As a sequel to the destruction of Jericho and Ai, a group
of Hivite cities, of which Gibeon was the chief, entered into
alliance with Joshua. The Israelite camp was only 19 miles
distant from Gibeon, an important strategic point, and the
elaborate preparations made by the Gibeonites to make their
cunning trick successful is an indication of their fear. When
Joshua made the discovery that he had been the victim of a
clever stratagem, he refused to go back on his pledge given
to the Gibeonites in the name of God. In the Bible there is
no divorce between religion and morality. The sanctions of
the ethical code are religious. The great prophets are in-
sistent on the need for the nation's honouring its obligations
even to a foreign oppressor, if an oath has been taken in the
name of God. Joshua, in an earlier age, held that to break
his word would be to dishonour God.

SAMSON—*Judges* xiv., xv., xvi.

To a host just emerging from the desert with neither siege
implements nor weapons the walled cities were impregnable.
Joshua's campaigns resulted only in the acquisition of unoccupied and sparsely populated districts. These he appor-

tioned among the tribes of Israel and adopted a policy of peaceful penetration.

The Israelites settled down side by side with their Canaanite neighbours. They avoided the great trade routes, in particular the coast highway between Egypt and the north, and resorted to guerilla warfare, led by their judges or deliverers, only under the threat of oppression and domination. Professor Garstang has shown that the periods of " rest " mentioned in Judges coincided with the periods of Egyptian suzerainty over Palestine, and the periods of anarchy with the periods of Egyptian weakness and apathy. He gives the following chronological scheme :—

Name of Leader B.C.	Space of Time.	Bible Story.	Political Situation
Moses 1447-07	40	Wandering	Domination of Egypt
Joshua 1407-1367	40	(a) Invasion (b) Penetration	(a) Egyptian apathy (b) Habiru revolt
Cushan 1367-59	8	Israel oppressed by Hittites	
Othniel 1359-19	40	Rest	Domination of Egypt
Eglon 1309-01	18	Oppression by Eglon king of Moab	Rebellion in Egypt
Ehud 1301-1221	80	Rest	Domination of Egypt by Rameses II.
Sisera 1221-01	20	Oppression of Sisera	Anarchy in Egypt
Deborah 1201-1161	40	Rest	Domination of Egypt by Rameses III. &c.
Midianites 1161-54	7	Midianite Oppression	Decline of Egyptian power
Gideon 1154-14	40	Rest	⎫
Abimelech 1114-11	3		⎬ Withdrawal of Egypt
Ammonites 1111-10	1	Oppression	⎪
Jephthah 1110-05	6		⎭
Philistines and Samson 20 ⎰ 1105-1065	40	Philistine Oppression	Philistine Domination

The Philistines, a non-Semitic people, came from some Aegean land, perhaps Crete, and moved towards Egypt by land and sea. Their first attack upon Palestine took place about 1230 B.C., but they were repulsed by Ben Anath, a Syrian sea-captain in alliance with Egypt. Israel was saved by Egyptian intervention. Garstang holds that a number of Philistines took service in the Egyptian army as mercenaries, garrisoning the five cities of Ashdod, Ashkelon, Gaza, Ekron and Gath, of which they later took possession on Egypt's withdrawal. In the time of Samson they appear in possession of these important cities on the Egyptian trade-route. Owing to the decline of Egyptian power the Philistines and the Israelites were left as the dominant peoples and a struggle between the two was inevitable. The Philistines had the advantage over the Israelites in that they knew how to work iron (1 Samuel xiii. 19-21). In the time of Samson they were regarded as the overlords of Israel (Judges x. 7), but there is no indication that their rule was oppressive or tyrannical.

Samson was a Nazirite, dedicated for life to God by his parents, perhaps before birth, so that he might be endowed by God with power to fight the nation's battles. He was forbidden to drink wine or to cut his hair in token of his consecration to the service of God. The scene of his exploits was the hill-country between the Maritime Plain and the mountainous plateau in which the Israelites were entrenched. Alive to the possibility of Philistine invasion Samson felt the call of God to use his great strength on behalf of his people. But he had no staying-power. He decided, contrary to the wishes of his parents and to the will of God, to ally himself with a Philistine woman. On the way to arrange his marriage he gave evidence of his great strength. He encountered a lion, which he slew by jerking back its head. He gave further evidence of strength in his quarrels with the Philistines who, at last, through the perfidy of his wife, discovered the secret of his power. " If thou weavest the seven locks of my head with the web and makest the whole fast, then I shall be weak and like any other man. And Delilah made him sleep and wove the seven locks of his head with the web and made it fast with the pin." The loom was a simple upright frame with the post in the ground.

Samson's strength did not lie in his hair but came from God and had long been on the wane. With his locks—the emblem of his consecration to God—shorn, he knew that his strength was gone. For disloyalty to God he was doomed to lose his sight and to grind corn for the Philistines. At a

festival to Dagon, the food-god of the Philistines, he was
brought forth for the sport of his enemies. The roofs of the
houses of the period were flat, with large logs of wood laid
across from one wall to the other. In the centre of the
Temple of Dagon there was a row of wooden pillars supporting beams on which rested the ends of the log-rafters,
and under the pillars were stones to prevent them from
sinking into the ground. Samson laid hold of two of the
central pillars and caused the collapse of the building, with
the result that the lords of the Philistines assembled within,
and the crowd gathered on the roof, met their death. He
saw the opportunity of striking a blow for his country, and
in his death made some amends for neglected opportunities
during his life. Had he proved loyal to God throughout
his life, what might he not have accomplished on behalf of
his people?

Saul made King—*1 Samuel* ix., x.

There are two accounts of the founding of the monarchy,
an event that profoundly affected the life of Israel for good
and for evil. They reflect the views held of the monarchy
at different periods. According to the earlier version Samuel,
an unknown seer at Ramah, recognised that the only method
of breaking the Philistine yoke was by the union of the
tribes under a king. The Philistines were superior in the
arts of war and a century ahead of the Israelites in culture.
They were equipped with weapons of iron and for long
dominated Israel. At the battle of Ebenezer they effected
the capture of the ark, which was returned owing to an outbreak of bubonic plague attributed to its possession. The
end of their 40 years' domination came with the victory of
Samuel at the second battle of Ebenezer, but they made a
quick recovery.

Samuel's problem was to find a suitable man for the
throne. Saul happened to visit Ramah, the seat of a
sanctuary, at a time when Samuel was about to offer
sacrifice, and when Samuel's eye fell upon this splendid
figure of a man he at once saw in him the future king.
Samuel anointed him. The ritual of anointing, possibly of
Egyptian origin, was intended to transmit to him the power
of God for future use. Samuel then gave him three signs.
He commanded him to join a band of wandering dervishes
who were subject to religious frenzy. In primitive times
inspiration was associated with the psychically abnormal,

ecstasy, frenzy, the trance, and there are still many who make the truth of a revelation dependent upon the manner in which the message comes. The three points to emphasise in the story are Samuel's self-forgetfulness and Saul's humility and changed personality. Had Samuel not responded to the divine voice he would have selected as king one of his own family or friends. After parting with Samuel we read that God gave Saul another heart. Saul had a new vision of himself and of his place in God's world, due to contact with the personality of the seer. " Soul grows in contact with soul," said Carlyle.

DAVID ANOINTED KING—1 Samuel xvi. 1-13.

After the interview with Samuel, Saul was a changed man. But he had not the grace of continuance. Success went to his head like new wine, and after the reins of power were in his hand the process of degeneration set in. Saul parted company with Samuel and dated his downfall from the day of separation.

In his search for a successor to Saul, Samuel set out for Bethlehem, and on arrival invited the inhabitants to take part in a sacrificial rite. Impressed by Jesse, he wondered if among his children there might be one fitted for the king-ship and invited them to join in the sacrifice and to perform certain ritual acts. He was tempted to make choice of Eliab because of his good looks, but passed him by as char-acter was of more importance than outward appearance. All the other sons of Jesse appeared before Samuel, but he considered none of them suitable. Almost without hope of finding a king, he casually asked Jesse if he had any more sons and received the information that the youngest, the herd-boy, was on the hills with the sheep. Samuel com-manded that he be brought, and when his eye fell upon the shepherd-lad with his straightforward, honest eyes, he knew that in him he had found the future king; and to the amaze-ment of the bystanders he consecrated him to the service of God. After contact with Samuel, David, like Saul, was a new creature, for we are informed that from that day forward the Spirit of the Lord came upon him.

" Man looketh upon the outward appearance but the Lord looketh upon the heart." David's brothers were apparently better fitted for the kingship than he. But David had been trained in a hard school, and as the result of his dangerous and strenuous life had developed a strong character. In this lesson the teacher will naturally give a vivid description of the Eastern shepherd's outfit and of the excitements of his life among the hills.

DAVID AND GOLIATH—1 *Samuel* xvii. 1-51.

Saul was so taken up with the dignity of his office that he forgot God and was unequal to the task of subduing the Philistines. In this story we see the Philistine and the Israelite armies encamped on two hills with a valley between them. When Moses' spies made survey of the country they felt as grasshoppers in presence of the Sons of Anak (Numbers xiii. 33), the descendants of an ancient race of giants. The presence of the Sons of Anak in Palestine is attested by pottery fragments of the eleventh dynasty (2000 B.C.), and Goliath, the Philistine champion, may have been descended on one side from these Anakim. About 9 feet in height, clad in heavy armour with a shield and shield-bearer, he was to all appearances invulnerable, and as he strutted out twice daily for 40 days he struck terror to the hearts of the Israelites.

David, because of his great trust in God, was prepared to accept the challenge of Goliath. "The Lord that delivered me out of the paw of the lion, and out of the paw of the bear," he said, "will deliver me out of the hand of this Philistine." The insult to God stung him into action. The weight of the unfamiliar armour offered by the king would, he knew, lay him prostrate at his enemy's feet. He felt that he must "be himself" and fight with familiar weapons. Carrying only his staff, his shepherd's bag and his sling, he ran down the hill and, as he crossed the stream, stooped to select five smooth pebbles. Although skilled in the art of slinging stones, he was taking no chances. "Even the man who trusts his God is in honour bound to prepare himself, so far as human foresight may, for all eventualities." God helps those who help themselves, and when a man has done everything humanly possible, he can leave the issue to Him.

DAVID: HIS BRAVE COMPANIONS—2 *Samuel* xxiii. 13-17.

2 Samuel xxi.-xxiv. contain a number of appendices from various sources, inserted possibly after the separation of the Books of Samuel and of Kings as we know them. In this lesson the teacher might discuss the things that bring men together and bind them together—birth in the same place,

education in the same school, interest in the same studies, attachment to the same political party, but above all devotion to the same person. David drew men to himself. He was the centre and leader, and there were two orders of honour in his army—one known as "the Three," the other as "the Thirty."

Among the stories told of these heroes is one of the loyalty of the Three to their chief at a time when the Philistines had such a grip upon the country that they garrisoned even Bethlehem. It was harvest-time and the sun was beating down upon the bare rocks of the Cave of Adullam. David, parched with thirst and home-sick, longed for a drink from the well of Bethlehem, his native place—surely a natural longing. Silently the Three slipped away, pierced the enemy's line, and returned with the water from the well by Bethlehem's gate. David was staggered by their deed. Perceiving the loyalty and affection of men who would seek to satisfy his longing at the risk of their lives, he felt that it was sacrificial water—too sacred to satisfy a vulgar thirst, and fit only for an oblation to God. He dare not sully it with his lips. The teacher should show that the value of things lies not in themselves but in the toil and the sweat, the suffering and the prayers of those who have secured them for us. What has been secured at so great a price we need to reckon as holy unto the Lord.

David's Kindness to Saul—1 *Samuel* xxvi. 1-12

David's popularity aroused Saul's jealousy, and David was forced into exile. Saul accused the priesthood of conspiring with David against him (1 Samuel xxii.) and ordered the execution of the priests of Nob to which the tabernacle had been transferred. Abiathar alone escaped and threw in his lot with David at Adullam. Spies kept Saul informed of David's movements, and on one occasion there was but a hill between the forces of the king and the handful of men about David. But the Philistines came up from the Maritime Plain and Saul was called away to cope with them. David took refuge in the Wilderness, that great howling waste that overlooks the shore of the Dead Sea, and on two occasions, if 1 Samuel xxiv. and xxvi. are not two versions of the same story, God delivered the king into his hand. "That the entry of the two heroes into Saul's camp is not impossible may be shown by comparison with the escape of the Maoris from the Gate of Pah at the end of the second Maori war in

1861. The Pah was surrounded by British troops bivouacked
on the ground, but the Maoris made their escape by night
without detection, leaving a cup of water beside each wounded
British soldier."   David refused to take the life of his
enemy.   The great spiritual truth in the story is that evil
cannot be overcome by evil but only by good.

David's Kindness to Mephibosheth—2 *Samuel* ix.

The same magnanimity that had marked David's dealings
with Saul up to the time of the latter's death, David continued to show to his children.   In particular he remembered
a promise he had made to Jonathan that, if he were made
king, he would deal kindly with Jonathan's family for
Jonathan's sake.   After his succession to the throne much of
his time was spent on active service owing to the Philistine
menace.   When, however, he had freed the country from this
yoke, then he had opportunity to fulfil his promise.   From
Ziba, one of Saul's servants, he learned that Mephibosheth,
son of his dead friend Jonathan, still survived and was living
by the ford Jabbok.

His nurse, in the excitement of the flight from the
Philistines, had allowed Mephibosheth, a child of five, to fall
from her arms, with the result that he was lame of his feet.

David, anxious to make good his promise, sent for Mephibosheth to be brought to his court.   Not only did he restore
to Mephibosheth the estate that had belonged to his grandfather Saul, but he also ordered Ziba and his servants to
cultivate it on his behalf.   David further gave instructions
that Mephibosheth and his little son, Micha, should stay at
his court as members of his own family.   " So Mephibosheth
dwelt in Jerusalem : for he did eat continually at the king's
table."   David took a risk in allowing any of Saul's descendants to live, as there was always the possibility of
a revolution for the purpose of establishing the old dynasty.
But he fulfilled his promise and showed his love for the dead
in a practical way.

The Return of the Ark—2 *Samuel* vi. 1-17.

The ark was a coffer or box which was kept in a tent or
sanctuary in times of peace and carried in front of the
Israelite hosts during military campaigns.   It was the symbol
or pledge of the divine presence.   Although in the early
period it was almost identified with God Himself (Numbers

x. 35-36), there are no good grounds for holding that it was regarded as the abode of God or that it bore any image or representation of the deity. Although the popular mind may have conceived that God dwelt in it, the imageless ark was a testimony to the exalted conception of God held by the Hebrews and made for the development of a spiritual religion. According to tradition, it was made by Moses to symbolise God in the midst of His people. To the writers of the Sixth and Fifth centuries B.C. its sanctity was due to the fact that it contained the Tables of the Law, and it was accordingly called "the Ark of the Covenant." Because of its association with God's service it was invested with divine power. It guided the oxen attached to the cart that carried it (1 Samuel vi. 7-12), and Uzzah, on touching it, dropped down dead. In primitive tribes to-day not infrequently the man who unwittingly breaks a taboo dies through fear of the vengeance to be exacted by an enraged deity.

On or near the site of the present Jerusalem the Amorites had a fortified city, the "City of Peace," at least as far back as 2000 B.C. This was wrested from the Jebusites by David about 1050 B.C. The removal of the ark to Jerusalem was a master-stroke of statesmanship, as it made the city the political and the religious centre of Israel. The great truth in the story is that neither individual nor nation can prosper without the divine presence. The teacher should mention that Psalm 24 was sung when the Ark was brought into the city, the doors being commanded to lift up their heads that the King of Glory might enter.

Solomon Builds the Temple—1 *Kings* v., vi.

The founding of the Temple took place about 966 B.C. The Canaanites had simple, unadorned temples at various holy places, e.g., Shechem and Bethshan, and Solomon no doubt felt that something more enduring than the tabernacle, as the abode of the Ark, was necessary. Solomon's predominant motive was religious, to erect a magnificent house for the Ark. His temple was originally a royal chapel not meant to supersede the other places of worship in the country. But it quickly became the chief shrine. "Under the shadow of the throne and supported by the royal bounty, the Temple inevitably gained prestige and importance with each succeeding generation. Its geographical position and magnificence also from the first exalted it above all the other sanctuaries in the land. . . . As it attracted more and more all members of the nation, it silently but powerfully emphasised the fact that one God, Jehovah, ruled supreme in Israel."

The Hebrews being unskilled as artists and artificers, the building was constructed by Phoenician architects after the model of the Egyptian temples, and so contained many symbols foreign to the religion of the Hebrews. The timber for building was landed from Lebanon at the port of Joppa and transported to Jerusalem, while the stone was quarried in the neighbourhood of the city. The building took 7 years to complete but was not large. It measured 90 feet in length by 30 in breadth. The walls were of white marble with gold decorations, their inside being lined with cedar overlaid with gold. The inner shrine was empty save for the Ark, and this emptiness made for the development of a spiritual religion. Unlike heathen temples it contained no image of the deity.

Any reconstruction of the building is conjectural. The actual sanctuary, regarded as the shrine of God, was divided into two parts, the Holy Place and the Holy of Holies. Within the Holy of Holies was set the Ark with two huge cherubim, each 15 feet high, overshadowing it. The cherubim were the upholders of the divine throne, and the Ark was placed under the two inner wings. In the Holy Place stood the Table of Shewbread, made of cedar and overlaid with gold. The shrewbread was "holy" or consecrated bread. Although amongst primitive peoples bread was set apart as the actual food of the deity, the "presence-bread" in Solomon's temple was not regarded as the actual food of God, but gave symbolic expression to the Hebrew recognition of God as the Giver of all material blessings. The teacher should discuss the motives that prompted Solomon to build the Temple and to leave the Holy of Holies empty save for the Ark.

SENIOR (First Year) — OLD TESTAMENT.

B.—HEROES OF ISRAEL.

TALES OF THE WILDERNESS WANDERING.

THE PASSOVER—*Exodus* xii.

Although the account of the Passover given in the Old Testament belongs to the seventh century B.C., there can be no doubt that the festival was very much older. As a feast it stands in a class by itself inasmuch as it was not only a national but a family affair, the meal taking place within the tent or house. Among Semitic pastoral tribes it was the custom to offer the firstlings of the flocks to God, and among agricultural tribes to offer the first-fruits of the soil. The Hebrews wished to leave Egypt to keep a festival to God and as Pharaoh refused God took the first-born of Egypt in exchange for the firstlings of the flocks that the Hebrews would have sacrificed.

On receiving permission to leave Egypt the Hebrews held a festival at which they sacrificed a lamb. The door-posts were sprinkled with the blood of the victim as a protection to the house against misfortune. A similar rite for the same purpose was practised in Arabia and Syria. Leaven, the symbol of evil, was excluded from the flat cakes eaten with the lamb. The bitter herbs served as a reminder of the miseries of Egyptian bondage but they may have been eaten originally to ward off evil. " Even in the eighteenth century modern Greeks thought of the plague as a horrible spectre which, during the night, marked with an indelible sign the houses which it would enter; but they believed that the one means of warding off its visit was the eating of garlic." To the Hebrews the Passover symbolised deliverance from Egyptian bondage and entry upon a new life.

THE BATTLE WITH AMALEK—*Exodus* xvii.

The Amalekites first make their appearance in the neighbourhood of Kadesh. At Rephidim, a broad plain to the north-west of Sinai, they engaged in battle for a whole

N

day against Israel. Joshua acted as leader of the Israelite hosts but Moses from the top of high ground within sight of the field of battle provided the stimulus to fight by holding up his rod as a divine sign. The Amalekites, in particular, were put under the "ban" because they had harassed the Israelites in the rear and destroyed the weak (Deuteronomy xxv. 17-19). They were at the head of the tribes already in possession of Canaan and the battle between them and the Israelites determined the future of both peoples. "It was the hatred of two rivals disputing a splendid prize which the one had previously possessed and still partially possessed, and the other was trying to get for himself by ousting him." Israel's victory gave her peace in the first stage of her advance on Palestine.

The Giving of Law—*Exodus* xix., xx.

After the exodus from Egypt the Hebrews sojourned for some time in the neighbourhood of Kadesh and then made their way to Sinai-Horeb, "the holy mount." The site of this mount is unknown. The tradition that identifies it with a mountain in the Peninsula of Sinai does not go back beyond the sixth century A.D. God had revealed Himself to Moses in the burning bush in Midian and some scholars place Mount Sinai in Arabia. Other scholars make reference to the statements in Deuteronomy xxxiii. 2, Judges v. 4, 5, Habakkuk iii. 3, and hold the view that Mount Sinai lay in the neighbourhood of Kadesh.

The Joseph tribe from Egypt probably united with some of their kinsmen in the desert and at the "holy mount" God formed them into a nation. He made Himself known, to the accompaniment of fire, earthquake and thunder, not only as the Deliverer from Egyptian bondage but as a God of righteousness. He renewed the covenant made with Abraham. The Hebrews accepted Him as their God, and pledged themselves to Him. Other peoples had their gods but they did not regard them as the only deities. To the Hebrews the gods of other peoples were of no importance. To them there was only one God whom it was their concern to know. The difference between Him and other gods was not merely in name but in character. While other gods made no ethical demands on their worshippers, Jehovah was a righteous God who demanded righteousness of His people. It was the knowledge of God as Righteousness that enabled Hebrew religion to survive the disintegrating influences of Canaan. "We fail to realise," writes Welch, "how much allegiance to one god has done for the moral culture of the race." The Israelites did not regard their allegiance to Jehovah as an obligation but as a privilege. "The sense of being in the power of one Will, which means well by them, is a deliverance rather than a duty. It has delivered them from the fear of the dark powers which lurk in the processes of nature, before which man found himself so helpless. It has unified their moral life to realise that there is One above all these who has a purpose with them."

There are different accounts of the giving of the Law. According to one account Moses wrote on tables of stone the commands of God. According to a later account the finger of God did the writing. There are three versions of the commandments (Exodus xxxiv., Exodus xx., Deuteronomy v.). While it is difficult to say which is the original, there is no doubt that ten commandments were given to Moses. The great prophets of the eighth and seventh centuries emphasise that they gave no new law, but the old law revealed at the Mount. The authority of the law of God is always referred back to the period of Moses.

THE MAKING OF THE TABERNACLE—*Exodus* xxv., xxxi.

There is almost universal concensus of opinion among scholars that the first five books of the Old Testament— known as the Pentateuch—belong in their present form to a period after the Jewish Exile (586 B.C.), and that they have been compiled from four documents belonging to different periods. The elaborate accounts of the Tabernacle with its furnishings and its priesthood belong to the latest of these four documents.

The earliest source informs us that Moses erected a "tent of meeting" or a "tent of revelation," pitched outside the camp. To this tent God descended in the pillar of cloud and revealed to Moses the messages that were to be communicated to the people. To it those who desired to worship God repaired. Within the tent lay the Ark, the symbol of God's presence. The tent was a perpetual reminder of God's abiding presence. It was set up in a conspicuous place and could be seen by every Israelite. The teacher should emphasise the need felt by men in all ages for definite places of worship. Moses worshipped God in every glory of earth and sea and sky but he erected the tent for daily communion. Our Lord worshipped God on the hilltop and by the lakeside but He was to be found in the synagogue on the Sabbath day.

THE GOLDEN CALF—*Exodus* xxxii.

While Moses was with God on the Mount, Aaron took his place as leader. As day succeeded day and Moses failed to return the people became anxious and impatient. Some suggested that he was dead, others that he was a deserter. Jehovah-worship was an imageless worship. Feeling the need of a visible sign of the divine presence some requested Aaron to fashion them a god like the gods of other peoples. Aaron in fear complied with the demand, and made them an image of a young bull in wood overlaid with gold. To this image sacrifices were offered and arrangements were made for a feast on a grand scale. Moses interceded with God on behalf of the sinful nation and on his return to the camp ground the image into powder, mixed it with water and compelled the Israelites to drink of it.

The worship of bull-images was a feature of Canaanite religion and from time to time certain of the Hebrews reverted to the degrading custom of representing God by an animal. In view of the prevalence of animal worship in Egypt, Canaan and elsewhere, the persistent weakness of the Hebrews for bull or calf worship is not surprising. Jeroboam erected golden bulls at Bethel and Dan as symbols of Jehovah, the god of power and vitality. Of the relationship of the worshipper to these symbols we know little. Hosea speaks of those who " kiss the calves," indicating that the worship included the kissing of the image.

TALES OF THE EARLY MONARCHY.

THE GENEROUS WARRIOR—1 *Samuel* xi.

The original territory of the Ammonites extended along the Jordan from the Arnon to the Jabbok, but they were forced by the Amorites to abandon the Jordan valley. They claimed from Israel the restoration of the land wrested from them by their Amorite conquerors. In the early years of Saul they formed a powerful nation and about a month after his anointing as king they laid

siege to Jabesh-Gilead, the chief city of the half-tribe of
Manasseh, and demanded such cruel terms that the inhabitants of the town requested a respite of seven days
to enable them, if possible, to find a deliverer. The loss
of the right eye would have rendered the warriors of
Jabesh useless for fighting purposes. Nahash, king of
Ammon, confident of his power, acceded to the request.
When the envoys of Jabesh-Gilead brought the tidings to
Gibeah, the people of that place set up a wail that reached
the ears of Saul at work in the adjoining fields. "What
aileth the people that they weep?" he asked. Whereupon,
being told the tidings of the men of Jabesh, Saul was so
incensed that he hewed a yoke of oxen in pieces and dis-
tributed the pieces amongst the Israelite tribes, threatening
vengeance upon those who failed to respond to his call
to action. The Hebrew warriors gathered at Bezek, some
16 miles to the north of Gibeah, opposite the fords of Jordan by Bethshan. Saul's threat caused the "dread of the
Lord" to fall upon them and they came out as one man.
Saul divided them into three companies each with a leader
and under cover of darkness led them down to the fords
of Jordan. The night was divided into three watches and
just before dawn in the morning watch the three companies made their attack and the men of Jabesh-Gilead
came forth to join in the pursuit of the fleeing Ammonites.

The victory over Ammon not only saved Jabesh but
established the reputation of Saul of the little tribe of Benjamin. The Israelites, flushed with success, demanded the
death of the men who had despised Saul at his coronation,
but as the Lord had wrought salvation Saul refused to
permit bloodshed in Israel. In his hour of triumph he
showed a magnanimity unusual in that age.

A Brave Young Prince—1 *Samuel* xiv. 1-16.

At the commencement of Saul's reign the Philistines
held the coast-line and the dominating strong-holds. Ex-
cavation has shown that they held even Bethshan in
northern Palestine, where they fastened the body of Saul
to the wall after his death. Their superiority was largely
due to their control of iron which gave them an advantage
almost comparable to that of rifles over bows and arrows.
Controlling the coastline they kept the Israelites from
obtaining iron supplies. "Now there was no smith found
throughout all the land of Israel: for the Philistines said,

Lest the Hebrews make themselves swords and spears: but all the Israelites went down to the Philistines, to sharpen every man his share, and his coulter, and his axe and his mattock."

Jonathan, Saul's son, took the lead in the war of independence. While his father was gathering his forces Jonathan made a successful attack upon the Philistines at Gibeah, but on the advance of the main Philistine army the Israelites fled to the caves and rocks. The Philistines divided themselves into companies for the purpose of looting, and Saul and Jonathan with a handful of followers fell back upon Gibeah.

From a precipitous rock called Seneh (tooth) Saul and Jonathan could see the Philistine garrison at the rock Bozez, guarding the pass. While Saul was brooding over his desperate plight Jonathan decided to launch an attack upon the Philistine sentinels almost single-handed. Accompanied by his servant he set out and attracted the notice of the Philistine guard who dared him to scale the cliff. He and his companion not only overpowered the sentry but all the others who came up the pass in single file with the result that the Philistine garrison, roused from sleep by the clash of arms, fell into a panic and fled.

THE REJECTION OF SAUL—1 *Samuel* xv. 1-31.

The Amalekites who had harassed Israel in earlier days were again active and Samuel, in the name of God, commanded Saul to put them " under the ban," to devote them to destruction. Saul, however, spared Agag, the Amalekite king, and the best of the cattle, excusing himself on the ground that the cattle were to be used for sacrificial purposes. For his disobedience there was pronounced upon him the doom of rejection as king. It has been suggested that Saul represented a more humane ideal than did Samuel but that is unlikely. Saul spared Agag to grace his triumph and he spared the best of the cattle for the feast associated with the sacrificial rites. His motive was selfish. The important point in the story is that Saul's downfall dates from the moment of his breach with Samuel, the prophet of God. " It was a sorrowful day for him when, from whatever motive, he parted from the prophet, who had called him from obscurity to the foremost place in the land. There are friends from whom when we wilfully depart, we go steadily down, haunted by the awful conviction that we are rejected, as it were, by God Himself."

TALES OF THE LATER KINGDOM.

HEZEKIAH AND THE ASSYRIANS—2 *Kings* xviii., xix.

After the death of Solomon the ten tribes which had been held together as a nation by Saul, David and Solomon, disrupted and two kingdoms, Israel and Judah, each with their own king, were formed. Assyria overran the northern kingdom of Israel in 722 B.C. and made it a province under an Assyrian governor. Ahaz, king of Judah, made an alliance with Assyria and thus preserved the existence of the southern kingdom as a semi-independent state. When Hezekiah came to the throne Assyria's forces were concentrated on her eastern frontier with the result that Hezekiah was able to reverse the religious policy of Ahaz and carry out religious reforms. He initiated the movement for the destruction of the local sanctuaries and the concentration of worship at Jerusalem. For a time he remained faithful to the treaty with Assyria but with the accession of Sennacherib to the Assyrian throne, he was persuaded by Egypt to join in a coalition against the Assyrian power.

Sennacherib after conquering Babylonia led his army into Palestine, overran Judah and laid siege to Jerusalem. In his record he says: "Hezekiah of Judah, who had not submitted to my yoke, I besieged, forty-six of his strong cities, fortresses, and small cities without number I took; Hezekiah himself in Jerusalem, his royal city, I shut up, like a bird in a cage."

Hezekiah offered to submit and paid a heavy tribute on the understanding that he should retain his capital. Sennacherib demanded unconditional surrender and the siege of Jerusalem was renewed. He attempted to frighten Hezekiah and his supporters into compliance but to no purpose. His main army at Lachish on the Egyptian border suffered disaster and he had to raise the siege of Jerusalem and beat a hasty retreat. The angel that smote the Assyrian host has been interpreted as a pestilence that decimated Sennacherib's forces. "In itself this is far from improbable. The host was ill-fed, since it was far from home, was involved in the desert between Egypt and Palestine, and had by this time eaten bare the country which lay behind it. The camping-ground it had reached was notoriously unwholesome, since it was among the low marshes in the neighbourhood of the present Suez Canal. The district was the home of plague and disease."

Isaiah counselled a policy of freedom from foreign alliances, and enjoined Hezekiah to put his trust in God. During the siege when two state officials came with a message of despair from the king he sent back the reply that God would deliver them. When the Rabshakeh (chief of the officers) sent his clever message for the purpose of undermining Isaiah's influence, Isaiah pictured Jerusalem as a girl laughing at the Assyrian power (2 Kings xix. 21) and gave renewed assurance that God would save the city. By his faith in God he gave the inhabitants of Jerusalem courage to stand fast until the besieging army was withdrawn.

Hezekiah's Illness—2 *Kings* xx.

In Isaiah xxxviii. a parallel account of Hezekiah's sickness is given in abbreviated form. Owing to the influence of Isaiah Hezekiah was one of the greatest of the kings of Judah. Not only did he remove the local sanctuaries from Judah but he purged the Temple at Jerusalem of all the emblems of Asshur, the god of the Assyrians. Success had attended all his schemes and there was a danger that he might attribute his exalted position to the strength of his own right arm. Hence his illness was a blessing in disguise, reminding him of the frailty even of kings.

Believing that his disease might prove fatal Hezekiah sent for his friend and counsellor, Isaiah. But the prophet offered no hope of recovery. "Set thy house in order," he said, "for thou shalt die and not live." This prediction like all prophetic predictions was conditional, not absolute. Judgment might be averted by prayer and repentance. Hezekiah prayed for recovery, reminding God that he had lived uprightly as in His sight and had not divided his allegiance between Him and other gods. After Isaiah had reached the middle part of the city he was given an assurance from on high that the doom that he had pronounced was revoked. The prophet turned back and commanded the king to put a plaster of figs upon his boil, but Hezekiah demanded, as a sign that he would recover, that the shadow on the dial of Ahaz should recede ten degrees. The dial introduced by Ahaz, as a result of his contact with Assyria, was probably in the form of a pillar mounted on a platform surrounded by steps. The shadow of the

pillar fell on a smaller or a larger number of steps as the
sun mounted or declined in the heavens. Either a partial
eclipse or a phenomenon purely local caused an alteration
in the length of the sun's shadow and thus God gave the
sign asked for by the prophet.

JOSIAH THE REFORMER—2 *Kings* xxii., xxiii.

Under Manasseh, son of Hezekiah, there was a religious
reaction. Manasseh, as vassal of Assyria which had renewed her grip upon Judah, had to recognise the gods of
his over-lord. In the temple-courts he set up altars to
" the host of heaven," the worship of the heavenly bodies
being characteristically Assyrian. Amon continued the
religious practices of his father.

With Assyria tottering to her fall Josiah, son of Amon,
felt that the time was ripe for religious reform. According to the biblical narrative there was discovered in the
Temple in the eighteenth year of Josiah (621 B.C.) a law-
book. In conformity with the laws in this book Josiah
carried out his reforms. The book is generally held to
be Deuteronomy v.-xxviii. which denounces certain abom-
inations introduced in Manasseh's reign and emphasises the
importance of the centralisation of worship at one place.
The probability is that the book was written during
Manasseh's reign as a protest against his religious policy,
was concealed in the Temple and brought to light when
the political situation made reformation possible. The
story of the finding of the book is one of the most dramatic
in the Bible and can be told to show the power of the
written word in human life.

Josiah made a bid for independence by clearing the
Temple of the symbols of " the host of heaven " and of the
goddess Astarte, forced on Judah by the Assyrian power.
Palestine was purged of all the emblems of heathenism and
the worship of Jehovah and of Jehovah alone, was restored. The local sanctuaries were suppressed and worship
was centralised at Jerusalem, so that it might be kept free
from corruption.

TALES OF THE EXILE.

THE DREAM OF NEBUCHADNEZZAR—*Daniel* iv.

It is almost universally admitted among Old Testament
scholars that the Book of Daniel was written about 165 B.C.

during the persecution of Antiochus Epiphanes who set up
the image of Zeus in the Temple at Jerusalem and endeavoured to exterminate the Jewish religion. The purpose of the book of Daniel is to encourage the Jews to
emulate Daniel, the ideal Jew, and to hold fast by their
traditions. The writer, says Welch, "was seeking to represent ideals, not to reproduce history. He used these
stories of life under the Babylonian kingdom in order to
say some things about the heathen world in which he and
his fellow Jews were living. The kingdom of Babylonia
had ceased to mean to him the kingdom of Nebuchadnezzar
with its capital on the Euphrates. It is the kingdom of
Assyria, of Persia, of Antiochus, of all the nations under
which the Jews are called to live; it is renewed in every
generation, as it has existed in every generation, and it
takes Protean shapes. It continually wins a temporary
allegiance, for it has the world and its rewards at its command. But, because it lives on force and appeals to men's
appetites, it never wins the hidden allegiances, and in every
generation it has been shortlived. Over against this kingdom stands the faith of the Jews. It has in it a wisdom
higher than the wisdom of the world, because it knows
Him whose purpose is being wrought on the face of the
world. . . . The writer believed that the peculiar glory of
his nation consisted in its refusal throughout its history
to barter its moral solidarity for outward advantage. And
in this belief he was true to all the prophetic tradition."

But there is no reason to doubt that, although the book
is late, the material contained in the first six chapters is
early. The background of these chapters is Babylonian.
That Daniel attained to high position in the state and
assumed a Babylonian name is quite in keeping with the
period to which he is assigned in the book. The Babylonian kingdom is to him the head of gold because it
rescued the Israelite exiles from submission to the
Assyrian yoke and gave them freedom of worship.

Nebuchadnezzar in his dream saw a large tree, its top
reaching to heaven, full of leaves and fruit. A holy one
from heaven appeared and commanded that the tree be
hewn down and the branches stripped off but the stump
left in the ground. It is evident that the dream referred
to an individual, as the holy one continued: " Let his heart
be changed from man's, and let a beast's heart be given
unto him." The court magicians and astrologers were
unable to interpret the dream. But God made known His

will to His faithful servant Daniel who could beat the
Chaldean magicians on their own ground. Daniel told the
king that the tree of his dream was himself, that madness
would overtake him, and that for seven years his portion
would be with the beasts of the field. The disease of
lycanthropy in which the sufferer imagines himself to be
an animal (wolf) was common. The purpose of the chapter is clear—to magnify the Jewish faith in contrast with
the religion of Babylon, and to show that the fate of
Nebuchadnezzar at the zenith of his power might overtake
Antiochus Epiphanes.

The Faithful Young Men—*Daniel* iii.

Nebuchadnezzar, to celebrate his victories, ordered an
image, 90 feet high, to be made and overlaid with gold.
The image was set up in the Plain of Dura, the river that
entered the Euphrates some six miles to the south of
Babylon. Orders were given that at the sound of the
sackbut (a triangular four-stringed instrument like a harp),
the psaltery (a stringed instrument like an inverted tri-
angle), the dulcimer (some form of bagpipe), and other
musical instruments, the assembled peoples were to fall
down and worship the image.

The three friends of Daniel, Shadrach, Meshach and
Abednego who had been given positions of trust and
authority in Babylonia refused to comply with the request.
They were bound in their court dress and cast into the
midst of a burning fiery furnace. They had no assurance
that like other victims of the king's wrath they would not
be burned to a cinder. " Mayhap our God will deliver us,"
they said, but if not, they were prepared to face the consequences rather than prove false to their religion. They
had counted the cost and were ready to face the furnace
even if nothing but ashes came out. They re-echoed the
faith of Job—" though God slay me, yet will I trust in
Him."

" As a story of moral courage and unfaltering faith in
God, Daniel iii. is unsurpassed in the world's literature.
Even for literary charm and emotional appeal it is a perfect model. The repetition and dramatic force make it a
pattern for the teacher in any age. . . . It was a supreme
gesture of faith that ' the Judge of all the earth does
right,' and that we are not concerned with consequences
but only with loyalty, and in doing right for its own sake."

There is a tradition that Antiochus Epiphanes erected a colossal statue of god at Antioch, and the purpose of the writer of this chapter was to hold up the three heroes of faith as an example, to encourage the Jews of his age to defy Antiochus and remain true to their God.

BELSHAZZAR'S FEAST—*Daniel* v.

Antiochus, the " Madman," as he was called, set up an image of Zeus in the Jerusalem Temple and compelled the Jews to offer sacrifice on pain of death. He stripped the Temple of its ornaments and used some of its golden vessels in his drunken orgies. He defiled the sacred rolls of the Law with grease from the flesh of the pig, an unclean animal to the Jew, and sacrificed swine in the Temple to render the building " profane." Many of the Jews died for their faith but many proved traitors in that they not only despised their own Law but endeavoured to induce their fellow-countrymen to take part in heathen festivals. Because Antiochus flourished like the green bay tree and escaped divine chastisement, many lost heart and faith.

The writer of the Book of Daniel, anxious to steady the faith of his people, told them a story of the past. He reminded them that the golden vessels had been removed by Nebuchadnezzar from the Temple of Jerusalem to the temple of Bel in Babylon, a city of enormous extent and strength, and almost impregnable, and to show his contempt for the Persian army that was laying siege to the city, Belshazzar, one of the successors of Nebuchadnezzar, gave a feast in keeping with the glory of his kingdom, using as drinking-cups the golden vessels removed from Jerusalem. A branch of the Euphrates passed through the city and while Belshazzar and his nobles were drinking themselves drunk, the Persians diverted the river along a new course and marched down the old river-bed without striking a blow. But before their arrival at the palace a ghostly hand wrote upon the wall the doom of Belshazzar. Both Herodotus and Xenophon state that a great feast was held on the night of the destruction of Babylon.

That the writer of the story is concerned with religious truth is obvious. His purpose was to provide a much-needed spiritual tonic for his people in trying circumstances.

Daniel and the Lions' Den—*Daniel* vi.

Darius, the new king of Babylon, set about the re-organisation of the kingdom. He had heard of the splendid service rendered by Daniel to his predecessors on the throne, and he set him in a position of trust and authority. The princes of Babylonia in their hate and jealousy of Daniel formed a plot with the result that Daniel was cast into a den of lions. In Babylonia lions were bred and preserved for the chase. Daniel came forth from the dungeon unhurt and Darius issued a decree to the effect that honour was to be paid to the God of Daniel. The story inspired the Jews to face the persecution of Antiochus and to resist his demands. The teacher should employ the lesson to teach the value of prayer. Indifferent to the decree of the king, Daniel prayed three times per day at his open window, as had been his custom. Communion with God meant more in his life than all the worldly honours heaped upon him, and a public declaration of his faith that might result in death was preferable to a policy of safe opportunism.

SENIOR (Second Year) — OLD TESTAMENT.

B.—HEROES OF LONG AGO.

In Ur of the Chaldees—*Genesis* xi. 31.

Mesopotamia, the land between the Tigris and the Euphrates, is known to have been the scene of an advanced civilization in early times. It was a fertile land owing to the fine climate and the richness of the soil deposited by the rivers in flood. At Ur, where excavations are being carried on by Woolley, a temple of date about 4300 B.C. has been unearthed, together with numerous other buildings. To-day a great deal is known about Ur and the life of its people. Round the city was a great wall and within it were temples built to the Moon-goddess, with sacristan, choir-master, etc. There was an excellent harbour to which ships brought cedar and pine, stone and marble, copper and gold. There was a system of banking, of issuing passports, and of insurance against sickness. There were directors of livestock, of dairying, of fishing, of transport. There were canals and irrigation works with machinery for pumping water. Along the canal banks grew palms, in the fields wheat and barley were grown, and there were huge sheep farms. Haran, some 500 miles farther north, to which Abraham's people migrated, was an important centre of traffic. It was also a centre for Moon-worship, the city being built in the shape of the crescent-moon. A Mohammedan legend states that Abraham's father was an idol-maker at Ur.

The priests, the most highly educated members of the community, controlled the worship of the temples and also all the various departments of public life, directing commerce, administering the law, and keeping records. They also acted as medical officers. The offerings made by the worshippers consisted of oxen, sheep, birds, fruit, oil, wine, etc., and sometimes human victims. The sacrifice was a gift to the deity and the more costly the sacrifice, the greater would be its value, it was believed, in the eyes of the god. At the time of his sacrifice the worshipper made confession of sin and offered prayer for divine help, desiring in his heart the forgiveness of the god.

THE CALL OF THE UNKNOWN—*Genesis* xii. 1-9.

Moon-worship failed to satisfy the spiritual cravings of Abraham, who saw the absurdity of the worship of the heavenly bodies. In response to the divine urge, he broke away from his people, and went forth, not knowing whither he went. He journeyed westward until he reached Shechem, a focus of all the great caravan roads, "making the city throughout all its history an influential commercial centre." Certain trees were regarded by the Canaanites as the abodes of gods, and at the sacred oak of Mamre, further south and near to Hebron, God revealed Himself to Abraham, giving him the assurance that one day the land would belong to his descendants. Many hear the call of the unknown, but not all respond to it as Abraham did, as the voice of God. His faith in a God whom no one recognised but himself, distinguishes Abraham from his contemporaries.

THE SONS OF ABRAHAM—ISAAC—*Genesis* xviii. 1-10; xxi. 1-6.

Isaac (laughter) was the son promised to Abraham and Sarah in their old age, Abraham being 100 years old and Sarah 91 at the time of his birth. God commanded that he be called Isaac, because Sarah had laughed at the idea of a child being born to such old people.

Isaac's play with Ishmael, son of Hagar, as a boy, aroused the jealousy of Sarah, with the result that Hagar and her son were sent into the wilderness. In the Old Testament Isaac is a subordinate figure to Abraham and Jacob. In Genesis xxvi. 5 the divine blessing is pronounced upon him, not for his own sake, but for the sake of Abraham, his father. Isaac was "yielding, easy-going, stationary, content to receive the promise without realising the extent or nature of the privilege." His service was rendered in "quietness and keeping still." This lesson provides an opportunity of speaking on the subject of entertaining angels unawares.

ISHMAEL—*Genesis* xxi. 8-21.

Ishmael ("May God hear") was son of Hagar by Abraham. Sarah ordered Abraham to cast out the child and mother. Abraham, though resentful at the loss of his first-born, gave way. God in a dream gave him the assurance that Ishmael would attain to greatness. So Abraham sorrowfully sent away mother and son with meagre provision for the journey. The two outcasts wandered in the desert in the neighbourhood of Beersheba until their water-supply gave out. Hagar, in exhaustion, cast the child under a bush and sat apart to await its death. But God heard the voice of the child and showed her a well of water from which to bring life to the dying boy. Ishmael in manhood settled in the wilderness on the south of Canaan and attained fame as an archer. The tribes descended from him settled on the east of Palestine, Edom, and the Gulf of Akabah. "The human passions and interests of Sarah and Abraham, of Hagar and Ishmael, the promptings, partly of natural affection, partly of religious feeling, under which they act, and the manner in which the hand of Providence guides and moulds the destinies of men, are all portrayed with the vividness and psychological truth which is generally characteristic of the Book of Genesis."

The Story of Rebekah—*Genesis* xxiv.

Rebekah was a great-niece to Abraham. According to Eastern custom the marriage arrangements were made not by Isaac but by Abraham's confidential servant, Eliezer. Abraham, apparently from Beersheba, sent his trusted servant to Nahor (Haran) to find a wife for his son, Isaac. The choice of a suitable woman was a fateful one as it involved the spiritual destiny of the race. During Eliezer's absence Abraham died and Isaac removed to Beer-Lahai-Roi. Laban is the typical Jew, shrewd and alive to his own interests. After inspecting the costly presents sent to open the marriage-negotiations and being satisfied as to his uncle's prosperity he was prepared to bargain with Abraham's representative. Rebekah consented to make the journey with Eliezer and on seeing her future husband covered her face with a veil, as was the custom of Eastern women on meeting strangers.

The picture of Eliezer, the faithful retainer, is beautifully drawn. After taking the most solemn and binding oath—with the hand under the thigh—he set out on his quest, in the full confidence that God had an interest in the matter and would grant him guidance. "His complete forgetfulness of self, his fidelity, his zeal and tact in carrying out the commands of his master, even though he be but a slave, and his childlike faith in God's leadership, are qualities that make men valuable members of society in every age." The story is a literary masterpiece and from its first telling must have found a special place in the Jewish heart.

Jacob Meets Rachel—*Genesis* xxix. 1-20.

Jacob, determined to be a better man, set out for Haran
and at the wells outside the city wall came into touch with
his uncle's shepherds. He received a welcome from Laban
who, recognising that he was attracted by Rachel, drove a
hard bargain. Jacob was a vagabond unable to provide a
dowry. He therefore contracted to work for seven years as
a shepherd in order to qualify as Rachel's husband. " And
Jacob served seven years for Rachel; and they seemed unto
him but a few days, for the love he had for her."

Jacob's Years of Service—
Genesis xxx. 25-30; xxxi. 1-9; 17-18; 20-32; 36-55.

After the marriage celebrations Jacob was permitted to
see his wife's face and discovered that he had been tricked
into marrying Leah, a woman with weak eyes and less hand-
some than her sister. Rachel had to be paid for by other
seven years of service. At the end of the second period of
service Jacob was anxious to return home but the unscrupulous Laban, loth to lose his valuable services, struck an apparently disinterested bargain. Jacob turned the arrangement to
his own advantage, securing by a piece of trickery the best
animals for his own flocks. Laban, envious of Jacob's prosperity and suspecting that he was being victimised, began to
display ill-will and changed Jacob's wages ten times. At last,
while Laban was away at the sheep-shearing, Jacob, after
consultation with his wives, took to flight. Laban, however,
satisfied that he had a claim on him, and annoyed at the loss
of the teraphim stolen by Rachel, set out in pursuit. The
teraphim were household images, possibly representations of
ancestors, used for purposes of divination. Laban, warned in
a dream not to take violent measures against his son-in-law,
overtook him on the borders of Gilead and entered into a
covenant with him.

Jacob had deceived his father and his brother. He was
himself deceived. God led him to serve a bigger rogue than
he himself had been, and Laban, by 20 years' cheating,
cheated the cheating out of him. He was beaten at his own
game and realised to the full the heinousness of his own sin.

Making up the Quarrel—*Genesis* xxxii. 3-21; xxxiii. 1-17.

On the borders of Gilead Jacob was within sight of his
home-land, and after 20 years' exile was face to face with
o

his old sin. What kind of a reception would he get from his brother Esau, now chief of an Arab clan, whom he had so cruelly wronged? He sent out scouts for news of his brother and received the information that Esau was approaching from Mount Seir with 400 men, independent chiefs with their followers prepared to fight for Esau as their emir. Jacob, dreading the vengeance of his brother, prepared a costly gift which he sent in advance, giving instructions to his servants that they were to assure Esau that Jacob recognised him as elder and chief. He crossed the brook Jabbok to meet his brother, sending his wives and children back to the other bank for safety.

At Peniel Jacob committed himself to God, fighting and agonising with God as in a wrestler's struggle. God changed Esau's heart and Jacob's name. In changing the name from Jacob (the Supplanter) to Israel (Prince of God) God did more than change the name. He set His seal of approval upon a changed nature. In exile Jacob had been undergoing a process of discipline and the last step in his schooling was the meeting with his injured brother. The Jacob who was forgiven by God and by Esau was a very different man from the lad who cried himself to sleep on the rocky slopes of Bethel the night he ran away from home.

Moses as Judge—*Exodus* xviii. 13-26.

Law, to begin with, is a matter of custom. Certain customs necessary for the survival of a tribe become fixed laws and are invested with divine sanction. Much of the Law in the Old Testament is of great antiquity and was probably the common property of Semitic peoples. In 1901 at Susa there was discovered the famous Law Code of Hammurabi, king of Babylonia about 2100 B.C.. An examination of this Code, the oldest hitherto discovered, shows remarkable resemblances between it and the Code of Moses. For example, in the Code of Hammurabi we read: "If a man hath caused the loss of another man's eye, then some man shall cause his eye to be lost," a law which appears in the Mosaic Code as "an eye for an eye." The similarity between the two codes is probably due to the common ancestry of the two peoples. The Hebrew Law-Code, however, is on a much higher ethical level than the Codes of their contemporaries, as a result of the operation of the Spirit of God. Moses as Law-giver was the mouthpiece of God. Israel looked back to him "as at once the organiser of Divine justice and the organiser of its due administration."

Moses, as Judge, sat outside his tent settling disputes. He brought them before God and gave a ruling in accordance with the divine leading. In the daily life of a nomad people there were innumerable occasions for dispute and the task of administering justice was too much for one man. Effect was given to a sugggestion made by Jethro that Moses should delegate the work. In this lesson the teacher should show the need for and the value of a legal system, discuss some of the cases that would come before Moses, and indicate the transformation that would be effected in the world to-day if the nations obeyed the law of God as revealed in our Lord.

JOSHUA'S ADVICE TO THE PEOPLE—*Joshua* xxiv. 1-31.

After the capture of the strategic strongholds the Hebrews effected the settlement in Canaan by a policy of peaceful penetration. Each tribe settled in its own territory and as many of the heathen strongholds remained unconquered, the Hebrews lived peaceably with their neighbours. No indication is given of the route by which Joshua removed his headquarters from Gilgal to Shechem, but his entry into Shechem (1370-67 B.C.) may be connected with a revolt against Egypt about which we read in the Amarna letters. There, writing to Pharaoh, Abd-Khipa, king of Jerusalem, reports that " Labaya and the Land of Shechem have given all to the Habiru." Whether the Habiru and the Hebrews are distinct from one another or not, it seems clear that Abd-Khipa identified them, and that the fortunes of both peoples " were for a time and in a measure interlocked."

Shechem, to which Joshua summoned the tribes before his death, was hallowed by venerable associations. There Abraham made his first encampment. There Jacob bought " a parcel of a field from the children of Hamor, where he had spread his tent." Near-by was Moreh, appointed by Moses for the national assembly. The danger that the Hebrews, living in peaceful contact with other tribes, would succumb to the debasing influences of Canaanite religion was a real one. Joshua, after tracing the hand of God in the national life in the past, put before the assembled tribes three choices. Would they serve the heavenly bodies, the gods worshipped by the forebears of Abraham, or the heathen deities of the Canaanite peoples among whom they had now settled, or would they serve Jehovah who had revealed Himself to the Patriarchs and delivered them from bondage and given them His law through Moses? Joshua impressed upon them the demands of God—holiness, truth, loyalty. The tribes made a tremendous decision. They confirmed their choice of Jehovah, the God of righteousness, and entered into a solemn covenant in ratification of their choice. Joshua's last service to his people was his pledge to serve God and the demand of a similar pledge from them.

DEBORAH—A MOTHER IN ISRAEL—*Judges* iv. 1-17.

During the last 50 or 60 years of Rameses II., a period of uninterrupted peace, the northern tribes of Israel established themselves in Canaan, and the other tribes equally prospered. In 1223 B.C., however, Merneptah, the Pharaoh, despatched an expeditionary force to the north, as large numbers of rovers and pirates had landed on the coast of Syria and were fomenting rebellion against Egypt. The inscription on Merneptah's victory stele, in which there occurs the first historical reference to Israel, reads : " The Hittite Land is pacified, Plundered is the Canaan with every evil, Carried off is Askalon, Seized upon is Gezer, Yenoam is made as a thing not existing, Israel is desolated, her seed is not, S. Palestine has become a defenceless widow for Egypt, All lands are united, they are pacified; Everyone that is turbulent is bound by King Merneptah."

After the withdrawal of the Pharaoh's troops, Sisera established himself firmly on the Plain of Acco, by alliance with the king of Hazor, and for 21 years, owing to internal troubles in Egypt, he exercised his tyranny. "This state of affairs plunged Israel in jeopardy, threatening with disruption the growing prospect of reunion at the very time when the tribes had attained their goal." To avoid meeting their masters on the highways the Israelites took to the side paths.

Deborah, "a mother in Israel," arose at this crisis, and sent out a summons to the Israelite tribes to unite against the tyrant, after discussing her plan of campaign with Barak and enlisting his help. Half the tribes responded to her call and gathered at Mount Tabor overlooking the Plain of Esdraelon. Sisera marshalled his forces at Taanach, on the other side of the Valley through which runs the Kishon. A Hebrew traitor advised Sisera of the impending Hebrew attack, and Sisera with his "chariots of iron"—wooden vehicles with two wheels, protected by iron plates, and with knives fitted to the axle-boxes—took the initiative and enticed the Hebrew warriors down to the Plain where his chariots could wreck havoc. As the result of a thunderstorm the Valley was converted into a bog in which the Canaanite chariots were rendered useless, and the Israelites secured an easy victory.

" Pursued and harassed in the retreat by Barak, the routed charioteers, making for Harosheth, would find the now swollen river between themselves and safety. An indescribable confusion of men and horses plunging into the dangerous ford to escape from the worse fury of the victorious Israelites completed the havoc of the day. The River Kishon swept them away."

Sisera, alone, fled on foot to Kedesh, to the tent of Jael, the wife of Heber, the Kenite. The Kenites, descendants of Abraham, frequently allied themselves with Israel. Jael with an iron peg and a wooden mallet, used by the women in pitching tent, slew Sisera. Possibly she was an Israelitess who felt the call to strike a blow for her people. Possibly she acted in defence of her honour, as Sisera had violated the women's quarters and committed a breach of law that merited death.

Gideon—A Patriot and Soldier.

The Reformer—*Judges* vi. 1-16, 28-31.

The Midianite oppression falls in the reigns of Rameses IV. and V., weak kings, under whom Egypt's Syrian Empire was lost. With the withdrawal of the Egyptian power, the peoples of Palestine became prey to the desert tribes who levied tribute on the tillers of the soil. As soon as harvest was ready, the marauders swooped down upon the threshing-floors.

The unity achieved by Deborah did not last. The Hebrew tribes were disunited and in danger of being absorbed by their Canaanite neighbours. In the north there was a belt of heathen strongholds from Bethshan to Megiddo in the Plain of Esdraelon, and continuing to Dor on the Mediterranean, and another belt in the south from Jebus, near the Dead Sea, to Gaza. With the withdrawal of the Egyptian garrison from Bethshan, the Midianites poured into the country by the Valley of Jezreel and overran the Plain of Esdraelon, and in the south the Amalekites reaped the corn-lands as far as Gaza. The raiders searched the hill-tops for corn, but as the grapes were not ripe, they failed to visit the vineyards. Threshing took place on the hill-tops by drawing oxen, harnessed to threshing-sledges, over the wheat, the ears of which were then thrown in the air to dispose of the chaff. During the years of oppression the Israelites were driven to the expedient of threshing the corn with sticks in the wine-presses cut in the rocks in the valleys.

Gideon, of the clan of Abiezrites, of the tribe of Manasseh, lived at Ophrah, identified by some with a place six miles from Shechem.   As he was threshing corn under the sacred tree, associated with the presence of God, and brooding over his countrymen's wrongs, there was given to him a manifestation of God, in the form of an "Angel of the Lord." As a sacrifice at that time was a communal feast in which God and man took part, he prepared a meal and poured out the broth to God.   The Stranger entered into a covenant with him by touching the food with a stick and thus reserving part of it as a sacrifice to God.   This was accepted by Gideon as a sign that he was chosen by God to deliver his people, and he erected there an altar to which he gave the name "God is peace."   In the name that he gave to the altar Gideon proclaimed beforehand the gift that he felt sure of from God. The altar was a thank-offering for a victory yet to be won. The important point in the story is that Gideon was conscious of God's power and help, and, assured of the divine call, acted without hesitation.

GIDEON'S VICTORY—*Judges* vii. 1-23.

Not only his own clan, but all the northern tribes rallied to Gideon's call.   The Leader purged his army of the doubters and the half-hearted.   By the simple but effective test of asking the remainder to drink he made another purge.   With the enemy at hand only the careless would risk lying down to drink from the stream.   "An Eastern courier, hardly pausing as he runs, merely bending on one knee, will whip up the water into his mouth with hand almost as rapidly as a dog can drink with tongue."

Gideon's military tactics were superb.   Through "listening-in" he knew of the uneasiness of the Midianites.   He divided his 300 trusted followers into three companies to deceive the enemy into believing that they were outnumbered. To each man he gave a ram's horn to be blown and a torch within a pitcher, the pitchers to be broken and the torches waved when the battle-cry "For God and Gideon" was raised.   The Midianites, aroused from sleep and unable to organise resistance, fled down the Jordan valley, but the hill tribesmen of Ephraim had secured the Jordan fords and the Midianites were caught in a trap.   Some were overtaken by the pursuers but some effected their escape.   Modest before his call, Gideon was equally modest in the hour of victory, ascribing the result to God.

In the interpretation of Gideon's character the teacher might note the following points :—

(1) His thoughtful, burning patriotism. Gideon does not return the angel's greeting with an empty courtesy. His question, rapped out so challengingly, " if the Lord be with me "—a question which transcends the particular and seems like the cry of suffering humanity—shows how his mind is working and what it works upon.

(2) His wisdom in the beginning of his action (*a*) in his own village, (*b*) against idol-worship, the source of the moral degeneration of his people.

(3) His prolonged, cautious, thoughtful hesitancy before decisive action (e.g., the fleece).

(4) The decisiveness of his action when his mind was made up. He was a supreme strategist and tactician in war.

(5) His persistence in pursuing his task till fruition— " faint, yet pursuing."

(6) His diplomacy in dealing with people, especially the disgruntled. " Is not the gleaning of the grapes of Ephraim? " is a fine example of the soft answer despite the ironic flavour.

(7) His ability to get to the heart of a problem, to separate the essential from the non-essential (e.g., the incident of Penuel and Succoth).

SENIOR (Third Year) — OLD TESTAMENT.

C.—HEROES OF LONG AGO.

SAMUEL—JUDGE AND KINGMAKER.

THE BOY SAMUEL—*1 Samuel* i. 24-28, ii. 18-19, iii. 1-10, 15-18.

THE theme of the Books of Samuel is the establishment of the monarchy and the transition from the period of disunity to the settled political organisation of David. Samuel was the last of the judges, the first of the prophets, and the founder of the monarchy. Apart from their historical value, the books of Samuel give us an idea of the development of Hebrew religion. God is placated by self-denial, such as abstinence from food. He appears in dreams. He reveals Himself through the media of Urim, Thummim and the Ephod. His Spirit is evidenced in frenzy, and He demands the annihilation of His enemies. The Books tell of the beginnings of the prophetic movement that exercised such a powerful influence upon the human race. It was Samuel who organised bands of prophets who tried to keep the monarchy true to God.

The Books open with the story of the early life of Samuel and an account of Eli's judgeship. The central sanctuary was at Shiloh, a sacred spot (Joshua xviii. 1; Judges xxi. 19). Hitherto the sanctuary that acted as protection for the Ark had been a tent, but now it is a permanent building with stone walls, a gateway and a draped roof. From this temple the ark was carried into the battlefield, where it was seized by the Philistines.

At the Feast of Tabernacles an animal was slain, part being burnt on the altar, part given to the officiating priests, and the remainder eaten by the worshippers. At the Festival, Hannah, childless, visited the sanctuary and vowed that if she were given a son she would dedicate him to the service of God. Such vows of consecration were common. At the age of two Samuel was weaned and brought to the temple to serve as attendant.

The word of the Lord was "rare." There was no open, i.e., frequent, vision. The fact that Eli had imagined Hannah to be intoxicated at the Festival indicates that the

Feast had degenerated into a drunken revel and that there
was an almost entire forgetfulness of God. Probably at the
age of twelve Samuel heard the call of God, a call to reform
the religious life of his time. " The influence of his godly
mother and his education by Eli produced a character admir-
ably fitted to guide the destinies of the nation in a religious
crisis."

DAVID AND JONATHAN—1 *Samuel* xviii. 1-4, xix. 1-2, xx.

David's victory over Goliath marked the turning point in
his career. The women sang his praises and the Philistines
regarded him as the real head of Israel (1 Samuel xxi. 11).
Naturally Saul's jealousy was aroused and he endeavoured
to rid himself of his dangerous rival by underhand methods.
That David acted with great tact and patience and made no
attempt to usurp the king's power is evidenced by his friendship with Jonathan, son and heir to the king. David's promotion from court-minstrel to the captaincy of the king's
body-guard—next position to that of commander-in-chief—
was rapid.

Jonathan loved David as his own soul. He was the
greater of the two friends. He had nothing to gain, from
a material point of view, from the friendship, but everything
to lose if David succeeded to the throne. He made a
covenant with David, perhaps by tasting his blood so that
they became blood-brothers. By the sign of the arrow he
saved David's life, communicating the information about
Saul's attitude. Then they bade one another a touching farewell. " The interview brings out all the peculiarities of
Jonathan's character—his little artifices, his love both for
his father and his friend, his bitter disappointment at his
father's ungovernable fury, his familiar sport of archery,
under cover of which the whole meeting takes place. The
former compact between the two friends is resumed, extending even to their immediate posterity; Jonathan laying such
emphasis on this portion of the agreement as almost to suggest
the belief that he had a slight misgiving of David's conduct
in this respect. With tender words and wild tears the two
friends parted, never to meet again in the royal home."

DAVID AND SAUL—1 *Samuel* xviii. 5-16, 28-30.

Saul's jealousy was not altogether unreasonable. The
kingship was a new institution in Israel and its stability

depended upon his military success. Unfortunately, Saul nursed his hate until David became an obsession. In a fit of passion, in his palace at Gibeah, he flung a javelin at the head of the minstrel, who knew from that moment the king's attitude, and could take counter-measures.

DAVID THE OUTLAW—1 *Samuel* xxii. 1-2, xxiii. 1-15, 19-21.

The Cave of Adullam lay in the Shephelah, the belt of hills between the great Maritime Plain and the central range of Judah. It was well known to David, being near the scene of his victory over Goliath. David took refuge there, along with a small band of retainers, the outstanding of them being Abiathar, son to Abimelech, priest of Nob, Abishai, David's nephew, and Gad, the seer. In return for maintenance he acted as guard over the flocks of the people in that region. Many of the farmers and shepherds owed their existence to David's protection of them from roving tribesmen.

Chief among the predatory bandits at this time were the Philistines, whose objective was the threshing-floors of Keilah. David's men, fearing the hostility of Saul if they came into the open, pressed him to remain in the security of the cave. David consulted the priest who drew lots, and, as the decision was to go, he believed that the message came from God. At the risk of his own life and the lives of his warriors, he saved Keilah, only to be repaid by treachery. The men of Keilah betrayed him to Saul, sending secret information of his presence within their walls. The use of the lot was one of the modes of divination practised by the Hebrews and their neighbours. It was believed that the lot was controlled by God and that the result coincided with His will. The lots were probably small tablets of stone or wood of different colours.

DAVID THE CHIVALROUS—1 *Samuel* xxiv. 1-22.

Chapters xxiv. and xxvi. are probably versions of the same story. In this account David, hiding in one of the numerous caves in the Engedi cliffs, was pursued by Saul, and God guided the king to the very cave in which David and his men were concealed. Saul, unsuspecting, lay down to sleep, and David, instead of running his sword through his heart, merely cut off a part of his cloak. After Saul's departure from the cave David boldly went after him, showed him the piece of his garment, and explained that he could well have taken his life. He hated to be at enmity with Saul and was determined, if possible, to heal the breach between them. Saul, in shame and remorse, proved that some remnants of his former goodness still clung to him. He made the hardest confession he ever made—that his magnanimous enemy was fitted to be king and would succeed to the throne instead of his own sons. He made a pathetic appeal to David to deal as generously with his descendants as he had dealt with him, and they parted friends.

DAVID THE KING—2 *Samuel* v. 1-12.

At Hebron David was acknowledged by the leaders of Israel, the northern area, as their king, thus becoming king of both Israel and Judah. The twelve tribes for the first time were united under one head. Jerusalem, in the Tel-el-Amarna tablets "the city of peace," was fortified by the Amorites by 2000 B.C. From the beginning of the period of the Judges (1230-10 B.C.) until captured by David it remained a Jebusite stronghold. The city was so well fortified that it could be defended by the blind and the lame. In making it his capital David took a great step on behalf of the recently formed kingship and on behalf of the national religion. There was animosity at the time between the northern and the southern tribes, and in making his capital the neutral city of Jebus, that belonged to neither north nor south, David revealed himself as a statesman of the first rank. Jerusalem, because of its strategic position, became both the religious and the political centre. The Millo was probably a fortified citadel at the north and vulnerable end of the town.

SOLOMON—THE WISE KING.

SOLOMON'S CHOICE—1 *Kings* ii. 1-4; iii. 5-15.

God revealed himself to Solomon, not by a prophet, but in a dream. Out of the gifts offered by God, Solomon chose wisdom. His prayer shows that he had a deep sense of the responsibility of those in high station, and realised that special gifts, conferred by God in answer to prayer, were necessary to enable him to distinguish between right and wrong.

THE REVOLT—1 *Kings* xii. 1-19.

At Solomon's death (937 B.C.) the twelve tribes which had been held together in a precarious unity under David

and his son, disrupted, ten tribes forming the northern kingdom of Israel and the remaining two forming the southern
kingdom of Judah.   These independent peoples resented the
heavy taxation imposed by Solomon for the maintenance of
his capital and the corvee system by which the taxes were
raised.   Rehoboam, an irresponsible autocrat, blind to the
advice of the statesmen of his father, not only refused con-
cessions but threatened the imposition of heavier taxation.

Jeroboam, foreman, in Solomon's time, of the forced levies
from Ephraim, became leader of the malcontents and had to
take refuge in Egypt.   His encounter with Ahijah by the
roadside shows that he had the support of the prophetic
party.   Hearing of the death of Solomon, he hurried home
and acted as spokesman of the oppressed tribes.   When
Rehoboam sent his tax-gatherer, Adoram, to collect the new
levies, the ten tribes rose in revolt and made Jeroboam their
king.   Because Rehoboam in his arrogance and folly forgot
that he ruled as a representative of God, he undid the work
of his father and grandfather in building up a united kingdom.

Elijah—The Fiery Prophet.

The Famine—1 *Kings* xvii.

After the revolt of the ten tribes changes of dynasty in
the northern kingdom were frequent.   Omri founded a
powerful dynasty which his son Ahab inherited.   As part of
the policy of alliance with Phoenicia, begun by Solomon and
continued by Omri, Ahab married Jezebel, daughter of
Ethbaal, king of Tyre.   This involved religious decline in
Israel, as Jezebel introduced the worship of the Tyrian Baal,
a temple and altar to Baal being erected in Samaria.   The
word Baal, meaning "lord" or "husband," was applied to
men and gods.   The Israelites had long been familiar with
Baal-worship in Canaan, the gods of the Canaanites being
fertility Baals.   The introduction of the Baal of Melkart of
Tyre was a different matter, as Melkart was the Moloch to
whom human victims without number were offered, and if
Baalism became the court-religion it would soon become the
national religion.   Elijah raised the issue between Baalism
and the worship of Jehovah, and showed that the two religions were mutually exclusive.   To Ahab he was an unpatriotic fanatic, because he placed "righteousness and religion before the exigencies of political statecraft."

About Elijah, the fiery prophet of the Old Testament,

there is an air of mystery. He appears and disappears like lightning. Of his origin nothing is known save that he was the Tishbite of the inhabitants of Gilead. Tishbe probably lay near Mahanaim in the territory of Gad. As a desert prophet Elijah had a profound contempt for the civilisation to the west of the Jordan, and regarded with horror the debasing influences of Baalism upon his fellow-countrymen. " His whole manner of life is meant to be a protest against a corrupt civilisation. . . . He has the fleet foot of a true son of the desert, and an iron frame that enables him to endure a forty days' fast. He dwells in the clefts of the Cherith, sleeps under a desert broom, lodges in the cave of Horeb, and haunts the slopes of Carmel. . . . He comes down from the hills of Gilead as the champion and prophet of Jehovah in the dark days of Israel's apostasy. He comes to bear witness to truths that ought never to have been denied in Israel. . . . He takes his stand upon old principles. He is the personified conscience of the nation."

In a country dependent entirely on its own resources for its food supply, the lack of rain entailed dreadful consequences. The withholding of rain was regarded as a sign of the divine displeasure. When Elijah intimated a drought, not only was it a scourge upon the people for their sins but a sign of the powerlessness of Melkart, claimed by his worshippers to be the source of fertility. To the brook Cherith, one of the tributaries of the Jordan, the ravens brought food for their young, and Elijah had his share.

When Cherith dried up, the prophet, at God's command, went to Zarephath, ten miles north of Sidon, and so removed from Ahab's power. A widow, reduced by famine to her last meal, gave him hospitality, and he miraculously increased her barrel of meal and her cruise of oil to meet their needs. When illness came and her son died he restored the boy to life.

The Priests of Baal—1 *Kings* xviii.

Ahab sent his messengers on a fruitless quest throughout the land for Elijah. For three years there had been neither rain nor dew, the famine being so severe that the country had to be scoured for provender for the king's stables. Unsuccessful in his search, at the instigation of his wife, the king took vengeance on the priests of Jehovah, driving them into hiding. Suddenly Elijah appeared and forced the issue by summoning the prophets of Baal to a contest be-

tween Baal and Jehovah on Mount Carmel. The issue of
rain or no rain would appeal to the imagination of the whole
community. It was a severe test for Elijah, who trusted
implicitly in God. It was a severe test for the Baal-
worshippers, as Melkart was supposed to rule the sun and
the rain, the crops and the harvests. Probably his representatives maintained that the long drought was due to the
neglect of his worship, and they gladly accepted Elijah's
challenge.

The priests of Baal gashed themselves with knives to
call Melkart's attention, and danced their religious dances
round the altar. At the hour for the evening sacrifice they
had failed as rain-makers and retired discomfited. Elijah's
biting remarks must have stung them to the quick. Elijah
stepped forward and rebuilt the broken altar of Jehovah that
had been in use in earlier times, making up its stones to
twelve to represent the twelve tribes of Israel. To make the
test complete and to avoid all suggestion of trickery he
ordered that the wood and the sacrifice be drenched with
water. He then uttered a few words of prayer and waited.
A storm of lightning rent the sky and consumed the sacrifice,
the wood and the water. The people acknowledged Jehovah
as God and massacred the priests of Baal for their deceit.
The lightning storm marked the end of the drought. Ahab
made for Jezreel to escape the downpour, and Elijah, in
imitation of the coming rain-storm, ran before his chariot for
a distance of 12 miles.

NABOTH'S VINEYARD—1 *Kings* xxi. 1-16.

Jehovah was a righteous God who demanded righteousness of His people. Consequently the Hebrews were demo-
crats. Their king ruled only as God's vice-regent and could
not exercise over his subjects such power as other monarchs
possessed. Great value was attached to possession of land,
and " when the little freeholder refuses to surrender his
ancestral property it never occurs to Ahab to impose his will
on his subject, either by force or by guile."

Ahab's crowning mistake was the seizure of Naboth's
vineyard under the influence of his wife's arguments about
the rights of kings. Ahab built a palace on the walls of the
city and desired a suitable domain. Naboth, refusing to
part with his ancestral inheritance, was murdered as the
result of Jezebel's plot, and his property was seized. Ahab,
walking in the vineyard, came face to face with Elijah, who

pronounced doom upon him and his unscrupulous wife for the crime committed against God.

Elisha—The Peace-Loving Man of God.

The Mantle of Elijah—2 Kings ii. 1-13.

Elijah on his return from Mount Horeb appointed Elisha as his successor, and from that time there appears to have been a change in his methods. The two prophets founded " guilds of prophets " to carry on the struggle against Baalism, with the result that by the eighth century B.C. Jehovah was universally recognised as the God of Israel. Elijah, like Enoch, was translated so that he should not see death, probably early in the reign of Jehoram.

At the sanctuary at Gilgal he was warned of his approaching end. He was summoned to die in the mountainous region of Nebo, the scene of the death of Moses, not far from the land of his boyhood. Desirous of sparing Elisha the pain of the parting ordeal, he entreated him to remain at Gilgal. But Elisha refused to leave him. Elijah set out for the Jordan via Bethel and Jericho, where he visited the prophetic guilds to deliver to them his final message. Fifty members of the guild at Jericho ascended the heights to watch him crossing the Jordan. After fording the river Elijah asked his faithful disciple if he had a last request to make. Elisha asked for an eldest son's portion of his master's spirit, i.e., a double portion (Deuteronomy xxi. 17). It was a hard request, as spiritual gifts are difficult to communicate, but Elijah gave him a sign whereby he would know if the request were granted. A whirlwind, associated in the Eastern mind with divine power, arose, accompanied by a storm of lightning, and when the storm subsided Elisha was alone. As a last tribute to his hero Elisha referred to him not only as his father but as the horsemen and chariot of Israel, meaning that he had been a power in Israel as great as her weapons of war. The great spiritual truth in the story of Elijah's translation is that his magnetic personality could not die, and " lest his followers become shrine-worshippers at his sepulchre, God took him."

Naaman—2 Kings v. 1-19.

Naaman is known only through this incident. He was probably a Syrian general of some repute. According to Jewish tradition he was the man who drew his bow at a venture at Ramoth-Gilead and inflicted the fatal wound on Ahab. His visit to Israel took place probably in the eighth year of Jehoram, Ben-hadad being king of the Syrian confederacy of states. The Black Obelisk of Shalmaneser II. of Assyria relates that Shalmaneser crossed the Euphrates eleven times to invade Syria and defeated an alliance of twelve kings, Ben-hadad being the leading king. No doubt Naaman took an active part in these campaigns.

He was a proud man and could not conceal his irritation at the insult offered to his country in the request that he dip in the muddy waters of the Jordan. The Abana had " the clearest water possible; in the morning a full, deep emerald green, in the evening a sapphire blue," and with the Pharpar, made Damascus the Paradise of the East. Yet Naaman was a remarkably fine character. He was beloved by his servants, even by the little captive Israelite maid, and he was held in high esteem by Ben-hadad, who provided him with £10,000 to purchase a remedy for his disease. As a result of his cure he embraced the religion of Jehovah. He expressed the desire for forgiveness for future attendance with Ben-hadad in the temple of Rimmon, an attendance imposed upon him by his official position. His request for two mules' burden of earth was natural in that age, as it was the universal belief that a god could be worshipped only on his own soil.

The story shows that Elisha had of a truth been given a double portion of Elijah's spirit. Although less spectacular, he was in many respects superior to his master. "His long career is marked by innumerable deeds of mercy. . . . He enters palaces not as an enemy, but as a friend and counsellor. Kings reverently address him as 'father.' " His influence extended beyond the confines of Israel as the king of Syria consulted him and offered him costly presents (viii. 7, 9). He cured Naaman, the general of a people who carried on guerilla warfare against Israel. "Even more than in palaces is he welcome in the homes of the people. . . . Most of his miracles are deeds of gracious and homely beneficence. Elijah began his career by predicting a famine in the land; Elisha begins his by healing a spring (ii. 21)." From first to last he was a man of God. Although neither Ben-hadad nor Jehoram nor Naaman thought of God as the Healer Elisha refused to admit Naaman into his presence until he had ascribed his cleansing to Jehovah. It is questionable if his leprosy was the disease known by that name to-day. The provisions in the Jewish Law (Leviticus xiii.)

for the treatment of cleansed lepers imply that recovery was by no means uncommon.

THE UNSEEN HOST—2 *Kings* vi. 8-23.

In this story Elisha appears as the moving spirit in the guerilla warfare with Syria. In order to control the route to Egypt the king of Syria had first to control Israel. He led a powerful army across the frontier and made his head-quarters in the neighbourhood of Samaria. He found it impossible to join battle with the Israelites, as the latter knew every foot of the ground and were not encumbered with heavy chariots which were unsuitable for hill-warfare. Further the king of Israel had a perfect espionage system and was advised in advance of the movements of the enemy's forces. Elisha was the super-spy. As a prophet he had points of contact all over the country and one of his sources of information may even have been the officer who denounced him to Ben-hadad.

Elisha was reported to be at Dothan, some 10 miles from Samaria, near the great caravan route. As the village stood on a hill and any hostile force could be seen by daylight, the Syrian troops encircled the town by night. In the morning Elisha's servant was smitten with fear as he saw the hedge of steel around the city. But Elisha, the fearless, communicated to him his own courage. The blindness with which the prophet smote the Syrian troops was not physical, but mental. It is possible that the prophet was disguised. It is more probable that as none of the enemy knew him the suspicion never entered their minds that this man in whom there was no trace of panic could be the prophet whom they sought. After delivering the Syrians into the hands of his king, Elisha gave instructions that they were to be entertained and allowed to go free. He overcame evil with good. The result of his magnanimity was peace, for " the bands of Syria came no more into the land of Israel."

The great truth in the story is that all things are possible to men of great faith. Elisha believed in the unseen spiritual forces. He knew that the hosts of God were greater by far than the hosts of the Syrians. The horses and chariots of fire symbolise the unseen defences. They describe the encircling power and protection of God. If it is true that seeing is believing it is no less true that believing is seeing, and Elisha transmitted to his servant his own faith. God opened the young man's eyes and he saw. In connection with this lesson the teacher might discuss the work of the League of Nations.

P

INTERIOR OF A CARPENTER'S SHOP AT NAZARETH.

Illustration for page 14.

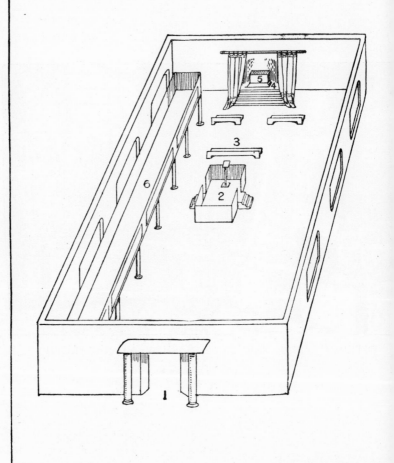

1 Porch Entrance.   4 The Apse.
2 Platform & Reading Desk.   5 The Ark.
3 Seats for Readers.   6 Women's Gallery.

A JEWISH SYNAGOGUE (Interior View)

Fig. 2.

Illustration for page 15.

INTERIOR OF A JEWISH SYNAGOGUE.

Fig. 3.   Illustration for page 15.

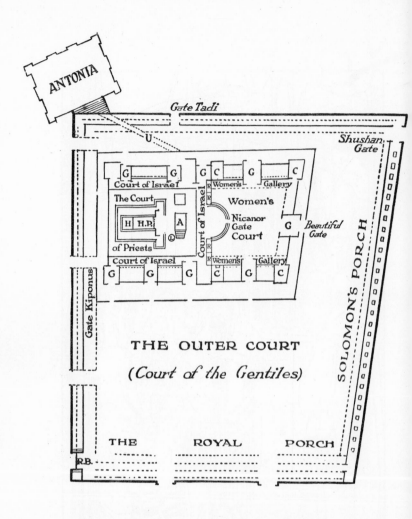

THE TEMPLE OF HEROD

A. *Altar;* **C.** *Chambers;* **G.** *Gates of the Sanctuary;* **H.** *Holy of Holies;* **H.P.** *Holy Place;* **L.** *Laver.* **R.** *Receptacles for Priestly Vestments.* **R.B.** *Royal Bridge to the Temple.* **U** *Underground passage to the Tower of Antonia.*

Fig. 4.   Illustration for page 16.

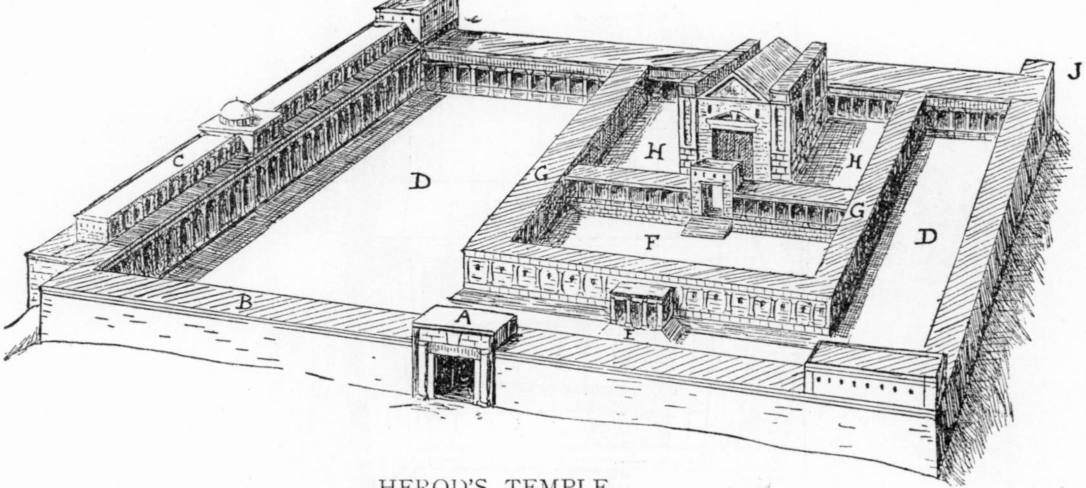

HEROD'S TEMPLE.

Fig. 5.

Illustration for page 16.

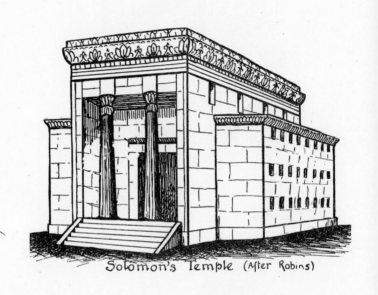

Solomon's Temple (After Robins)

Fig. 6.   Illustration for pages 17, 175.

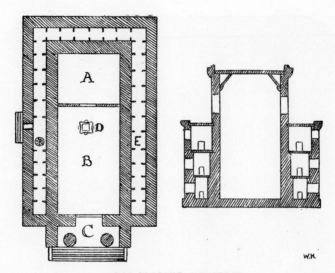

SOLOMON'S TEMPLE.
(A) Holy of Holies; (B) Holy Place; (C) Porch; (D) Altar; (E) Chambers.

Fig. 7.   Illustration for pages 17, 175.

SOLOMON'S PORCH.

Fig. 8.   Illustration for page 18,

A Galilean Fishing Boat.

Fig. 9.

Illustration for page 27.

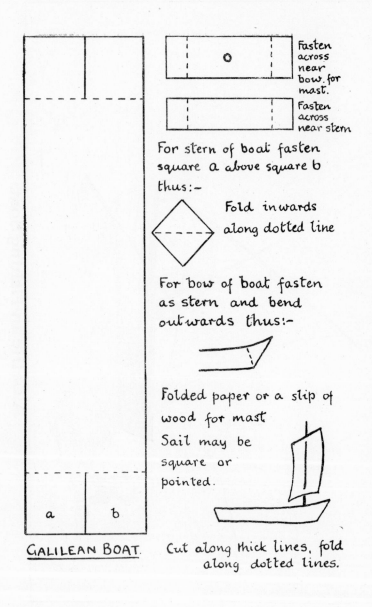

Fasten across near bow. for mast.

Fasten across near stern

For stern of boat fasten square a above square b thus:-

Fold inwards along dotted line

For bow of boat fasten as stern and bend outwards thus:-

Folded paper or a slip of wood for mast
Sail may be square or pointed.

GALILEAN BOAT.

Cut along thick lines, fold along dotted lines.

Fig. 10.   Illustration for page 27.

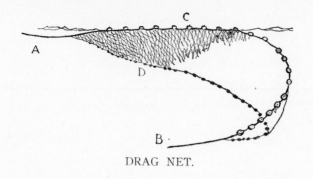

DRAG NET.

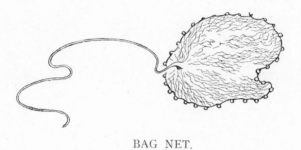

BAG NET.

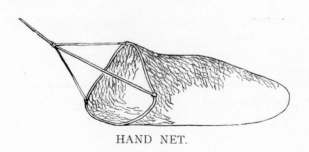

HAND NET.

GALILEAN FISHING NETS.

Fig. 11.   Illustration for page 27.

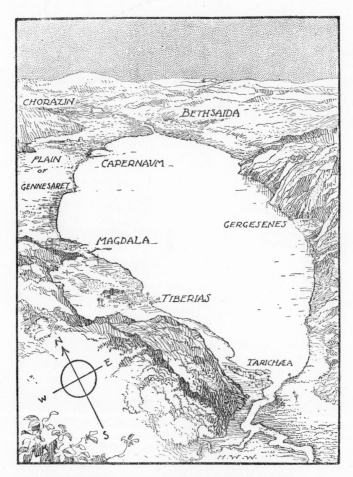

BIRD'S-EYE VIEW OF SEA OF GALILEE.

Fig. 12.   Illustration for page 28.

GALILEE FISHERMEN AT WORK.

Fig. 13.

Illustration for page 36.

H.w. whanslaw.

JEWISH RABBI READING THE LAW.

Fig. 14.   Illustration for page 38.

PHYLACTERIES.

Fig. 15.
Q

Illustration for page 38.

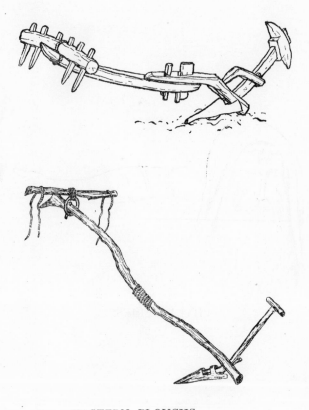

EASTERN PLOUGHS.

Fig. 16

Illustration for page 51.

Interior of Eastern Peasant's House.

Illustration for page 51.

Fig. 17.

A PEASANT'S MEAL IN THE EAST.

Fig 18.   Illustration for page 51.

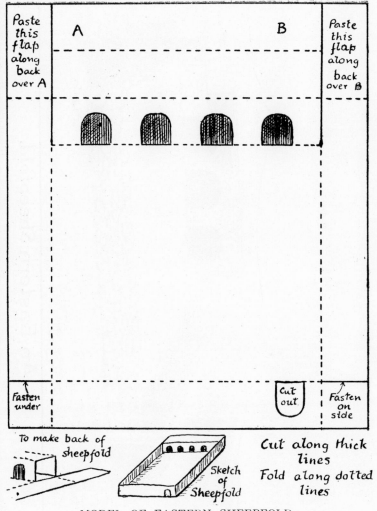

Paste this flap along back over A

A

B

Paste this flap along back over B

Fasten under

Cut out

Fasten on side

To make back of sheepfold

Sketch of Sheepfold

Cut along thick lines
Fold along dotted lines

MODEL OF EASTERN SHEEPFOLD.

Fig. 19.

Illustration for page 52.

An Eastern Sheepfold.

Illustrations for pages 52, 57.

Fig. 20.

PHARISEES AND PEASANTS.

Fig. 21.   Illustration for page 53.

THE LOST SON.

Fig. 22.

Illustration for page 55.

EASTERN LAMPS.

Fig. 23.   Illustration for page 55.

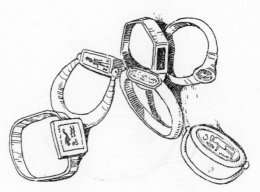

EASTERN SIGNET RINGS.

Fig. 24.

Illustration for page 55.

AN EASTERN HOUSE.

Fig. 25.

Illustration for page 63.

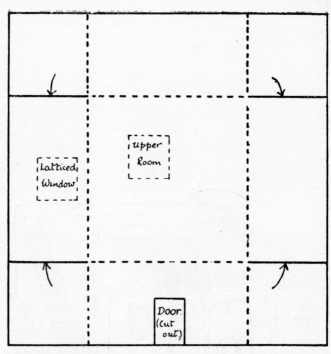

Inside the diagram:

↓ ↓

Upper
Room

Latticed
Window

↑ ↑

Door.
(cut
out)

EASTERN HOUSE. Cut along thick lines
Fold along dotted lines
Paste and fold corner squares under sides.

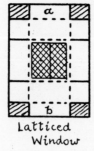

a

b

Latticed
Window

Latticed Window
and Upper Room.
Cut away shaded
corners. Fold and
fasten in same way
as house. Flaps a
and b are used to
fasten room on roof
and window on side.

a

b

Upper
Room.

Fig. 26.

Illustration for page 63.

A ROMAN CENTURION.

Fig. 27.   Illustration for page 65.

EASTERN PEASANTS AND BEGGAR.

Fig. 28.

Illustration for page 65.

ALABASTER JARS FOR PERFUME OR OIL.

Fig. 29.

Illustration for page 66.

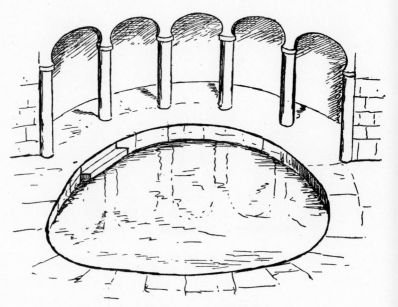

THE POOL OF BETHESDA.

Fig. 30.

Illustration for page 68.

HALL OF THE JEWISH SANHEDRIN.

Fig. 31.
R

Illustration for page 71.

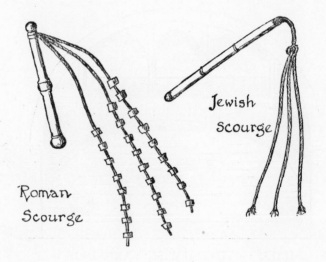

Jewish
Scourge

Roman
Scourge

Fig. 32

Illustration for page 72.

16. Pilgrim St. London. E.C.

A ROCK-HEWN TOMB, WITH ROLLING STONE.

Fig. 33.

Illustration for page 74.

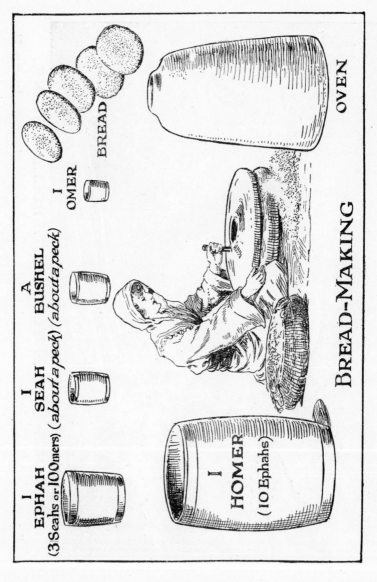

BREAD-MAKING

Fig. 34.

Illustration for page 76.

LABOURERS IN A VINEYARD.

Fig. 35.   Illustration for page 77.

AN EASTERN INN.

Fig. 36.

Illustration for page 80.

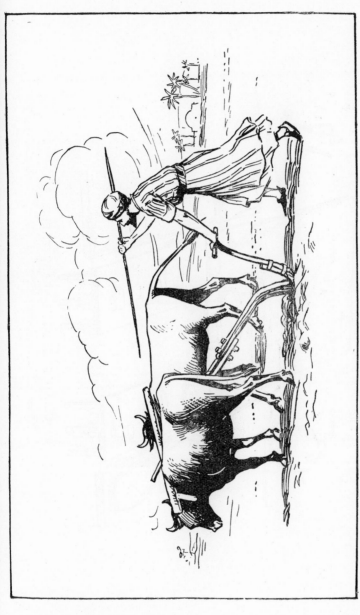

Ploughing with Oxen.

Fig. 37.

Illustration for page 81.

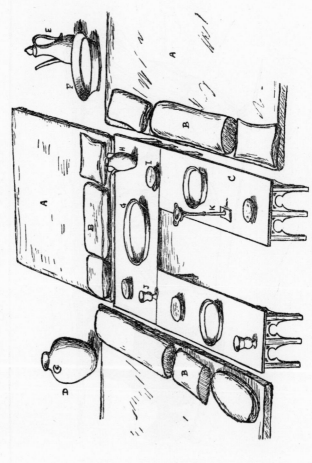

TRICLINIUM (JEWISH FEAST TABLE).

Fig. 38.

Illustration for pages 91, 96.

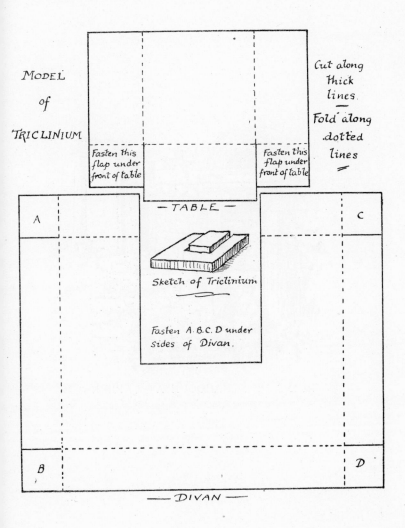

MODEL

of

TRICLINIUM

Cut along
thick
lines.

Fold along
dotted
lines

Fasten this
flap under
front of table

Fasten this
flap under
front of table

A

C

— TABLE —

Sketch of Triclinium

Fasten A. B. C. D under
sides of Divan.

B

D

— DIVAN —

Fig. 39.

Illustration for pages 81, 96.

RUINS OF SYNAGOGUE AT CAPERNAUM.

Fig. 40.

Illustration for page 93.

EWER AND BASIN.

Fig. 41.　　　　　　　　　　　　Illustration for page 96.

A City Man's House, showing the Upper Room

Fig. 42.

Illustration for page 98.

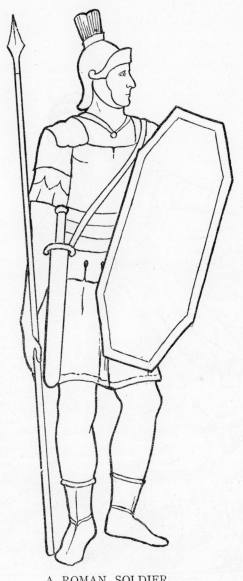

A ROMAN SOLDIER.

Fig. 43.   Illustration for pages 99, 123.

The Sower

Fig. 44.

Illustration for page 113.

H. W. WHANSLAW

EASTERN CHILDREN PLAYING AT WEDDINGS.

Fig. 45.   Illustration for page 113.

WATER JARS, JUG, BASIN AND SANDALS.

Fig. 46   Illustration for page 113.

Damascus, showing the Great Omayyade Mosque in the foreground, where the head of John the Baptist is believed to be buried. (The mark **x** indicates the position of the street called Straight, Acts ix. 11)

Fig. 47.
S

Illustration for page 141.

Tarsus.

EASTERN DUNGEON BELOW PRISON FLOOR.

Fig. 49.   Illustration for page 144.

ROMAN SLAVE GALLEY.   ALEXANDRIAN CORN-SHIP.

Fig. 50   Illustration for page 145.

ROMAN CORN-SHIP.

Fig. 51.

Illustration for page 145.

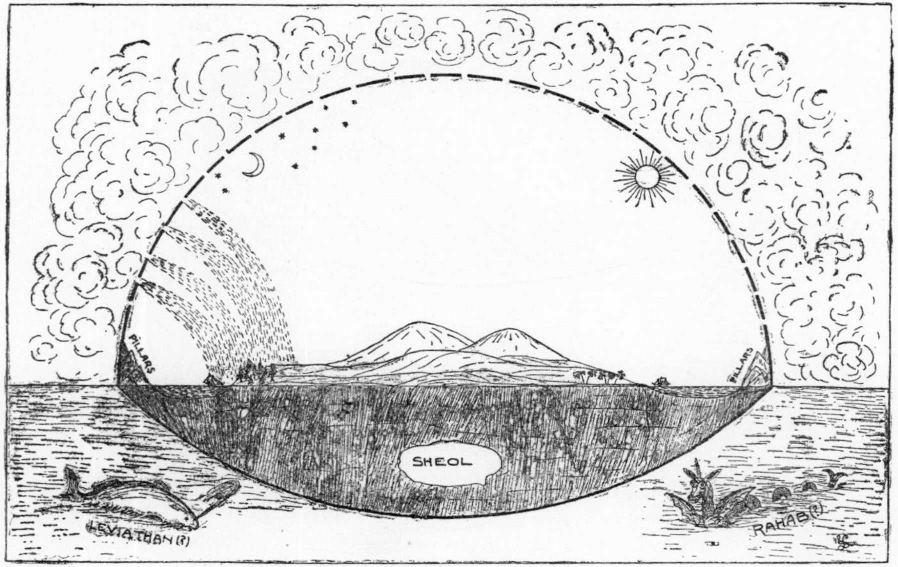

THE BABYLONIAN IDEA OF THE UNIVERSE.

Illustration for page 146.

Fig. 52.

THE TEMPLE OF BEL.

Fig. 53. Illustration for page 150,

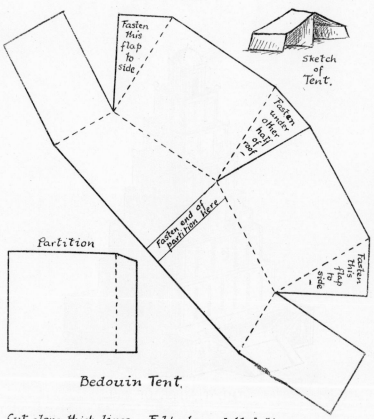

Fasten this flap to side

Fasten under other half of roof

Sketch of Tent.

Fasten end of partition here

Partition

Fasten this flap to side

Bedouin Tent.

Cut along thick lines. Fold along dotted lines.

Fig. 54.

Illustration for page 151.

An Arab Encampment.

Fig. 55.

Illustration for page 152.

WELL AND WATER TROUGH.

Fig. 56.

Illustration for page 152.

AN EASTERN CARAVAN.

Fig. 57.   Illustration for page 154.

VISIT OF A SEMITIC FAMILY TO EGYPT.

Fig. 58.   Illustration for page 154.

VISIT OF A SEMITIC FAMILY TO EGYPT.

Fig. 59.   Illustration for page 154.

AN EGYPTIAN GRANARY.

From a Wall Painting discovered at Thebes.

Fig. 60.

Illustration for page 154.

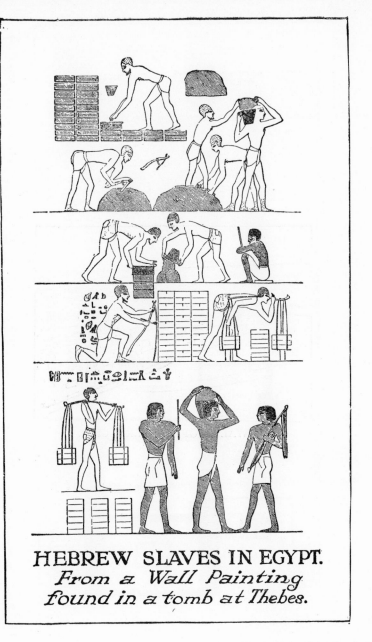

HEBREW SLAVES IN EGYPT.
From a Wall Painting found in a tomb at Thebes.

Fig. 61.

Illustration for page 156.

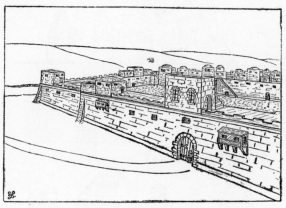

WALLS OF EASTERN CITY.

Fig. 62.   Illustration for page 162.

WALLS AND GATEWAY OF AN EASTERN CITY.

Fig. 63.
T

Illustration for page 162.

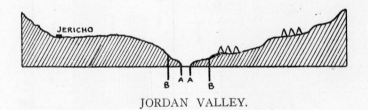

JORDAN VALLEY.

Fig. 64 Illustration for page 163.

DAGON.
The Fish god of the Philistines.
From a bas-relief on the walls of the Palace of Assur-nasir-pal, King of Assyria.

Fig. 65.   Illustration for page 167.

A PHILISTINE WARRIOR.

Fig. 66.   Illustration for page 169.

THE ANOINTING OF DAVID.

Fig. 67.

Illustration for page 171.

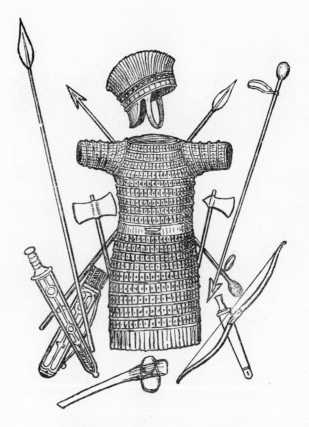

ANCIENT ARMS AND ARMOUR.

Fig. 68.   Illustration for page 172.

THE CAVE OF ADULLAM.

Fig. 69.

Illustration for page 173.

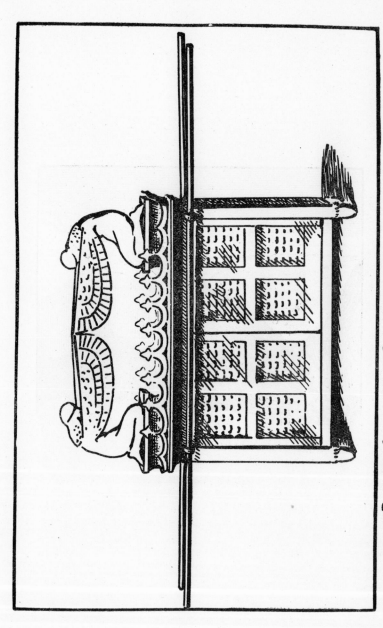

Probable form of the Ark of the Covenant.

Fig. 70.

Fig. 71.

THE TABERNACLE.

Illustration for page 179.

A BRAVE YOUNG PRINCE.

Fig. 72.

Illustration for page 181.

ASSYRIAN SOLDIER.

Fig. 73.   Illustration for page 183.

ASSYRIAN KING IN HIS CHARIOT.

Fig. 74.

Illustration for page 183.

THE SURRENDER OF LACHISH.

Fig. 75.

Illustration for page 183.

POSTURES FOR PRAYER IN THE EAST.

Fig. 76.

Illustration for page 185.

ALTARS ON HIGH PLACES.

Fig. 77.

Illustration for page 185.

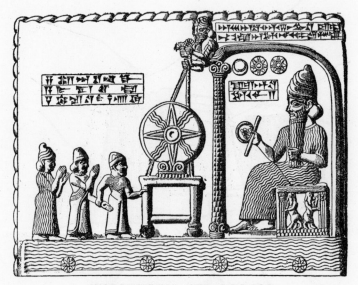

WORSHIPPING THE SUN-GOD.

Fig. 78.

Illustration for page 190.

AN EASTERN WELL

Fig. 79.

Illustration for page 192.

U

WOMEN AT THE WELL.   Illustration for page 192.

Fig. 80.

Winnowing Corn with a Fan.

Fig. 81.   Illustration for page 197.

A Primitive Wine Press.

Fig. 82.

Illustration for page 197.

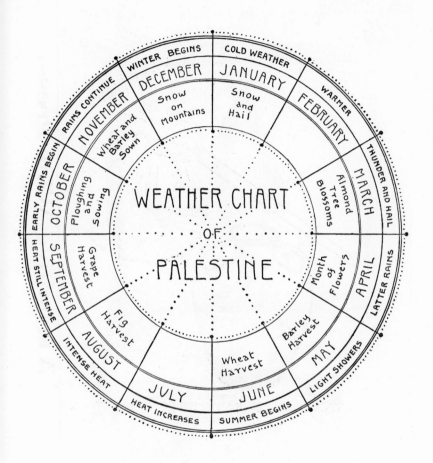

Fig. 83.

Illustration for page 197.

EASTERN TORCH, RAM'S HORN TRUMPET AND
WATER-PITCHER.

Fig. 84.

Illustration for page 198.

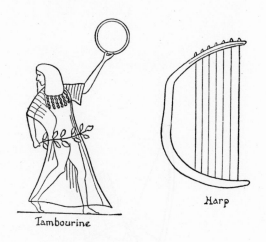

Tambourine

Harp

Grand Egyptian Harp.

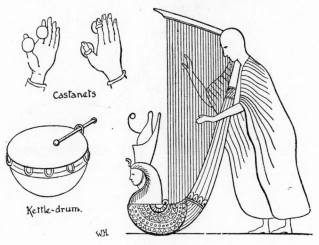

Castanets

Kettle-drum.

W.H.

MUSICAL INSTRUMENTS.

Fig. 85.

Illustration for page 201.

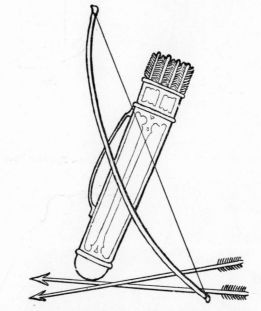

AN EASTERN QUIVER, BOW AND ARROWS.

Fig. 86.

Illustration for page 201.

Baal

Baal stone.

Fig. 87.
X

Illustration for page 204.

MOLOCH. (Molech)

A Canaanitish god

Human sacrifices were offered to this god.

Fig. 88.　　　　　　　　　　　　Illustration for page 204.

ELIJAH AND THE RAVENS.

Fig. 89.   Illustration for page 205.

PRIMITIVE LOG-BOAT.   A CORACLE.

Fig. 90.   Illustration for page 145.

FORDS OF THE RIVER JORDAN.

Fig. 91.

Illustration for page 163.

"THY TOUCH HAS STILL ITS ANCIENT POWER."

Fig. 92. Illustration for pages 60, 111.

HAMMURABI RECEIVING THE LAWS FROM
SHAMASH, THE SUN-GOD.

Fig. 93.   Illustration for page 178.

BLACK OBELISK OF SHALMANESER II.

Fig. 94.   Illustration for page 208.

GENERAL INDEX

INDEX OF BIBLICAL REFERENCES

xix. 1-2—201.
xx.—201.
xxii. 1-2—202.
xxiii. 1-15—202.
xxiii. 19-21—202.
xxiv. 1-22—202 f.
xxvi. 1-12—173 f.

2 Samuel.

v. 1-12—203.
vi. 1-17—174 f.
ix.—174.
xxiii. 13-17—172 f.

1 Kings.

ii. 1-4—203.
iii. 5-15—203.
v.—175 f.
vi.—175 f.
xii. 1-19—203 f.
xvii.—204 f.
xviii.—205 f.
xxi. 1-16—206 f.

2 Kings.

ii. 1-13—207.
v. 1-19—207 f.
vi. 8-23—208.
xviii.—183 f.
xix.—183 f.
xx.—184 f.
xxii.—185.
xxiii.—185.

Daniel.

iii.—187 f.
iv.—185 ff.
v.—188.
vi.—189.

Matthew.

i. 18-25—82 ff.
ii. 1-12—83 ff.
ii. 13-15—90 ff.
ii. 19-23—90 ff.
iii. 1-6—19 ff.
iii. 13-17—61.
iv. 1-11—25 ff.
viii. 5-13—95 f.
ix. 9-13—30 ff.
ix. 27-31—36.
xii. 9-13—64 f.
xii. 22-30—42 f.
xiii. 1-23—113 f.

xiii. 31-32—76.
xiii. 33—76 f.
xiii. 44—51 f.
xiii. 45-6—77 f.
xiv. 22-33—47 f.
xv. 21-28—10, 41 f.
xvii. 1-13—43 f.
xx. 1-16—77 ff.
xxi. 1-11—60 f.
xxi. 14-16—60, 111 f.
xxv. 1-13—49 ff.
xxv. 14-30—114 f.
xxvii. 32—112.
xxvii. 57-60—108 ff.

Mark.

i. 6-11—24 ff.
i. 16-20—27 ff.
i. 21-28—93 f.
i. 29-38—93 f.
i. 40-45—37 ff.
ii. 1-12—63 f.
ii. 13-22—30 ff.
ii. 23-iii. 6—64 f.
iii. 7-12—118 f.
iv. 1-20—113 f.
iv. 26-29—119 f.
iv. 30-34—76.
iv. 35-41—46 ff.
v. 1-20—92 f.
v. 21-43—62 f.
vi. 35-46—40 f.
vii. 24-30—41 f.
viii. 27-ix. 1—43 f.
ix. 2-10—43 f.
ix. 14-29—45 f.
ix. 33-7—60, 111 f.
x. 13-16—60, 111 f.
x. 17-27—120 f.
x. 32-4—97 f.
x. 46-52—65 f.
xi. 1-11—69 f.
xi. 15-19—70 f.
xii. 1-12—121 ff.
xii. 13 ff.—2.
xiv. 1-11—112, 123 ff.
xiv. 12-26—112, 125 ff.
xiv. 32-52—98 f, 128 ff.
xiv. 53-4—132 ff.
xiv. 66-72—132 ff.
xiv. 55-65—134 ff.
xv. 1-20—134 ff.
xv. 22-41—100 ff.
xv. 42-47—107 f.
xvi.—138 f.

Printed in Great Britain by
LINDSAY & CO., LTD., 17 Blackfriars Street, Edinburgh.